Memorial Tributes

NATIONAL ACADEMY OF ENGINEERING

NATIONAL ACADEMY OF ENGINEERING
OF THE
UNITED STATES OF AMERICA

Memorial Tributes

Volume 11

THE NATIONAL ACADEMIES PRESS
Washington, D.C. 2007

International Standard Book Number-13: 978–0–309–10337–4
International Standard Book Number-10: 0–309–10337–1

Additional copies of this publication are available from:

The National Academies Press
500 Fifth Street, N.W.
Lockbox 285
Washington, D.C. 20055

800–624–6242 or 202–334–3313 (in the Washington metropolitan area)

http://www.nap.edu

Printed in the United States of America

CONTENTS

v

CONTENTS

FOREWORD

THIS IS THE ELEVENTH VOLUME in the series of *Memorial Tributes* compiled by the National Academy of Engineering as a personal remembrance of the lives and outstanding achievements of its members and foreign associates. These volumes are intended to stand as an enduring record of the many contributions of engineers and engineering to the benefit of humankind. In most cases, the authors of the tributes are contemporaries or colleagues who had personal knowledge of the interests and the engineering accomplishments of the deceased.

Through its members and foreign associates, the Academy carries out the responsibilities for which it was established in 1964. Under the charter of the National Academy of Sciences, the National Academy of Engineering was formed as a parallel organization of outstanding engineers. Members are elected on the basis of significant contributions to engineering theory and practice and to the literature of engineering or on the basis of demonstrated unusual accomplishments in the pioneering of new and developing fields of technology.

The National Academies share a responsibility to advise the federal government on matters of science and technology. The expertise and credibility that the National Academy of Engineering bring to that task stem directly from the abilities, interests, and achievements of our members and foreign associates, our colleagues and friends, whose special gifts we remember in these pages.

W. Dale Compton
Home Secretary

Memorial Tributes

NATIONAL ACADEMY OF ENGINEERING

Hubert I. Aaronson

HUBERT I. AARONSON

1924–2005

Elected in 1997

"For contributions to the understanding of
diffusional phase transformation in commercial steels."

BY JOHN P. HIRTH

HUBERT I. AARONSON, an international leader in the materials field, died December 13, 2005, after a lengthy illness. He continued working as R.F. Mehl Professor Emeritus at Carnegie Mellon University until the very end.

Born in New York City on July 10, 1924, Aaronson moved in 1936 to Jersey City, where he completed high school. Although his father and advisors discouraged him from going into engineering, his sister, Barbara, supported his goal. Hub envisioned great advances in engineering and he enrolled at Carnegie Institute of Technology (CIT), now Carnegie Mellon University, determined to become an engineer.

At the end of his second year, Hub was called into the service. He wanted to enter the U.S. Army Air Corps, and, helped by his comrades and others, he was able to do so. However, when he realized he was scheduled to enter bombardier school for B-24 Liberators, which had a poor survival rate, he showed up a week early at the B-17 training school instead. The bureaucracy absorbed this unprecedented change, and Hub went on to fly many B-17 missions during World War II.

When he resumed his studies after the war, he not only did very well in his classes, but also became editor of the campus newspaper. He completed his B.S., M.S., and Ph.D. in metallurgical engineering at CIT in 1948, 1954, and 1954, respectively.

His thesis advisor was the eminent metallurgist, R.F. Mehl. Hub remained at CIT as a research metallurgist until 1957, working with Mehl, G.M. Pound, and C. Wells. He then became a research scientist at Ford Scientific Laboratory (1958–1972), a professor at Michigan Technological University (1972–1979), R.F. Mehl Professor at Carnegie Mellon University (1979–1992), a scientist at the Naval Research Laboratory (1992–1996), and finally R.F. Mehl Professor Emeritus (1996–2005).

Hub was a giant in the field of phase transformation, to which he made many seminal contributions. One of his major contributions was defining and understanding the role of microstructure in phase transformations. In 1951, F.C. Frank had demonstrated the importance of ledges in the growth of crystals from vapor. Hub recognized the potential for similar effects in transformations in solids. In classic early work with K. Kinsman and M. Adams, he demonstrated that bainitic and other plate-shaped transformations proceeded by the motion of what he called "growth ledges." Atomic-level ledges, or steps, which had dislocation content as well, relieved strains that would otherwise appear at interfaces between reactants and products. Hub called these defects structural ledges. In later work with a number of his students, he verified the nature of these defects by transmission electron microscopy and by computer simulations.

Hub engaged in a long, vigorous debate with J.W. Christian on the details of bainitic transformation. Hub's view was that the diffusional composition change during the transformation accompanied the motion of ledges, while Jack Christian argued that the step structure (and accompanying shear) occurred first. Their views have been largely reconciled in the new millennium.

Hub also made significant contributions in alloy thermodynamics, the role of alloying elements in "hardenability" (retardation or enhancement of the rate of transformation) in steels, the mechanism of nucleation of new phases, interfacial energies, and the mechanism of massive transformation. His work had a substantial impact on the selection of materials for automobiles and Navy ships.

Hub was elected to the National Academy of Engineering in 1997, and he received many awards in recognition of his accomplishments. These included Fellow, R.F. Mehl Medalist, C.H. Mathewson Medalist, Educator Award, and Hume-Rothery Medalist from the Minerals, Metals, and Materials Society (TMS); Fellow and Albert Saveur Achievement Award from ASM International; and Honorary Member of the Japan Institute of Metals. He participated widely in international conferences as keynote speaker, conference organizer, and editor of conference proceedings.

Hub had a tremendous influence on his students and associates, and he was beloved by all of them. A stern taskmaster, but a friendly and helpful advisor and collaborator, his vision and optimism were inspiring, and his supportiveness was legendary. On three different occasions, his students organized symposia honoring him. He regularly held lavish dinner parties for his students, often reserving an entire restaurant for the occasion. He held similar events to entertain visiting scientists and speakers, often paying for them himself. He also funded portions of conferences he organized, particularly to help students to attend.

In a sense, his work was his hobby. He remained a bachelor throughout his life and worked long and unusual hours. Unless he had to attend a function or deliver a lecture, his day began at about 3 p.m. and ended around 5 a.m. Students and colleagues who wanted to see him had to fit in late afternoon appointments. Even Ford Scientific Laboratory accommodated his schedule and made special arrangements for him to work through the night.

He took vacations at posh resorts, often beaches, and lived the high life. He read assiduously, especially in military history. Indeed, this interest led him to work at the Naval Research Laboratory for four years after his retirement from Carnegie Mellon University.

Hub Aaronson was an internationally respected colleague, a valuable collaborator, a successful teacher, and a warm friend to many in the materials field. He will be missed, but his contributions will live on.

He is survived by his sister, Barbara A. McMurray, of Lafayette, Indiana.

James G. Baker

JAMES G. BAKER

1914–2005

Elected in 1979

"Innovation and design of optical devices for diverse,
unusual, and exacting requirements."

BY WILLIAM T. PLUMMER AND STEPHEN D. FANTONE

JAMES GILBERT BAKER, renowned astronomer and optical physicist and longtime associate in research at the Center for Astrophysics of Harvard and Smithsonian Observatories, died at his home in Bedford, New Hampshire, on June 29, 2005. He was 90 years old.

Jim was born in Louisville, Kentucky, on November 11, 1914, the fourth child of Jesse B. Baker and Hattie M. Stallard. After graduating from duPont Manual High in Louisville, he attended the University of Louisville, where he majored in mathematics; an astronomy professor, Dr. Moore, often allowed him to use his telescopes. Jim also fabricated mirrors for his own telescopes and helped form the Louisville Astronomical Society in 1931. While he was still a student, he met his future wife, Elizabeth Katherine Breitenstein, of Jefferson County, Kentucky. In 1935, he received a B.A. and was a Woodstock Society medalist.

In 1936, Jim received his M.A. in astronomy at the Harvard College Observatory and was appointed a Junior Fellow (1937–1943) of the prestigious Harvard Society of Fellows. During an Astronomy Department dinner in 1942, the director of the observatory, Dr. Harlow Shapley, asked him to give an impromptu talk. According to *The Courier-Journal Magazine*, immediately following the talk "Dr. Shapley stood up and proclaimed an on-the-spot departmental meeting and asked for a vote on recommending Baker for a Ph.D. on the basis of the 'oral exam' he had just finished. The vote was unanimous."

At Harvard College Observatory, Jim collaborated with Donald H. Menzel, Lawrence H. Aller, and George H. Shortley on a landmark series of papers on the physical processes in gaseous nebulae. In addition to this theoretical work, Jim began designing a set of astronomical instruments with increasing resolving powers and wide field angles. In 1945, he was co-author, with George Z. Dimitroff, of *Telescopes and Accessories*. His design for the Baker-Schmidt telescope and the Baker Super Schmidt meteor camera were notable accomplishments.

In 1941, while still a graduate student, Jim was awarded a small research contract by U.S. Army Col. George W. Goddard to develop a wide-angle reconnaissance camera at the Harvard College Observatory. The next year, this project was expanded to produce huge quantities of an f/2.5 lens capable of covering a 5x5-inch photographic plate. More than 100 other projects were subsequently developed, with lenses up to 12 inches in diameter.

As director of the Observatory Optical Project at Harvard University from 1943 to 1945, Jim spent thousands of hours doing calculations on a Marchant calculator to produce his aerial cameras. He provided the optical designs, supervised the optical and machine shops, and risked his life operating cameras in early test flights that carried these photographic systems in unpressurized compartments. During this time, he also began a long consulting career with the Perkin Elmer Corporation. When World War II ended, Harvard University decided to terminate its war-related projects, and Jim's lab was moved to Boston University. The lab later became the basis of ITEK Corporation.

Jim was an associate professor and research associate at Harvard from 1946 to 1949. In 1948, he received the Presidential Medal of Merit for his work in the Office of Scientific Research and Development during World War II, as well as an honorary doctorate from the University of Louisville. That year, he also moved to California to spend two years as a research associate at Lick Observatory. He returned to Harvard in 1950.

To speed up the tedious process of design calculations, Jim introduced numerical computers into the field of optics. His ray-trace program was one of the first applications run on the

Harvard Mark II (1947) computer. He developed his own methods of optimizing the performance of his designs. During the 1960s and 1970s, the development of optical computer programs became a family affair when Jim's children developed programs, under his direction, to support his increasingly sophisticated work.

Jim was involved not only with cameras, but also with concepts for camera delivery systems. As chairman of the U.S. Air Force Scientific Advisory Board (1953–1954), he recognized that meeting national security requirements would entail using aircraft at extreme altitudes and optical designs of even greater resolving power. The concept of the U-2 system, consisting of a plane and a camera that functioned as a unit to create panoramic, high-resolution aerial photographs, was developed to meet those requirements. Jim formed Spica Incorporated in 1955 to perform the necessary optical design work. His final aerial camera design was a lightweight 36-inch f/10 system. Jim also designed the aircraft's periscope, which enabled pilots to see their flight path.

He continued to serve on the President's Foreign Intelligence Advisory Board and the Land Panel of the Killian Committee. Jim designed the Baker-Nunn satellite-tracking camera to support the Air Force's early satellite-tracking and space-surveillance networks, and, thanks to his foresight, a dozen of these cameras were in place around the world when Sputnik was launched in October 1957. For the next three decades, these cameras were used to determine the precise orbits of spacecraft. By 1958, Jim was almost solely responsible for all of the cameras used in photoreconnaissance aircraft. He himself figured the aspheric surfaces of the most demanding optical components, usually in his basement workshop.

Jim continued to advise top government officials as reconnaissance systems evolved during the 1960s and 1970s, and he helped create the camera systems used in the SR-71 Blackbird, the Air Force high-speed reconnaissance plane, which was in use from the 1960s to the 1990s. He also designed some of the lenses and camera systems for the Air Force Samos Satellite Program.

In 2000, in recognition of his work as an advisor to the U.S. Air Force and the National Reconnaissance Office, he received the Pioneers of National Reconnaissance Medal with the following citation: "As a young Harvard astronomer, Dr. James G. Baker designed most of the lenses and many of the cameras used in aerial over-flights of 'denied territory' enabling the success of the U.S. peacetime strategic reconnaissance policy." In 2002, the U.S. Air Force awarded him the Space Pioneer Award.

In 1966, Jim began a long, productive consulting relationship with the Polaroid Corporation. Dr. Edwin Land had persuaded him that only he could design the optical system for his new SX-70® Land camera, which was introduced in 1972. For the next 35 years, Jim also designed other remarkable, high-volume commercial products. He was most notably responsible for the mathematical design of the Quintic® focusing system for the 1986 Polaroid Spectra camera system, which involved a revolutionary combination of two free-form aspherics to adjust focus by a lateral rotation across the optical axis.

Jim maintained his affiliation with Harvard Observatory and the Smithsonian Astrophysical Observatory until he retired in 2003. After retirement, he continued to work at his home on a new telescope design he told his family he should have discovered in 1940.

Jim received many honors and awards during his long career. In 1958, he was made a fellow of the Optical Society of America (OSA), and, in 1960, he was elected president of OSA for one year, during which he helped establish the *Applied Optics* journal. He was the only individual to receive all four primary OSA awards in optics: the Adolf Lomb Award, Frederick Ives Medal, Joseph Fraunhofer Award, and David Richardson Medal. In 1993, he was made an honorary member of OSA. In 1976, he was the recipient of the Alan Gordon Award and, in 1978, the Gold Medal, the highest award of the International Society of Optical Engineers (SPIE). In 1953, the American Philosophical Society awarded him the Magellanic Medal. The Franklin Institute awarded him the 1962 Elliott Cresson Medal for his many innovations in astronomical optics.

Jim was an elected member of the American Academy of Arts and Sciences (1946), National Academy of Sciences (1965), American Philosophical Society (1970), and National Academy of Engineering (1979). He was also a member of the American Astronomical Society, the International Astronomical Union, and the Astronomical Society of the Pacific. He published more than 30 professional papers and received more than 50 U.S. patents.

A friend, a gentleman, a scholar, a patriot of the highest integrity, and a truly inspirational engineer of uniquely difficult and important accomplishments, Dr. James G. Baker will be greatly missed by all who knew him. He is survived by his wife, Elizabeth; his four children, Kirby Alan, Dennis Graham, Neal Kenton, and Brenda Sue; and seven grandchildren.

LYNN S. BEEDLE

1917–2003

Elected in 1972

*"For contributions to steel structures research and design practice,
especially plastic design and residual stress effects."*

BY JOHN W. FISHER

LYNN S. BEEDLE, University Distinguished Professor Emeritus of Civil Engineering, Lehigh University, died on October 30, 2003, at the age of 85.

Lynn was born on the San Francisco side of the Golden Gate Strait in Orland, California, on December 7, 1917, one of seven children of Granville and Carol (Simpson) Beedle. He grew up in the San Francisco area and was influenced by the construction and opening of the Golden Gate Bridge, which was completed in 1937. His attendance at the opening of the bridge and his observations during its construction contributed to his decision to focus on civil engineering as an undergraduate at the University of California, Berkeley. Lynn received a B.S. in civil engineering with a minor in architecture from the University of California, Berkeley in 1941.

After a short term of employment as an engineer at the Todd-California Shipbuilding Corporation in 1941, Lynn was commissioned as a naval officer at the beginning of World War II and began his military service as a student in naval architecture at the U.S. Navy Postgraduate School. His career in the Navy included instructor at the Postgraduate School of the U.S. Naval Academy in Annapolis, Maryland; officer-in-charge of research on underwater explosions at the Norfolk Naval Shipyard in 1942; an assignment in the U.S. Navy Bureau of Ships in Washington, D.C.; participation in the 1946 Bikini atoll atomic bomb tests as deputy officer in charge of the Ship Instrumentation Group there until 1947.

After the war, Lynn joined the faculty at Lehigh University as a research instructor in civil engineering. He received his M.S. in 1949 and Ph.D. in 1952, both from Lehigh. He was appointed assistant professor in 1952, full professor in 1957, and Distinguished University Professor in 1978. He became associate director of Fritz Engineering Laboratory in 1952 and director in 1960; he continued to serve the laboratory with distinction until 1984. He became Professor Emeritus in 1988.

As director of the Fritz Engineering Laboratory, he led research on the behavior and design of steel structures. His first textbook, *Plastic Design of Steel Frames* (John Wiley & Sons), was published in 1958. He was editor and co-author of the American Society of Civil Engineers (ASCE) Manual 41, *Plastic Design in Steel*, which was published in 1961 and revised in 1971. He led the Lehigh team as editor of *Structural Steel Design*, published by Ronald Press in 1964. He was also editor in chief of several editions of *Structural Stability: A World View* and *The Planning and Design of Tall Buildings*, a monograph in five volumes published by McGraw-Hill. Altogether, Lynn was the author or co-author of more than 200 papers, articles, and books.

Lynn's stellar reputation and his promotion of research at Lehigh attracted graduate students from all over the United States and more than 30 other countries. He made it a point to meet with graduates of Lehigh during his many travels abroad.

In 1944, after the collapse of the Quebec Bridge during construction, the Structural Stability Research Council was organized to develop knowledge about the behavior and strength of compression elements. Lynn was director of the council for 23 years, from 1970 to 1993.

In 1969, Lynn founded the Council on Tall Buildings and Urban Habitat and served as director until he became Director Emeritus in 2000. Through his leadership and passionate dedication, the council brought together architects, structural engineers, construction workers, environmental experts, sociologists, and policy makers in an effort to provide a rationale for the construction of high-rise structures.

Lynn received many accolades and awards from local, national, and international organizations. Lehigh recognized his achievements with the Alfred Noble Robinson Award in 1952 and the R.R. and E.C. Hillman Award in 1973. In 1972, he became the first Lehigh faculty member elected to the National Academy of Engineering. Other notable awards were the ASCE Research Prize in 1955 and the Ernest E. Howard Award in 1963. The American Institute of Steel Construction awarded him the T.R. Higgins Lectureship Award in 1973 and the Geerhard Haaijer Award for Excellence in Education in 2003. The Franklin Institute awarded him the Frank P. Brown Medal in 1982.

In 1977, Lynn was elected an Honorary Member of the International Association of Bridge and Structural Engineers; in 1979, he was elected an Honorary Member of ASCE, and in 2002, he was given the ASCE Opal Award for Lifetime Achievement in Management. He was the first recipient of the International Contributions Award from the Japan Society of Civil Engineers in 1994. In 1995, the American Association of Engineering Societies honored him with the John Fritz Medal, one of the highest awards in the engineering profession. The University of California, Berkeley named him Distinguished Engineering Alumnus in 2000. In 1999, Lynn was recognized by *Engineering News Record* as one of the top 125 contributors to the construction industry during the 125-year period from 1874 to 1999.

Lynn's activities and awards brought Lehigh University significant recognition from around the world. It was largely through his efforts that funds (mostly from abroad) were raised for the Fazlur Khan Chair in Structural Engineering and Architecture and Bruce G. Johnston Chair in the P.C. Rossin College of Engineering and Applied Science.

Lynn lived to see three awards established in his honor. At a black-tie dinner in New York in 2002, the Council on Tall Buildings and Urban Habitat announced the establishment of the Lynn S. Beedle Achievement Award to be given annually to an individual for service to the building profession and the council. Also in 2002, the Structural Stability Research Council established the Lynn S. Beedle Award to be given to a leading stability researcher or designer from anywhere in the world for significant contributions to the field. In 2003, the Department of Civil and Environmental Engineering at Lehigh University established the Lynn S. Beedle Distinguished Civil and Environmental Engineering Award with Lynn as the first recipient.

Lynn is survived by Ella, his wife of 57 years; five children, Lynn Jr., Helen, Jonathan, David, and Edward; a brother, Richard, and two sisters, Carol Healy of Seattle and Jane Hildebrand of Chicago; nine grandchildren and one great grandchild.

DONALD S. BERRY

1911–2002

Elected in 1966

"For transportation and safety technology."

BY RAYMOND J. KRIZEK

DONALD S. BERRY, Professor Emeritus of Civil Engineering at Northwestern University, died in Kenosha, Wisconsin, on December 16, 2002, at the age of 91. A consummate transportation engineer, Professor Berry helped create transportation engineering programs at three universities and was responsible for pioneering interdisciplinary graduate studies in transportation engineering at Northwestern.

Don was born on January 1, 1911, in the middle of a blizzard on a ranch near Vale, South Dakota. He attended high school in Rapid City, South Dakota, and graduated from the South Dakota School of Mines in 1931. His graduate studies took him to Iowa State University, where he received an M.S. in 1933, and the University of Michigan, where he completed his Ph.D. in transportation engineering in 1936.

During his graduate studies at the University of Michigan, he met the girl who was to become his wife for more than six decades. At a student dance one evening, Don met a young lady named Helen Mitchell, an M.S. student in history, and that was the beginning of their romance. After their first date, Don told his roommate he had met the girl he was going to marry. Don and Helen were married on October 30, 1937, in Washington, D.C., Helen's hometown. Their honeymoon consisted of the trip from Washington to Evanston, where the couple set up home-making in an apartment. In the ensuing years they had two daughters, Judy (1940) and Jeane (1946).

Donald Berry's professional career was devoted to education and research in traffic and transportation engineering. After spending 12 years as a transportation engineer and then director of the Traffic Division at the National Safety Council in Chicago, he embarked on a career in academia. As a professor, he helped organize graduate programs in transportation engineering at the University of California, Berkeley (seven years), Purdue University (two years), and Northwestern University (22 years). The 10 to 15 M.S. and 2 to 4 Ph.D. graduates each year from Northwestern University went on to occupy many key positions in federal, state, and local transportation agencies, on university faculties, and in consulting firms. From 1962 to 1968, Don was chairman of the Department of Civil Engineering at Northwestern. Over the years, he directed in-service training programs in traffic and transportation engineering in many parts of the United States and several foreign countries, including Venezuela, Spain, South Africa, Thailand, Israel, and the Philippines.

Even before Don Berry became a university professor, he was an educator. During World War II, he was selected by the FBI to teach courses in major cities throughout the country on controlling transportation and traffic in the event of blackouts, air raids, or wartime damage. Later he worked in Washington for the Office of Civil Defense.

Don always brought the practical world of transportation into the classroom. He was a teacher who made every academic concept real and established bridges linking research to practice. He built cooperative education programs connecting the university to key public agencies, allowing students to finance and broaden their education by working at these agencies and conducting research as a part of their work. He strongly encouraged his students to join and participate in the activities of professional societies, including attendance at meetings of the Institute of Traffic (now Transportation) Engineers (ITE) and Transportation (formerly Highway) Research Board (TRB).

Don created a family of graduate students whom he nurtured to professional maturity, setting academic, professional, and personal standards that are being promulgated to this day. Because of his interest in students as people, his classroom was a diverse and interesting place to study transportation. He never returned from a professional meeting without bringing into the classroom what he had learned about practical problems and ideas, and his students grew professionally and intellectually as a result.

Don was very active in TRB and served on numerous committees, including a term as chairman of the Executive Committee in 1965. He also served on various committees of ITE, American Society of Civil Engineers (ASCE), American Society for Engineering Education, National Safety Council, and several special assignments. His research produced more than 100 papers on numerous subjects related to traffic and transportation engineering. He initiated much of the early work relating speed to accidents and contributed materially to the development of chemical tests for intoxication. His inquiring mind took him into many other areas, and his explorations led to regulations and traffic operational developments that are now accepted as basic principles.

Dr. Berry received many honors and awards during his lifetime. One of the most prestigious was his election to the National Academy of Engineering (NAE) in 1966; he was the first transportation educator to become an NAE member. He was awarded an honorary Doctor of Engineering degree by the South Dakota School of Mines in 1964. In 1967 he was the recipient of the Sesquicentennial Award from the University of Michigan, and he became a Walter P. Murphy Professor at Northwestern University. In 1972 he received the Theodore M. Matson Memorial Award from ITE and the James Laurie Prize in Transportation from ASCE. Five years later, in 1977, he was given the College of Engineering Professional Achievement Citation from Iowa State University. After retirement in 1979, he received a Lifetime Achievement Award from the Transportation Division of the Illinois Section of ASCE in 1992 and the Wilbur S. Smith Distinguished Transportation Educator Award in 1993. On the day he died, a package arrived in the mail awarding him lifetime emeritus status in NAE.

Dr. Berry was a registered civil engineer and was active in many professional societies. He was a fellow of ITE and a fellow and honorary member of ASCE. In addition, he belonged to Sigma Xi, Tau Beta Pi, Chi Epsilon, and Phi Kappa Phi.

He was an active member of Saint Matthews Episcopal Church in Evanston, Illinois. After his retirement, he joined the North Shore Senior Center, where he taught classes in defensive driving for ten years. He was also a member of the Commission on Aging for the city of Evanston, and he enjoyed playing duplicate bridge, golf, and ping-pong.

Don is survived by two daughters, Judy Stasik of Kenosha, Wisconsin, and Jeane Borkenhagen of Lincoln, California, eight granddaughters and nine great grandchildren, and a sister, Elizabeth Hagman, of Royal Oak, Michigan. Helen, his wife of 63 years, died in 2000.

Don Berry was a man of admirable integrity and loyalty, a leader in engineering and higher education, and a dear friend to all who knew him. We are all richer because Don shared his life with us, and we miss him greatly. As a mentor, friend, and inspiration, his legacy is the hundreds of trained professionals, including many university professors, who will carry his message throughout the world for many years to come.

John M. Bogdanoff

JOHN L. BOGDANOFF

1916–2003

Elected in 1975

"For leadership in the introduction of stochastic processes into mechanical and civil engineering analysis."

BY HENRY T.Y. YANG

JOHN "JACK" BOGDANOFF was a pioneer in basic mechanics, materials, dynamics, fracture and fatigue, and stochastic processes for solving large-scale, complex engineering problems. Born on May 25, 1916, in East Orange, New Jersey, he passed away on July 20, 2003, in West Lafayette, Indiana.

Jack obtained a B.S.M.E. from Syracuse University in 1938, an M.S. from Harvard University in 1939, and a Ph.D. from Columbia University in 1950. While at Columbia, he studied with Professor Raymond Mindlin. Jack's stellar career began as a test engineer in engine performance, vibration and stress analysis, and advanced design at Wright Aeronautical Corporation in Woodridge, New Jersey, from 1939 to 1946. From 1946 to 1950, he was an instructor and assistant project engineer in civil engineering at Columbia University, where he taught courses in statics and dynamics and in vibration.

Most of Jack's professional life was spent at Purdue University. Beginning in 1950, he was professor of engineering sciences; he taught courses in statics, dynamics, materials, vibration, elasticity and control systems, vectorial mechanics, analytical mechanics, and statistical analysis of engineering systems. During the 1950s, Jack and Professor Frank Kozin and a few other Purdue colleagues, formed the Midwest Applied Science Corporation (MASC). Their major project, the Land Locomotion Project, for the U.S. Army Tank and Automotive Center in Warren, Michigan, involved the design of vehicle suspensions that could respond to vibrations caused by variations in ground height. Louis J. Cote, a colleague at Purdue, was a major collaborator on the project. MASC undertook many more projects until 1968. In 1962, Professors Bogdanoff and Kozin founded (and were co-directors) of the Center for Applied Stochastics, which was partially supported by a grant from the National Science Foundation (NSF). Principal investigators associated with the center were Wilbert M. Gersch, Anshel J. Schiff, and Arnold L. Sweet, all professors in the School of Aeronautics, Astronautics, and Engineering Sciences at Purdue. During this time, undergraduate and graduate courses were developed to introduce students to the concepts of probability and statistics. Research topics included stochastic differential equations, stochastic stability, metal fatigue, soil subsidence, system identification, column buckling, heat transfer, and fluid turbulence.

Jack was associate head of what was then called the School of Aeronautics, Astronautics, and Engineering Sciences from 1967 to 1971 and was head of the school from 1971 to 1972. Subsequently, he was a professor in the school, which was renamed the School of Aeronautics and Astronautics, until his retirement in 1986. In his 36 years at Purdue, Jack was instrumental in building the engineering and science program into one of the strongest programs in the world. He also made extraordinary contributions to the program in aeronautics and astronautics, which is now also one of the very best in the world.

Jack's research led to significant contributions to computer modeling of fatigue and cumulative damage. He identified critical energy-related engineering problems of national significance and developed several pioneering theoretical studies of earthquake response for the world's largest fossil fuel power plant. The work was supported by a multi-million-dollar grant from NSF and the Tennessee Valley Authority. Jack was the principal investigator (PI), with Hsu Lo as co-PI, on the first phase of the project; he was PI, with Henry Yang as co-PI, on the second phase. He also introduced the use of stochastic methods of analysis for solving large-scale, complex engineering problems. As was stated in Purdue's memorial resolution, "Professor Bogdanoff was a structural dynamicist ahead of his time." Among his key contributions was "Theoretical Study of Seismic Response of the Paradise Cooling Tower," one in a series of papers on the topic, presented to the 6th World Conference on Earthquake Engineering held in New Delhi during the 1970s. The papers were focused on the steam-generator support structures, natural-draught cooling towers, tall chimneys, and coal-conveying structures of the fossil fuel plant at Paradise, Kentucky, the site of the major Tennessee Valley Authority power plant. A major goal of the study was to identify vulnerable aspects of the power plant to inform future designs. Professor Bogdanoff's research team included five professors, Hsu Lo, Henry T.Y. Yang, Anshel J. Schiff, C.T. Sun, and Kenneth Kayser, and several graduate students. The work resulted in six Ph.D. theses and many publications.

After his retirement from Purdue in 1986, Jack remained an internationally recognized authority on dynamics and applied stochastics. His pioneering research is a critical platform for continuing studies in structural dynamics that have far-reaching impacts. Some of his closest long-term friends and colleagues included NAE members Paul Chenea and Robert Naka and prominent Purdue colleagues George Hawkins, Hsu Lo, Paul Lykoudis, Edward Trabant, Frank Kozin, Shien-Shiu Shu, Jack Goldberg, Joe Modrey, and Al Orden from the University of Chicago. Jack's friendship with both Al Orden and Joe Modrey began at Wright Aeronautical during World War II.

Jack was a fellow of the American Association for the Advancement of Science and the American Society of Mechanical Engineers (ASME), and he was elected to the National Academy of Engineering in 1975 for "leadership in the introduction of stochastic processes into mechanical and civil engineering analysis." He was a committee chair for ASME and associate editor of the *Journal of Applied Mechanics*, co-editor of the *Proceedings of the First Symposium on Engineering Applications of Random Function Theory and Probability*, with Frank Kozin, and author of more than 75 papers published in such prestigious journals as the *International Journal of Mechanical Science*, *Journal of Terramechanics*, *Journal of the Acoustical Society of America*, *Journal of Applied Mechanics*,

Journal of Sound and Vibration, Journal of the Engineering Mechanics Division of ASCE, and the *American Institute of Chemical Engineers Journal.*

Jack was also an industry consultant for many corporations, including Chatham Electronics Corporation, Allison Division of General Motors, Baker Manufacturing Company, Aeroproducts Operations, Houdaille-Hershey Corporation, Graver Tank and Manufacturing Corporation, KSMB Systems, Inc., and Kozin-Bogdanoff and Associates, Inc.

Professor Bogdanoff was an inspiration to his students and colleagues. Known as a strict teacher who required the highest level of performance from his students, he was also an enthusiastic, generous mentor who contributed original and innovative ideas that inspired both colleagues and students. An early riser, Jack bicycled three miles to work before 7 a.m. every morning. One of his hobbies was woodworking, another area in which he was highly skilled.

He will be dearly remembered by generations of engineers. His Ph.D. students who have gone on to stellar careers in academia and industry include Tsu-Teh Soong (1962), Samuel P. Capen Professor of Engineering Science at SUNY Buffalo; Arnold L. Sweet (1964), professor of industrial engineering at Purdue University; Michael C. Bernard (1965), Professor Emeritus, Georgia Institute of Technology; Anshel J. Schiff (1967), consulting professor (retired), Stanford University; Siong Siu Luo (1970), chairman and CEO, Gate Trade, San Francisco; James V. Carnahan (1973), adjunct professor, UIUC; Kenneth Kayser (1973), CTO, BIAS Power Technologies, Roanoke, Virginia; William Kreiger (1977), Chevron Corporation, San Ramon, California; and Bong Kim (1982), vice president, Hyundai Electronics, South Korea.

Jack was predeceased by Ruth, his beloved wife of 45 years. He is survived by his son, Paul Bogdanoff, his daughter, Sue Cole, and granddaughter Aleksa Bogdanoff.

BRUCE ALAN BOLT

1930–2005

Elected in 1978

"For application of the principles of seismology and applied mathematics to engineering decisions and public policy."

BY DAVID BRILLINGER, JOSEPH PENZIEN,
AND BARBARA ROMANOWICZ

BRUCE ALAN BOLT, Professor Emeritus of Seismology at the University of California, Berkeley, died suddenly of pancreatic cancer at Kaiser Permanente Medical Center in Oakland, California, on July 21, 2005.

Professor Bolt was born on February 15, 1930, in the small town of Largs, New South Wales, Australia. He attended East Maitland Public School, Maitland Boys' High School, Newcastle Technical College, and the University of Sydney (at Armidale) where he majored in mathematics and physics and received a B.Sc. with honors in applied mathematics in 1952. After a year at Sydney Teachers' College (Diploma of Education) he taught mathematics and physics at Sydney Boys' High School. He was then appointed to the faculty in the Mathematics Department at the University of Sydney, where he received an M.Sc. and Ph.D. in 1955 and 1959, respectively. In 1972, he was awarded a D.Sc. by the University of Sydney.

After completion of his Ph.D. in elastic wave theory, he won a Fulbright scholarship to Lamont Geological Observatory at Columbia University in 1960 and to Cambridge University (U.K.) in 1961. There he met the late Perry Byerly, Professor of Seismology at University of California, Berkeley (UCB), which led to an invitation to a chair in seismology at UCB in 1963.

From 1963 to 1993, he was professor of seismology in the Department of Geology and Geophysics at UCB and director of the UCB seismographic stations from 1963 to 1989. In his early years at UCB, while pursuing his interests in the study of earthquakes and the earth's deep structure, Professor Bolt also developed strong research interests with other faculty members in structural and geotechnical engineering, and from 1983 to 1993, he was professor of civil and environmental engineering. Upon retiring from UCB in 1993, he received the university's highest honor, the Berkeley Citation. He then became Professor Emeritus of Seismology and professor in the graduate school. He continued to engage in academic activities until his death on July 21, 2005.

As a lecturer and senior lecturer at the University of Sydney, Professor Bolt developed expertise in applied mathematics, statistics, and geophysics, and he continued to make valuable contributions in these areas throughout his career. His strongest desire was to understand natural phenomena and to describe them mathematically and statistically. He wrote numerous innovative papers pertaining to the deep earth, dispersion, free oscillations, seismology, and statistics. His first published paper, in 1957, was a note in *Nature*, followed by a note in *Geophysical Journal of the Royal Astronomical Society*, on seismic observations of the 1956 atomic explosions in Australia. In 1960, he published a paper with John Butcher on the dispersion of seismic waves. This paper signaled the beginning of his involvement with large data sets and digital computing.

His creative use of statistical methodologies, influenced by Harold Jeffreys, led to the estimation technique of revising earthquake epicenters that is still in use today. He developed the method of robust regression some 10 years before others in the field. His many contributions to seismology, including the development of earth models, involved finite-element methods, elastic wave-propagation theory, broadband and digital recording, strong-motion array development, data collection and interpretation, attenuation relations, and earthquake statistics.

Professor Bolt published almost 200 research papers and wrote six and edited eight textbooks on earthquakes, geology, and computers, among other topics. His numerous publications include four very popular books: *Earthquakes: A Primer* (1978); *Inside the Earth: Evidence from Earthquakes* (1982); *Earthquakes and Geological Discovery* (1993); and *Earthquakes* (5th ed., 2003).

In recognition of Professor Bolt's contributions to seismology, he was elected a fellow of the American Geophysical Union and the Geological Society of America, Associate of the Royal Astronomical Society, London, in 1987, and Overseas Fellow of Churchill College, Cambridge University, in 1980. He was president of the Seismological Society of America in 1974 and editor of its *Bulletin* from 1965 to 1972, president of the International Association of Seismology and Physics of the Earth's Interior from 1980 to 1983, president of the Consortium of Organizations for Strong-Motion Observation Systems (COSMOS), and president of the California Academy of Sciences (its medallist in 1989).

In addition to his many contributions to seismology, Professor Bolt made invaluable contributions to the field of earthquake engineering through his teaching of basic seismology to graduate students in structural and geotechnical engineering, his research characterizing strong ground motions for engineering design purposes, his consulting role on important engineering projects, and his participation on numerous panels, boards, and commissions. He was also an active participant in the UCB Earthquake Engineering Research Center.

Professor Bolt's consulting work was focused primarily on setting seismic criteria for new and retrofitted designs of critical structures, such as dams, nuclear power plants, large bridges, underground structures, and pipelines. These structures included the Aswan Dam, Diablo Canyon Nuclear Power Plant, Golden Gate Bridge, Bay Area Rapid Transit (BART) underground stations, BART transbay tube, and the Alaska Pipeline. His consulting work in 2005 included characterizing the controlling seismic sources and assessing tsunami risk for the design of a suspension bridge crossing the Messina Strait between Italy and Sicily. The main span of this bridge will be 3,300 meters long, more than twice the length of the main span (1,280 meters) of the Golden Gate Bridge.

Setting seismic design criteria for critical structures involves identifying seismic-source zones, conducting seismic hazard analyses, generating site-specific response spectra and corresponding free-field ground motions, characterizing the spatial variations of ground motions, and predicting future fault offsets. In addition, he participated in the evaluation of the seismic performance of structures. With his strong background in applied mathematics and mechanics, he was able to communicate effectively with structural and geotechnical engineers on seismic-design and damage assessments.

The numerous seismic-related panels, boards, and commissions on which Professor Bolt served include the California Department of Water Resources Consulting Board, California Department of Transportation Seismic Advisory Board, San Francisco Bay Conservation and Development Commission Engineering Criteria Review Board, Metropolitan Transportation Commission Engineering and Design Advisory Panel, Golden Gate Bridge Seismic Instrumentation Panel, and the California Seismic Safety Commission (CSSC). As a member and chair of CSSC, he participated in the sponsorship of numerous bills that eventually became law in California and have greatly improved seismic hazard mitigation throughout the state.

In recognition of Professor Bolt's many contributions to earthquake engineering, he received the Earthquake Engineering Research Institute 2000 George W. Housner Medal, the California Earthquake Safety Foundation 1995 Alfred E. Alquist Medal, and was elected to the National Academy of Engineering (NAE) in 1978. His NAE citation reads: "For the application of the principles of seismology and applied mathematics to engineering decisions and public policy."

Having served as chair of the UCB Academic Senate (1992–1993) and, for many years, as president of the Faculty Club, Professor Bolt seemed to know everyone on the Berkeley campus. In addition, he developed close relationships with a myriad of scientists and engineers worldwide. Whenever he met one of his many close friends, he extended a warm greeting with a big smile. His personal character was admired by everyone who had the pleasure of knowing him, and he will be greatly missed by his friends, colleagues, and students.

Professor Bolt is survived by his wife Beverley (nee Bentley) of Berkeley, California; three daughters, Gillian Bolt Kohli of Wellesley, Massachusetts, Helen Bolt Juarez of Fremont, California, and Margaret Bolt Barber of Orinda, California; a son, Robert Bolt of Hillsborough, California; a sister, Fay Bolt of Sydney, Australia; and 16 grandchildren.

HARVEY BROOKS

1915–2004

Elected in 1968

"For technical contributions to solid-state engineering and nuclear reactors; leadership in national technological decisions."

BY JOHN HOLDREN AND VENKATESH NARAYANAMURTI

HARVEY BROOKS, Gordon McKay Professor of Applied Physics, Emeritus, in the Division of Engineering and Applied Sciences and Benjamin Peirce Professor of Technology and Public Policy in the Kennedy School of Government at Harvard University died of natural causes at his home in Cambridge, Massachusetts, on May 28, 2004. He was 88 years old and is survived by his wife Helen and their four children, Alice, Katharine, Kingsley, and Rosalind, and by two grandchildren.

Harvey was born in Cleveland, Ohio, on August 5, 1915. He graduated from Yale in 1937 in mathematics and studied physics as a Henry Fellow at Clare College, Cambridge, England, and at Harvard, where he got his Ph.D. in 1940 under the direction of Nobel Laureate John Van Vleck. He was a Junior Fellow in the Harvard Society of Fellows from 1940–1942 and a staff member in the Harvard underwater sound laboratory from 1941 to 1945. He joined General Electric in 1946 and served there as Associate Head of the Knolls Atomic Power Laboratory.

In 1950 Harvard established the Division of Engineering and Applied Physics with Van Vleck as its first Dean. Van Vleck in turn invited Harvey back to Harvard as Gordon McKay Professor of Applied Physics in 1950. At Van Vleck's retirement, Brooks succeeded him as Dean in 1957 and served in that post until 1975. During this period, Harvey made several notable contributions to the fundamental theory of semiconductors and the band structure of metals. He founded the *International Journal of Physics and Chemistry of Solids* in 1957 and served as its editor-in-chief for nearly two decades. During his tenure as dean, the Division of Engineering and Applied Physics made many significant faculty appointments in the applied sciences and engineering.

In addition to his work in industrial and academic research, administration, and teaching in science and engineering, Harvey pursued an exceptionally vigorous and productive career of practice and scholarship in science and technology policy. He served as a member of the President's Science Advisory Committee (PSAC) for Presidents Eisenhower, Kennedy, and Johnson and forever after was one of the shrewdest observers and chroniclers of the craft of science advice to the President.

He was one of the principal developers of the concept and methods of technology assessment and could take (although he never claimed) much credit for the establishment of the Congressional Office of Technology Assessment in 1973, which operated with great success for 22 years until its demise in a fit of congressional budget-cutting in 1995.

Harvey was a member of the National Academy of Engineering, the National Academy of Sciences, the Institute of Medicine, and the American Academy of Arts and Sciences, serving the American Academy as President from 1971 to 1976. He participated in and chaired an immense number of committees and panels in the academy complex, where the highlights of his service included instrumental roles in the founding of both the International Institute for Applied Systems Analysis in Vienna and the International Centre of Insect Physiology and Ecology in Nairobi. From 1975 to 1980 he co-chaired the largest and most complex committee effort ever undertaken by the National Research Council, generating the prescient and influential study of America's energy future, *Energy in Transition 1985-2010.*

Harvey's prodigious output of scholarly articles and chapters on science and technology policy, extending over five decades, conveyed a striking proportion of the seminal ideas that shaped this field. He was, for this whole period, the best known, most widely read, most respected scholar in the world in the science and technology policy field—the acknowledged chief architect and dean of the discipline.

Harvey's cross-cutting interests at the intersection of science and technology with policy were abundantly reflected in his trajectory at Harvard. He shepherded the newly formed, IBM-funded Program on Technology and Society from 1968 to 1972, and when he stepped down as dean of engineering and applied science in 1975 he became Benjamin Peirce Professor of Technology and Public Policy in the Kennedy School of Government. The following year he founded the Kennedy School's Program in Science, Technology, and Public Policy in 1976 and directed it until his retirement in 1986. That program still flourishes today, guided in substantial part by Harvey's ideas.

Harvey was the recipient of the Ernest O. Lawrence Award of the Atomic Energy Commission, the Philip Hauge Abelson Prize of the American Association for the Advancement of Science, and many other honors awards including six honorary doctorates.

For all of his erudition, experience, and distinction, though, Harvey was absolutely without arrogance or affectation. He invested tremendous effort in improving the thinking and writing of his students and colleagues (who were often tempted to publish the densely reasoned commentaries he produced on their drafts and throw the drafts away). Harvey cared about science and technology, about policy, about teaching, and about the intersection of these in making the world a better place. He never cared about who got the credit.

A much beloved scientist, engineer, dean, public intellectual, and advisor to three presidents and generations of policy practitioners and scholars, Harvey Brook had a lasting impact. He is sorely missed.

Richard M. Carlson

RICHARD M. CARLSON

1925–2004

Elected in 1990

*"For significant contributions to the application of
composite materials to operational helicopters."*

BY WILLIAM F. BALLHAUS JR.

R ICHARD M. CARLSON, retired chief of the Advanced Systems Research and Analysis Office, U.S. Army Aviation and Missile Command, Ames Research Center, died at his home in Saratoga, California, on July 12, 2004. He was 79 years old.

Dick was born in Preston, Idaho, on February 4, 1925. His grandfather was a doctor who supported his interest in aviation—it was the Lindbergh era—by sending him, at age 10 or 12, on a flight from Salt Lake City, Utah, to Los Angeles to visit relatives. The plane, a Fokker, with wooden wings, was operated by TWA, predecessor of Trans Continental and Western Air. The experience made a big impression on Dick, who enrolled in the University of Washington after high school and participated in the U.S. Navy V-12 Program for reserve officer candidates. He earned a Bachelor of Science degree in aeronautical engineering in 1945.

Following graduation, Dick was commissioned as an ensign in the U.S. Navy; he served as an aircraft maintenance officer for 10 months in the Pacific. One of his assignments, at Pearl Harbor, was disposing of surplus aircraft, many of them brand new, a task he did not relish, especially after he learned that some engines and other parts found their way into the hands of unscrupulous profiteers. After completing his service, Dick re-

41

turned to the University of Washington and, in 1948, was awarded a master's in aeronautical engineering. Afterward, he gained valuable research experience working in the 12-foot pressure tunnel at Ames, then a part of NACA (National Advisory Committee for Aeronautics), predecessor of the National Aeronautics and Space Administration (NASA), at Moffett Field, California. He gained his initial industry experience in fixed-wing engineering at Convair and Douglas Aircraft in Southern California.

In 1950, Dick joined Hiller Aircraft Corporation, Menlo Park, California, as a structures engineer, and, in just three years, he was manager of the Aerostructures Department. He worked closely with the company founder, Stanley Hiller Jr., a pioneer in helicopters (who died on April 20, 2006); at the same time, Dick attended Stanford University, where he earned a Ph.D. in engineering mechanics in 1960.

Dick's involvement with rotary-wing aircraft began while he was at Hiller, where he was instrumental in providing technology and design contributions to a generation of helicopters, particularly the early application of composite structures, and in developing unique aircraft configurations (e.g., tilting thrusters). Aircraft he worked on include the UH-12B, Hiller Hornet (HJ-1), Navy One-Man Helicopter (XROE), H-23D, UH-12E, X-18 Tilt Wing, OH-5A, and XC-142 Tilt Wing.

In 1964, when Hiller was sold, Dick joined Lockheed California Company in Burbank, where, as an engineer in the Advanced Design Division, he was responsible for aerodynamics, dynamics, structures, and weights development analyses for the AH-56 Compound Helicopter (Cheyenne). While continuing to encourage the development and use of composites in vertical take-off and landing (VTOL) aircraft (for example, for the AH-56 propeller, tail rotor, and structural panels), Dick was assigned to support fixed-wing projects related to C-5A wing problems, L-1011 empennage, and development of the supersonic transport (SST) and to serve as a consultant to the Advanced Development Projects activity, also known as the Skunk Works. He worked with many engineering luminaries, such as Kelly Johnson and Jack Real, and was an advisor to Howard Hughes. He directed pre-design activities on the Canadian "Bush Pilot" and Dutch navy's anti-submarine warfare (ASW) versions of the Model 286 helicopter; the U.S. Army Composite Aircraft Program; the U.S. Air Force Combat Aircrew Rescue Aircraft; and the Light Intra-theater Transport.

From 1958 to 1974, while commuting from southern California during his Lockheed years, he was a lecturer at Stanford, where he developed and taught a full helicopter curriculum at the undergraduate and graduate levels, covering VTOL aerodynamics, dynamics, aeroelasticity, and design. He enjoyed his academic experience and was dedicated to it. When he finally relinquished his duties, he enlisted other rotorcraft experts to lecture.

After leaving industry in 1972, Dick went to work for the U.S. Army at Ames. Beginning as chief of the Advanced Systems Research Office, U.S. Army Air Mobility Research and Development Laboratory, he rose to the position of laboratory director in 1976, assuming responsibility for all rotorcraft research activities for the Army and directing programs at Ames, Lewis, and Langley Research Centers and at Fort Eustis. He was the leader for technology development programs for the advanced digital-optical control system, advanced rotorcraft transmission, the Advanced Composite Airframe Program, and the Crew Station Research and Development Facility at Ames. His influential role in the research and development program of the XV-15 tilt-rotor aircraft was integral to the foundation of the V-22 Osprey, the third VTOL aircraft (after the helicopter and jet lift) to attain production status.

Dick retired from the government in 1995 but continued his professional career as an Army emeritus volunteer and as a designated engineering representative (structural) for the Federal Aviation Administration (FAA), a position he held from 1952 until his death. Among his many awards and honors, were a Presidential Rank of Meritorious Executive Award and three Army Meritorious Civilian Service Awards. He was the author of 25 technical papers on circular frames, helicopter rotor-blade structural analysis, and the use of composite material in rotorcraft structures.

He was an honorary fellow of the American Helicopter Society (AHS), which awarded him the Alexander Klemin Award (for notable achievement in the advancement of rotary-wing aeronautics), Paul E. Hauter Award (for significant contributions to the development of VTOL aircraft other than helicopters), and Alexander Nikolsky Lectureship Award (for exceptional achievements in V/STOL aircraft engineering and development). He served with distinction as a member of the original Aircraft Industry Association W-76 Committee on CAA/FAA Structural (Fatigue) Certification of Aircraft, the AHS Technical Council, the NATO-sponsored Advisory Group for Aerospace Research and Development Structures and Materials Panel, and three-terms on the Congressional Advisory Committee on Aeronautics. In addition, he was a member of the U.S. Department of Defense/NASA Aeronautical/Astronautical Coordinating Board Subcommittee for VTOL Aircraft and the NASA Special Advisory Subcommittee on Manned Aeronautical Flight Research.

Dick was elected a member of the National Academy of Engineering in 1990. He was also a fellow of the American Institute for Aeronautics and Astronautics; a fellow of the British Royal Aeronautical Society; a member of the Swedish Society of Aeronautics and Astronautics; the Army Aviation Association of America; and Sigma Xi, the Scientific Research Society. He was a registered professional engineer (mechanical) in California.

Dick was a mentor to a legion of practicing engineers and aviation professionals. He liked to "walk the boards" and meet engineers. He was interested in their work and was always looking for promising young talent. He was also very interested in developments in VTOL overseas and was involved extensively in international research on rotary-wing aircraft conducted jointly by the U.S. Army and France, West Germany, Italy, and Israel.

Dick was widely recognized as a leader in the development of aviation technology. His lifetime of technical achievement spanned some 50 years, and his impact on the aerospace technology field in industry, government, and academia is practically unmatched. His personal contributions to the field of rotorcraft technology greatly advanced and continue to benefit the domestic and international VTOL community. Dick's guidance and direction for technology development in the Army gave the United States a substantial lead in the rotorcraft field.

Dick is survived by his wife Venis Carlson; a son, Richard Carlson Jr., of Santa Cruz, California; two daughters, Judith Anderson of Eureka, California, and Jennifer Peterson of San Jose, California; and two grandchildren.

George Carrier

GEORGE F. CARRIER

1918–2002

Elected in 1974

"For leadership in the development and application of mathematical methods for the solution of engineering and geophysical problems."

BY FREDERICK H. ABERNATHY AND ARTHUR E. BRYSON

GEORGE FRANCIS CARRIER, Emeritus Professor of Applied Mathematics at Harvard University, died of esophageal cancer at the Beth Israel Deaconess Hospital in Boston, Massachusetts, on March 8, 2002.

He was born in Millinocket, Maine, on May 4, 1918. His father was a chemical engineer and manager of the Great Northern paper mill in Millinocket. As a teenager, George was a guide in his beloved Maine woods; he worked summer jobs at the mill without his father's knowledge. Following in his father's footsteps, he attended Cornell University, where he received an M.E. in 1939 and a Ph.D. in 1944, working with Professor Norman Goodier. An accomplished clarinet and ocarina player, he organized a swing band at Cornell; he also was houseman at a local pool hall.

When George contracted tuberculosis and had to spend a year in a sanitarium, he studied books on advanced mathematics. He then returned to graduate school where he taught courses in drawing and mechanisms and the first advanced course in applied mathematics for engineers at Cornell. Two students in the latter course, Julian Cole and Ivar Stackgold, said they first heard about asymptotic perturbations and similarity in that course and believed that experience had shaped their careers (they both became distinguished professors of applied mathematics).

George began his technical career in 1944 as a research engineer working for Professor Howard Emmons on the flow of compressible fluids. George helped design and build a high-speed cascade wind tunnel for the study of jet engine turbines and compressor blades. He was a good experimenter, but his extraordinary mathematical-modeling and analysis capabilities set him apart. When Emmons proposed him for a faculty position but was overruled by the rather formal Professor Richard von Mises who thought George was "too much of a wise guy," he went off to Brown University, where he quickly set the academic world on fire.

Stories of George's exploits at Brown abound. He worked with 14 Ph.D. students and is reported to have given a fall course on complex variables that ended by Thanksgiving. In response to complaints, he gave the entire course again by the end of the term. After only five years, he was promoted to full professor.

In 1952, he was invited back to Harvard (von Mises had retired) as the Gordon McKay Professor of Mechanical Engineering. In 1972, he was appointed the T. Jefferson Coolidge Professor of Applied Mathematics. He had 24 Ph.D. students at Harvard, many of whom went on to pursue distinguished careers in applied mathematics. He became an emeritus professor in 1983 but continued to do research.

George was widely considered one of the best applied mathematicians the United States ever produced. He loved applied problems with complex mathematical models, for which he found ingenious approximations and asymptotic results. He had a quick mind and remarkable physical intuition, which made him a much sought after consultant. He could listen to the description of a problem and come up with the solution or an effective approach to the solution in a few minutes. Almost every summer for 40 years, he was a consultant to either the Los Alamos National Laboratory or the Space and Defense Group at TRW in California; both organizations considered him the ideal consultant. Among his many accomplishments at TRW (according to his former Ph.D. student and co-author Frank Fendell) were: (1) showing how a spinning spacecraft could be controlled with a tuned liquid damper (jointly with John Miles of UCSD);

(2) showing how to contend with vortexing during rapid drainage of a propellant tank; and (3) showing how ceiling sprinkler systems might kill people by keeping smoke near the floor. His good friend and distinguished aerodynamicist, Hans Liepmann of Caltech, described him as "the greatest problem solver ever!"

George's favorite subject was wave propagation, and in the 1960s, he taught a graduate course with this description: "Haphazardly selected superficial (but advanced!) investigations in the propagation of waves in various media." The dean objected, but George persisted, arguing that the description was absolutely accurate. Harry Yeh, a distinguished oceanographer, told of how George stimulated his and others' research on tsunamis by pointing out, among other things, that even the Pacific Ocean is too small for a tsunami to evolve into a soliton (solitary wave) through dispersive effects. George provided analytical solutions with simple geometry for the tsunami run-up problem that could be used to check computer simulations with more complicated geometries. George also showed that the eye-formation is a critical feature of the thermal ocean-air interaction in hurricanes.

George was elected to the National Academy of Sciences in 1967 and to the National Academy of Engineering in 1974. He received the President's Medal of Science in 1990 with the following citation: "For his achievement and leadership in the mathematical modeling of significant problems of engineering science and geophysics and their solution by the application of innovative and powerful analytical techniques." He also received many other awards and honors, including the Dryden Medal of the American Institute of Aeronautics and Astronautics, Fluid Dynamics Prize of the American Physical Society, Timoshenko Medal and Silver Centennial Medal of the American Society of Mechanical Engineers, National Academy of Sciences Award in Applied Mathematics and Numerical Analysis, Von Karman Medal of the American Society of Civil Engineers, Von Karman Prize of the Society of Industrial and Applied Mathematics, and Von Neumann Lectureship of the Mathematics Societies.

He served with distinction on 27 committees and panels of the National Research Council of the National Academies, including the Executive Committee of the Assembly of Mathematical and Physical Sciences, Naval Studies Board, Executive Committee of the Assembly of Engineering, and Advisory Board of the Office of Mathematical Sciences. He was also an associate editor of the *Journal of Fluid Mechanics* and the *Quarterly of Applied Mathematics.*

George authored or co-authored more than 110 technical papers on fluid mechanics, solid mechanics, heat transfer, radiation, stochastic systems, oceanography, and mathematical techniques. In these papers and in his consulting work, he made outstanding contributions to the understanding of tsunamis, hurricanes, wave diffraction, and singular-perturbation theory. He also co-authored three books with Carl E. Pearson, *Functions of a Complex Variable: Theory and Technique, Ordinary Differential Equations,* and *Partial Differential Equations.*

George had boundless energy, a cheerful nature, and was master of his emotions. He knew how to put a fractious committee at ease with a lighthearted remark. He had no appetite for prestige, position, or wealth. He was unfailingly honest, always did what he thought was right, and was quick to admit when he was wrong or made a mistake. He chose to work on technical problems for their usefulness and for the fun he could have. Despite his extraordinary accomplishments, he managed to remain modest and "human."

George was also known for his high jinks. On one occasion, he arranged to have the dean of engineering arrested for a parking violation during the annual Christmas party. On another occasion, during a seminar on guided missiles, he and a prestigious MIT professor "arrested" the speaker and carried him out of the room for revealing "classified information." He was admired as much for his good nature as for his work, and although by his own admission his jokes often deserved only a groan, his humor was affectionate, without malice and contagious.

He loved gardening and building things at his home in Wayland, playing catch with his sons, and dancing with his wife in the living room to a Benny Goodman record. His work habits included watching Perry Mason on TV. A few minutes into the show he would take out a yellow pad of paper and begin writing equations at a furious pace. That way he was able to enjoy Perry

Mason for 40 years, according to his son Mark, because he could never remember "who done it."

His wife Mary (nee Casey) died on July 5, 2006. She and George were a devoted couple for nearly 60 years of married life. They are survived by three sons, Kenneth of Ithaca, New York; Robert of Wayland, Massachusetts; and Mark of Eugene, Oregon; and two grandchildren, McKenzie and Katrina of Eugene, Oregon.

MARVIN CHODOROW

1913–2005

Elected in 1967

"For microwave tube research and development."

BY JAMES F. GIBBONS AND CALVIN F. QUATE

Marvin CHODOROW, Emeritus Professor of applied physics and electrical engineering, who had been at Stanford since 1947, died peacefully at his home on campus on October 17, 2005, of natural causes. He was 92 years old.

Chodorow was born in Buffalo, New York, on July 16, 1913. He received his bachelor's degree in physics from the University of Buffalo in 1934. In 1936, while in graduate school at the Massachusetts Institute of Technology (MIT), he met a social worker, Leah Ruth Turitz, whom he married in 1937. He obtained his doctorate in physics from MIT in 1939. His thesis introduced what is now known as the "Chodorow potential," which is recognized as a seminal solution of Schroedinger's equation for electrons in metals.

Chodorow's early career was spent as a research associate at Pennsylvania State College (1940–1941), physics instructor at the College of the City of New York (1941–1943), and senior project engineer at Sperry Gyroscope Company (1943–1947), where he worked with Sigurd and Russell Varian, Ed Ginzton, Bill Hansen, Myrl Stearns, Don Snow, and Fred Salisbury. In 1948, this small group of engineers and physicists founded Varian Associates in Palo Alto, California.

In 1947, Chodorow left Sperry for Stanford, where he joined the Physics Department as an assistant professor; he became an associate professor in 1950 and a professor in 1954. Beginning in 1954, he also held a professorship in the Department of Electrical Engineering. From 1959 to 1978, he directed the Microwave Laboratory (renamed the Edward L. Ginzton Laboratory in 1976).

From 1962 to 1968, Chodorow was executive head of the Division of Applied Physics at Stanford. In 1968, at the instigation of Chodorow and Hugh Heffner, a separate Department of Applied Physics was created, with Chodorow as department chair; at the same time, he maintained his position as director of the Microwave Laboratory. In 1975, he became the Barbara Kimball Browning Professor of Applied Physics.

Chodorow was a major contributor to the development of the klystron tube, a device that generates and amplifies high-frequency electromagnetic waves. Klystron tubes are essential components for radar systems, particle accelerators, satellite communications systems, and many medical devices. In describing Professor Chodorow's contribution, Wolfgang K.H. Panofsky, Director Emeritus of the Stanford Linear Accelerator Center (SLAC) and a close friend of Chodorow's, said:

> Marvin was the leading figure in transmitting the lore of klystrons [from Sperry] to the Stanford community. In doing this, he deserves most of the credit for the spectacular increase in klystron tube power, which was achieved during the 1940s, from watts to megawatts. He supervised Ph.D. students for about four decades, with most of the students still serving Stanford or the local industrial community. He was a person of enormous kindness, willing to help anyone who approached him for assistance. He is clearly one of the "godfathers" of the whole field of microwave technology at Stanford.

The main focus of Chodorow's research was on the theory and design of microwave and traveling-wave tubes. His work led to the development of a series of devices crucial to the most sophisticated radar systems built in the United States and throughout the world. Later versions were used as power sources for the two-mile-long SLAC atom smasher and for medical accelerators currently used to treat 100,000 cancer patients each day in the United States alone. "The linear accelerator and storage rings that are the heart of SLAC's research still today rely critically on the use of very high power klystrons," said current SLAC Director Jonathan Dorfan. "The legacy remains central to the success of accelerator research worldwide."

Chodorow also worked in microwave acoustics and quantum electronics with professors Calvin Quate and Bertram A. Auld, building an acoustic microscope that uses sound waves (instead of light or electromagnetic waves) to provide images of living cells in action.

Although he continued to conduct research and teach well past the then-mandatory retirement age of 65, Chodorow was feted at a "retirement" party in 1978. On that occasion, Stanford vice president and Provost William F. Miller called him "one of those who brought on the first blooming of the university after World War II [leading] Stanford to national and international standing as one of the great universities of the world."

Professor Edward L. Ginzton, then chairman of the board of Varian Associates, pointed out that the Varian Physics Building and Hansen Laboratories at Stanford had been paid for largely with royalties from klystron. Ginzton added: "Microwaves are indispensable to our society for communications, television, the navigation of ships and aircraft, and for defense. Most of these systems would not be practical today were it not for the contributions [Chodorow] has made."

"Marvin was a visionary," said Theodore H. Geballe, Theodore and Sydney Rosenberg Professor of Applied Physics and Professor of Materials Science and Engineering, Emeritus. "With humor and charm, he left an indelible mark on the university by creating a whole new department.

Chodorow foresaw the arrival of the golden age of solid-state (now condensed-matter) physics and tried to convince his colleagues to make new appointments in the field of solid-state physics. Geballe continued his tribute to Marvin with the following anecdote:

As he told Mac Beasley and me one day while driving to a faculty retreat, he was finally given authorization, but only for one billet. His problem was that
he had two promising candidates and couldn't
choose between them. In order to comply with the
Physics Department's strict limit of only one appointment in physics, he was given permission to make
both appointments, but the second would have to
be in a new division (of applied physics). Marvin did
just that. His two promising candidates were Art
Schawlow, winner of the 1981 Nobel Prize in Physics, and Cal Quate, renowned, among other things,
as a developer of the atomic force microscope. In
1961, Art went to Physics and Cal to the new division.

In succeeding years, Chodorow recruited other luminaries,
including Arthur Bienenstock, Walter Harrison, and Geballe.
"Marvin's intense interest in his colleagues and his undisguised
pleasure in their achievements made the Ginzton Lab a special
place and a strong contributor to Stanford throughout the '60s
and '70s," Geballe recalled. "His colleagues, both in Applied
Physics and beyond, had a deep affection for Marvin for his personal contributions to the lives of every person he touched."

Professor Chodorow remained a consultant to Varian Associates from its founding until his retirement. One of the first companies in what was to become Silicon Valley, Varian specialized
in manufacturing high-powered klystrons that enabled the research and development of linear accelerators around the world
and the successful treatment of cancer through radiation.

Chodorow was a lecturer at the Ecole Normale Superieur in
Paris (1955–1956) and a Fulbright Fellow at Cambridge University (1962–1963). The University of Glasgow gave him an honorary doctor of laws degree in 1972. His other awards include the
W.R.G. Baker Award from the Institute of Radio Engineers (1962)
and the Lamme Medal from IEEE (1982). Chodorow was co-
author, with Charles Susskind, of *Fundamentals of Microwave Electronics*, published in 1964, and about 40 technical articles. He
also held at least a dozen patents.

Chodorow was a fellow of IEEE, the American Physical Society, and the American Academy of Arts and Sciences, and a member of the National Academy of Engineering, National Academy of Sciences, American Association for the Advancement of Science, American Association of University Professors, American Association of Physics Teachers, and Sigma Xi.

Marvin's influence reached far beyond the university. He was an advisor to the Office of Naval Research and a consultant to the U.S. Department of Defense, MIT Lincoln Laboratory, RAND Corporation, and other companies. He was also an active supporter of human rights for exiled Soviet scientists and for arms control.

In addition to his scientific and academic contributions, colleagueship, and many close professional friendships, Marvin had wide-ranging interests. He brought an endless engaged curiosity to colleagues in a large variety of fields and loved to talk about almost anything. He was especially interested in politics, history, and economics, fields in which he had many good friends. He was a self-educated connoisseur of wine and food, an enthusiastic and knowledgeable world traveler, and an accomplished bridge and poker player. He was a passionate follower of Stanford football and basketball. He had a wonderful sense of humor.

He is survived by his wife, Leah Ruth Turitz Chodorow, an active community leader, volunteer, and well-known gracious and beloved hostess; daughters, Nancy Julia Chodorow, a psychoanalyst, of Cambridge, Massachusetts, and Joan Elizabeth Chodorow, an actress, of Venice, California; and two grandchildren, Rachel Chodorow-Reich of Oakland, California, and Gabriel Chodorow-Reich of Washington, D.C.

Note: This tribute borrows heavily from a more detailed article written by Ms. Dawn Levy for the *Stanford Report*. The authors are grateful to her for permission to use substantial portions of her work.

Leland C. Clark, Jr.

LELAND C. CLARK JR.

1918–2005

Elected in 1995

"For inventions and contributions covering biosensors, artificial organs and blood, and their medical applications worldwide."

BY HARDY W. TROLANDER

LELAND C. CLARK JR., retired vice president of Synthetic Blood International, died at the home of his daughter, Rebecca, in Cincinnati, Ohio, on September 25, 2005. He was 86 years old.

Clark was born on December 4, 1918, in Rochester, New York, and attended elementary and secondary schools in Attica, New York. A marginal student, he surprised everyone, including himself, by getting a perfect score in science on what was the first administration of the Regents Exam in New York State. From that moment on, he applied himself fully with a clear view of his goal. After high school, he attended the co-op program at Antioch College, from which he graduated in 1941 with a B.S. in chemistry. This was followed by a National Research Council Fellowship at the University of Rochester, which led to a Ph.D. in biochemistry and physiology, awarded in 1944.

Clark then returned to Antioch to become an assistant professor of biochemistry and chairman of the Biochemistry Department in the Fels Institute on the Antioch campus. In essence, he founded the department and remained its head until 1958. From 1955 to 1958, he was also a senior research associate in pediatrics and surgery at the University of Cincinnati College of Medicine, Cincinnati, Ohio.

In 1958, Clark left Ohio to become associate professor of biochemistry, Department of Surgery, University of Alabama Medical College, in Birmingham, Alabama. In 1961, he became professor of biochemistry, and he remained there until 1968. He then returned to Ohio and was named professor of research pediatrics at the Children's Hospital Research Foundation in Cincinnati, a position he held until 1991. Clark was named University Distinguished Service Professor of the University of Cincinnati in 1984 and research professor of biological sciences at Antioch in 1991.

In 1992, Clark was a founder of Synthetic Blood International Inc., of San Diego, California, whose primary mission was to develop his earlier invention of a fluorocarbon-based artificial blood, safe for human use. As the company's vice president of research and development, he conducted and oversaw the research in laboratories on the Antioch campus. One of Clark's early contributions was a large-capacity, all-glass bubble-defoam oxygenator and pump, one of the earliest successful heart-lung machines.

Perhaps his major contribution was the invention of the Clark membrane oxygen electrode. The device was first reported in a landmark paper delivered on April 15, 1956, at a meeting of the American Society for Artificial Organs during the annual meetings of the Federated Societies for Experimental Biology. The importance of this invention was immediately recognized, and when the paper was published, it became one of the most often cited papers in the life sciences. The electrode, in its original form, has been in use throughout the world in a broad range of applications requiring precision measurement—for water quality, many medical and pharmacological situations, and food production.

Clark later envisioned a new form of polarographic sensor that used an enzymatic reaction to produce a polarographically measurable reaction product from an otherwise polarogaphically insensitive material. The first manifestation of this sensor was in the form of an electrode capable of instantaneous, very accurate measurement of glucose in human blood. Based on Clark's electrode, a variety of enzyme electrodes were developed for a multiplicity of medical, food processing, and environmental measurements.

Clearly, Clark's vivid imagination and his ability to combine chemical, electrical, and mechanical principles led to the development of a wide range of devices, from large-scale heart-lung machines for human open-heart surgery to microelectrodes for making measurements within the human brain. His creative range was truly unique.

Clark was elected to membership in the National Academy of Engineering (NAE) in 1995 and was awarded the NAE Fritz J. and Dolores H. Russ Prize in 2005. His citation reads "For bioengineering membrane-based sensors in medical, food, and environmental applications."

Clark's many awards and honors include the NIH Research Career Award (1962); Distinguished Lecturer Award, American College of Chest Physicians (1975); Honorary Doctor of Science, University of Rochester School of Medicine and Dentistry (1984); Horace Mann Award for Service to Humanity, Antioch College (1984); Heyrovsky Award in Recognition of the Invention of the Membrane-Covered Polarographic Oxygen Electrode (1985); American Association for Clinical Chemistry Award for Outstanding Contributions to Clinical Chemistry (1989); American Heart Association Samuel Kaplan Visionary Award (1991); enshrinement into the Engineering and Science Hall of Fame (1991); Pharmacia Biosensor's Sensational Contributions to the Advancement of Biosensor Technology Award (1992); and the Daniel Drake Award for Outstanding Achievements in Research, University of Cincinnati College of Medicine (1993).

In the 1970s, Lee Clark invited Fred Hoover (a successful inventor and NAE member) and me to his house for a demonstration. With a couple of wires, a meter and a battery at hand, Lee filled a glass with water and some sugar, connected everything up, and placed the wires in the liquid. He then added some glucose oxidase and immediately the meter indicated that a current was flowing between the two wires. I treasure the memory of that demonstration. It was typical Lee Clark, essentially simple yet conveying a powerful message—the first ever bioelectrode was clearly in the offing.

Dr. Clark was preceded in death in 1988 by his wife, Eleanor, who assisted him in his work throughout his career. Though not originally trained as a scientist, she was a very bright woman who learned not only the basic science, but also the intricacies of writing grant and patent applications.

He is survived by his daughter, Susan Clark Wooley, and granddaughter, Laura Wooley; daughter, Joan Tornow, son-in-law, John Tornow, and grandsons, Nick and Alex Tornow; daughter, Linda Noyes, son-in-law, Dave Noyes, and grandson, David Friend; daughter, Becky Clark, and grandson, Chris Gerrard; and younger brother, Woodums Clark. The Tornows live in Takoma, Washington, and the Wooleys, Noyes, and Clarks live in Cincinati, Ohio.

Franklin S. Cooper

FRANKLIN S. COOPER

1908–1999

Elected in 1976

"For originality in speech instrumentation and its application to human communication, including aids for the handicapped."

BY KENNETH N. STEVENS

FRANKLIN S. COOPER, pioneer and educator in the field of speech science, died on February 20, 1999, at the age of 90 in Palo Alto, California. He was one of the founders, and for most of his career president or research director, of Haskins Laboratories.

Born on April 29, 1908, in Robinson, Illinois, Frank grew up with his mother and grandparents on his grandfather's farm in central Illinois. He attended a rural elementary school and supplemented his education by reading the books in his grandfather's library, including an old physics textbook. In high school, he pursued his early interest in physics and also became interested in electrical engineering. Frank won the competitive examination in his county, which earned him a scholarship to the University of Illinois worth $210 for four years. For financial reasons, however, he postponed his entry to the university and spent a year teaching in a one-room elementary school with just a few students. He found dealing with discipline problems and lukewarm interest from his students very frustrating.

Frank entered the University of Illinois in 1927 and completed a B.S. degree in engineering physics in 1931. He remained at the university until 1934 with a teaching fellowship and doing some graduate research in the Physics Department. From 1934 to 1936, he worked at Massachusetts Institute of Technology

(MIT) on a project setting up a newly designed vacuum spectrograph (with P.G. Kruger) and another project in medical radiology (with R. Evans). In 1935, he got a summer job at the General Electric (GE) Research Laboratories in Schenectady, New York. That summer he also spent some weekends back in Cambridge finishing the Evans project.

That same summer, he met Caryl Haskins and became interested in a project of Caryl's on the biological effects of fast electrons, as an alternative to x-ray radiation. This project became the basis for Frank's doctoral thesis at MIT. At about this time, Caryl Haskins and Frank formed Haskins Laboratories, a private, not-for-profit research group that would conduct research in biophysics. In the early days, Haskins Laboratories was located primarily at Union College in Schenectady, but it also had some involvement with Harvard and MIT. Frank's work at the laboratories was focused on radiation therapy.

In 1935, Frank married Frances Edith Clem, whom he had known as a girl some years earlier; their relationship had been rekindled when Edith came for a visit to Schenectady. Edith died in 1991.

After completing his doctorate in 1936, Frank was recruited as a full-time scientist/engineer at GE Research Laboratories, where he worked on high-voltage insulation, a project that involved testing various chemical compounds to develop an improved compressed-gas insulator. At the same time, he continued to pursue his interest in nuclear methods for radiation therapy at Haskins Laboratories and published several papers on this topic.

During World War II, from 1941 to 1946, Frank served as a liaison officer and senior liaison officer in the Office of Scientific Research and Development (OSRD). His interest in speech began near the end of World War II, when OSRD requested that Haskins Laboratories coordinate a program for the development of prosthetic devices, including a reading machine, for blinded veterans. This project sparked Frank's interest in the process of human speech communication—an interest that was to be the focus of his research for the rest of his life.

Early in his work on speech communication, Frank realized

that human speech was not just a concatenation of sounds, one for each phoneme. Experiments that he and his colleagues carried out in the 1950s and 1960s showed that the acoustic manifestation of a phoneme was dependent on the context in which the phoneme occurred. For example, the same sound could be interpreted as one consonant when followed by one vowel and another consonant when followed by a different vowel.

Frank's background as a physicist and engineer was evident in the device he developed for synthesizing speech-like sounds, called the pattern playback. He understood that research on speech was interdisciplinary, and he recruited scientists from a variety of fields to work at Haskins Laboratories. Under Frank's guidance, researchers used the pattern playback to study how human listeners extract cues from speech waves and organize them into linguistic units. Several classic papers emerged from Frank's collaboration with Pierre Delattre, a linguist at the University of Colorado, and Alvin Liberman, an experimental psychologist at the University of Connecticut.

These early experiments were the basis for a variety of speech-perception studies at research laboratories around the world. They also led to the development of rules for controlling a speech synthesizer from a phonetic transcription; thus, the original goal of a reading machine for the blind became a reality. Frank was a leader in the development of the reading machine, and his early work catalyzed similar research at several other laboratories.

This seminal research on speech perception was carried out by a small group of researchers at Haskins Laboratories, which was then located in midtown Manhattan. In the summer of 1970, the laboratories moved to New Haven, Connecticut, where a formal connection with Yale University was established. For Frank, this was an important linkage that led to closer interaction with students, particularly in linguistics and psychology, from both Yale and the University of Connecticut.

At about the time of the move to New Haven, Frank began to conduct research on speech production, which brought him closer to understanding the linguistic units that underlie speech sounds. Researchers under his direction used cineradiography, electromyography, and other techniques to examine the movement of articulators, including the larynx. Haskins Laboratories attracted scientists from around the world to this research. For example, Frank arranged for a series of young Japanese otolaryngologists to work with staff and students on projects using electromyography and other techniques to understand how the muscles of the larynx and other articulators are coordinated during speech production. Over the years, Haskins Laboratories produced a cohort of researchers who have contributed to our understanding of the production, acoustics, and perception of speech.

Drawing on his background in physics and engineering, combined with his insights into linguistics, psychology, and physiology, Frank developed a unique research style. He was instrumental in bringing the interdisciplinary study of speech perception and production into the domain of quantitative science. As president and research director of Haskins Laboratories for many years, his gentle encouragement engendered enthusiasm for research and led to direct associations with many academic institutions in the Northeast.

In addition to his administrative and research activities, Frank served on a number of academic and scientific boards and committees, including the National Advisory Neurological and Communicative Disorders and Stroke Council, an advisory panel on the White House tapes, and for a number of years, the visiting committee of the Department of Linguistics of MIT. He was also an adjunct professor of phonetics at Columbia University.

He is survived by two sons, Alan of Palo Alto, California, and Craig of Nellysford, Virginia, four grandchildren, and five great grandchildren.

Leo S. Crane

L. STANLEY CRANE

1915–2003

Elected in 1978

"For pioneering the application of modern and creative engineering concepts to more productive railroad equipment and operations."

BY WILLIAM J. HARRIS JR.

STAN CRANE was born in Cincinnati, Ohio, on September 7, 1915. He died in a hospice in Boynton, Florida, on July 15, 2003.

Stan attended the Engineering School of George Washington University in Washington, D.C., and earned the degree of Bachelor of Science in Engineering in 1938. While he was still an undergraduate, he was elected to Tau Beta Pi, the engineering honorary fraternity.

In 1934, he began work as a laboratory assistant at Southern Railroad, where he continued working after graduation. At that time, the railroad industry was facing serious financial problems. The economy was in a depression, and, as highways and trucks were improved, railroads were facing growing competition for transportation services. When Stan Crane joined Southern Railroad, he believed they could beat the competition by using diesel locomotives, which could pull longer and heavier trains. As a result of Stan's hard work and leadership, Southern was the first Class I railroad to achieve complete conversion to diesel power. Engineers working for Southern Railroad raced to replace cars that could carry 40 tons of cargo with cars that could carry 100 tons of freight. Diesel locomotives pulling trains with 100 of these 100-ton cars dramatically improved transportation services.

Until that time, railroad track had been assembled by bolting together 39-foot long sections of rail. These steel track sections were laid on cross ties of wood or concrete and held down on the cross ties by spikes or other fasteners. Then crushed rock or other materials were laid on the ground to ensure good drainage and good support for the crossties and rail. With the advent of longer and heavier trains, it was necessary to increase the strength and stability of track. This was accomplished by welding many sections of rail together and fastening the welded sections to the cross ties. The longer sections of rail not only provided more stability, but also required less maintenance. Southern Railroad was a pioneer in the introduction of welded rail and a significant contributor to the development of track-laying and maintenance technology. The operation of long, heavy trains also necessitated that locomotive engineers be retrained. Southern Railroad developed training programs based on research and operations experience. As Stan's career developed, all of these issues fell within the limits of his responsibility. He was promoted to assistant chief mechanical officer, then to vice president of engineering and research, then to executive vice president of operations.

Nothing in Stan's education signaled his unique leadership qualities, but from the beginning, he displayed a capacity to identify the nature of problems and the resources necessary to address them. Exchanges between Stan Crane and his senior staff were more like the sharing of views in an extended family than typical boss/employee exchanges. Stan had the presence of a father figure and the ability to infuse the discussion with the excitement of a doctoral examination. He knew how to generate excitement for solving the problems of the hour.

Stan's progression from laboratory assistant was duly noted by other companies faced with making the same improvements, and the Pennsylvania Railroad recruited Stan Crane to serve as director of industrial engineering. After just two years, however, Southern Railroad won him back, and Stan renewed his climb to the top of the company. He was soon named president and chief executive officer (CEO).

Southern had an inflexible requirement for retirement at age 65. At that time, Stan left to become chairman and CEO of

Conrail, a group of railroads in the Northeast that had gone into bankruptcy, had been reassembled as a single operating property, and were facing significant economic losses. Stan Crane was ideally suited to rescuing them. Not only was he highly regarded by executives in the industry, but he also had a management style that generated dedication and enthusiasm for achieving common objectives. His achievements at Conrail were extraordinary. In a single year, he transformed a railroad that was losing hundreds of millions of dollars per year into a profitable venture. The following year, the company earned even more, despite very difficult times.

When he became head of Conrail, all of the company's stock was owned by the U.S. Department of Transportation, but Stan was convinced that Conrail should be operated as a private company. Ultimately, Conrail was divided into two separate elements, one that merged with Norfolk Southern Railroad and one that merged with Seaboard Coastline Railroad. The Conrail segments of both continue to make significant traffic and economic contributions to their parent companies.

Throughout his decades of accomplishment, Stan was a strong supporter of the research program of the Association of American Railroads (AAR), which had a facility in Chicago where new components were tested to ensure that they met performance requirements. To expand the program, he worked cooperatively with the Federal Railroad Administration (FRA) to establish a research facility in Pueblo, Colorado, dedicated to improving the efficiency and safety of railroad operations in general. Stan was deeply involved in efforts to mark all freight cars with machine-readable identifiers and develop a reliable way of communicating the order of cars as they approached the switching yard so they could be efficiently sorted and reassembled in trains moving toward their proper destinations.

In 1970, when FRA decided to close down the Pueblo facility, Stan Crane was instrumental in persuading FRA to keep it open. Eventually, all AAR research was transferred to Pueblo, which still uses test tracks and test equipment to improve the safety and efficiency of rail transportation.

Stan was the recipient of many awards in recognition of his

contributions to the railroad industry: *Modern Railroads* named him Railroad Man of the Year in 1983 and 1987; *Financial World* awarded him the Silver Award of CEO of the Decade and named him Chief Railroad Executive of the Year; the Pennsylvania Chamber of Business and Industry named him Business Leader of the Year in 1987; the Women's Transport Seminar gave him the Philadelphia Award; the Cooperstown Conference gave him the Right Hand Man Award; Syracuse University awarded him the Salzberg Memorial Medallion; *Industry Week* gave him the Excellence in Management Award; the National Defense Transportation Association gave him an award for excellence; the St. Louis Railway Club named him Man of the Year; the Transportation Association of America gave him the Seley Award; and the American Society of Traffic and Transportation honored him with the Joseph C. Scheleer Award. Stan was elected to the National Academy of Engineering in 1978.

William B. Davenport, Jr.

WILBUR B. DAVENPORT JR.

1920–2003

Elected in 1975

"For Contributions to communications engineering and education and for leadership in continuing engineering education."

BY LEO L. BERANEK

WILBUR B. DAVENPORT, Professor Emeritus of Communication Science and Engineering at the Massachusetts Institute of Technology (MIT), died on August 28, 2003. He was born in Philadelphia, Pennsylvania, on July 27, 1920.

Wilbur received the degree of Bachelor of Electrical Engineering in 1941 from the Alabama Polytechnic Institute, Auburn, Alabama. He matriculated that fall at MIT and received the Master of Science degree in 1943. From 1943 to 1946, he was ensign and lieutenant junior grade in the U.S. Naval Reserve. When he completed his active military service, he returned to MIT and, in 1950, received the Doctor of Science degree. His first published paper, "Statistical Errors in Measurements on Random Time Functions," co-authored by R.A. Johnson and D. Middleton, appeared in the *Journal of Applied Physics* in April 1952. The paper was the first in a series on statistical theory.

Wilbur was made an assistant professor of electrical engineering in 1949, when Harold Hazen was chairman of the department. When the Lincoln Laboratory was founded in 1951, Wilbur was invited to be one of its first members as a group leader. In 1955, he was named associate division head, and two years later he became division head, a title he held for three years.

In 1960, Gordon Brown, head of the Department of Electrical Engineering, asked Wilbur to become a professor of electrical engineering. In 1961, he appointed Wilbur associate head of

77

the Research Laboratory for Electronics (RLE), a position he held for two years. At RLE, while working on a project to make radio communications secure, Wilbur was involved in the development of "spread-spectrum" techniques, which were highly classified at the time but much later became common in cordless telephones. His principal publication during that period was "An Experimental Study of Speech-Wave Probability Distributions" in the *Journal of the Acoustical Society of America*. In 1963, he returned to Lincoln Laboratory as assistant director to supervise the work of a half dozen graduate students, including two military officers, on spread-spectrum techniques, called, at MIT, NOMAC (noise modulation and correlation).

In 1971, Wilbur was appointed associate head of the Department of Electrical Engineering and the next year, director of the Center for Advanced Engineering Study, a position he held until 1974. At the time, the faculty was trying to determine which courses should be offered in computer hardware and software, which were burgeoning new technologies. Some members of the department were already involved in Project MAC; several project leaders at Lincoln Laboratory had helped develop the TX(0) computer and then left to form the Digital Equipment Corporation; another group had left to join Bolt Beranek and Newman Inc., which developed and built the beginnings of the Internet. Faculty members were also in constant communication with engineers at IBM Corporation.

As the number of students and faculty in the department increased, largely because of computers, some faculty members recommended that computer sciences be made a separate department. The situation was suddenly complicated when Louis Smullin announced that he would step down as head of the Department of Electrical Engineering in June 1974, and a search committee was established to seek a replacement. During its interviews and studies of the candidates, the committee concluded that the person selected had to be acceptable to both computer scientists and electrical engineers. The dean of engineering and MIT officers decided that Wilbur was the most qualified and acceptable to the department faculty as a whole, and he was appointed chairman in 1974.

In an interview with the *MIT TECH* newspaper, Wilbur described his job: "The role of a department head is to work with the faculty to develop a curriculum that meets the needs of the graduating students. He must get along with people who are his intellectual peers and with people who are of different ages. He must be concerned with the teaching of the human side of engineering, the world in which the engineer lives. Implementing all aspects of engineering education is difficult because the department's objectives must be met without costing itself out of existence."

The debate about making computer sciences a separate department continued, however. Opponents argued that a new department would create new walls and would be a bad move. Supporters contended that it was irrational that students in computer science be required to take the core courses of electrical engineering. Wilbur felt that curriculum reform, rather than two departments, was the way to go. A consensus was reached that more integration of the diverse disciplines in electrical engineering would be a healthier course of action. To reflect that consensus, the department was renamed the Department of Electrical Engineering and Computer Science. Wilbur remained department head for four years but finally resigned, "Over the last few years I have begun to feel ground down by all the problems. Happily there are enough competent people around that I can relax knowing that the department will be in good hands." He remained on the faculty as a professor.

Wilbur served on a number of national committees. He was consultant to the Office of the Special Assistant to the President for Science and Technology from 1961 to 1973, a member of the Carnegie Commission on the Future of Public Broadcasting from 1977 to 1979, and a member of the Air Force Scientific Advisory Board from 1976 to 1979. He was also a director of the GenRad Corporation from 1974 to 1982.

Among his publications were two books that received international attention, *An Introduction to the Theory of Random Signals and Noise,* with W.L. Root (McGraw-Hill, 1958, republished, 1987), and *Probability and Random Processes* (McGraw-Hill, 1970, reissued 1987).

In 1982, Wilbur and his wife, Joan, moved to Honolulu, where he became visiting professor of electrical engineering at the University of Hawaii at Manoa; he remained in that position until 1987, although he returned to Hawaii to teach in spring terms from 1989 through 1993. From 1984 to 1987, he was a member of the Executive Committee, Pacific International Center for High Technology Research, in Honolulu.

In 1987, the Davenports returned to the mainland and settled in Sunriver, Oregon, where Wilbur was an active member of the Public Works Committee of the Sunriver Owners Association. From 1988 to 1990, he was a member of the Industrial Advisory Committee of the Department of Applied Physics and Electrical Engineering, Oregon Graduate Center, in Beaverton, Oregon. From 1994 to 1995, he was a trustee of the Sunriver Preparatory School. During this time, he and his wife also traveled extensively throughout Europe, Canada, and the United States, including Alaska. As a hobby, he enjoyed doing lapidary work along with a number of his friends.

Wilbur received numerous honors, including fellowship or membership in the Institute of Electrical and Electronics Engineers (IEEE) (1958), National Academy of Engineering (1975), American Academy of Arts and Sciences (1977), and American Association for the Advancement of Science (1979). He received a Certificate of Commendation from the U.S. Navy in 1960 and the Pioneer Award of the IEEE Aerospace and Electronic Systems Society in 1981.

Wilbur was an engineer of the highest capabilities and integrity who always gave of himself wholeheartedly. He inspired confidence in his peers and earned their highest respect. The Davenports spent many happy hours at their cabin on Lake Winnipesaukee in New Hampshire with family and friends swimming, waterskiing, sailing or hiking in the nearby mountains. He is survived by his wife, Joan, now living in Medford, Oregon; a son, Mark, of Turlock, California; and a daughter, Sally Clevenger, of Bellbrook, Ohio.

W. KENNETH DAVIS

1918–2005

Elected in 1970

*"For contributions to the development of
nuclear power technology and its industrial application."*

BY HAROLD K. FORSEN AND WILLIAM L. FRIEND

W. KENNETH (Ken) DAVIS, a leader of the World Energy Council, former vice president of the National Academy of Engineering, former Deputy Secretary of Energy, and Bechtel Corporation executive, and one of the nation's most distinguished chemical engineers, died on July 29, 2005, at the age of 87 at his home in San Rafael, California.

Ken was born in Seattle, Washington, but moved when he was young to the San Francisco Bay Area. He began his education at the University of California, Berkeley, where he studied chemistry before transferring to Massachusetts Institute of Technology (MIT) to become a chemical engineer. He received his B.S. and M.S. from MIT in chemical engineering in 1940 and 1942, respectively.

In 1947, after working for several years in the research department of what is now the Chevron Oil Company doing process design and the development of synthetic rubber, he joined Ford, Bacon & Davis (FB&D) in Chicago, a company that had won the contract to build the nation's first nuclear engineering laboratory at Argonne, Illinois. Thus began Ken's career in the newly emerging field of nuclear energy.

Ken left FB&D in 1949 to begin an academic career at the University of California, Los Angeles (UCLA). Encouraged by Llewellyn Boelter, now dean at UCLA, who was a close professional friend whom he met at Berkeley, Ken took a position at

UCLA in the engineering school, with the challenge that he develop courses in nuclear engineering. Early in his career at UCLA, he was asked by his former associates at Chevron to rejoin them to work on a large radiation project for the Atomic Energy Commission (AEC), so he took a one-year leave of absence. Ken's work on the classified accelerator project, which later became the Lawrence Livermore National Laboratory, stretched his leave from the university to three years. Upon his return to UCLA, he was promoted to full professor.

In 1954, Ken was recruited to join the AEC, which was charged with managing the development of the nuclear navy and civilian nuclear power. He began as assistant director and then, for four years, director of the Reactor Development Division. Civilian nuclear power was the driving force in the development of the division, and Ken Davis was its champion.

Ken became a corporate vice president at Bechtel Corporation in 1958 and was instrumental in developing the company's role in the rapidly emerging civilian nuclear industry. He was the first manager of Bechtel's Scientific Development Division, which was organized to provide the company with capabilities in applied research, development, and advanced engineering and the application of these skills, particularly in the electric power sector. By this time, Ken was known as "Mr. Nuclear"—one of the world's truly outstanding engineers. He retired from Bechtel in 1981 to become Deputy Secretary of Energy during the Reagan administration.

In 1970, Ken was elected to the National Academy of Engineering; he served on the NAE Council from 1972 through 1981, the last three years as vice president of the organization. During those years, he was also president of the American Institute of Chemical Engineers (1981), fellow and director of the American Nuclear Society, chair and president of the Atomic Industrial Forum and Atlantic Council of the United States. He then moved to the world stage as vice chair of the World Energy Council and chair of the U.S. Committee for the World Energy Council. Ken's remarkable achievements were essential to the development of peaceful uses for nuclear energy. On the less technical side, Ken was a member of the Commonwealth Club of San

Francisco and the Cosmos Club in Washington, D.C., and a Life Member of the Sierra Club.

Ken's many awards over the years included the Arthur S. Flemming Award (1956); AIChE Professional Progress Award (1958), Robert E. Wilson Award (1969), and Founders Award (1983); the American Nuclear Society's Walter H. Zinn Award (1983) and Henry DeWolf Smyth Nuclear Statesman Award (1993); the Atomic Industrial Forum Oliver Townsend Award (1981); and the Secretary of Energy's Gold Medal (1983). Ken was also a participant in many National Research Council studies and a member of many advisory boards during several federal administrations.

An avid and excellent skier and expert rock climber, Ken was one of a group of three climbers to make the first ascent of the Royal Arches route at Yosemite's North Dome (1936). Later in his life, he went on two high treks in the Himalayas.

Ken's wife, the former Margaret Bean, an accomplished pianist and composer, died in 1998 after 57 years of marriage. The couple had three children and five grandchildren.

Ken Davis was surely one of the "fathers" of the nuclear age and an influential leader, technologist, and statesman. Today, nuclear energy generates about one-fifth of the nation's electricity, and considering the effects and consequences of global warming, we are likely to become increasingly dependent on safe, reliable nuclear power. In large measure, we will have Ken Davis to thank for it!

Ken is survived by his second wife, Ann Nilsson Davis of San Rafael; a brother, Keith Davis of Grand Lake, Colorado; two daughters, Kerry Davis of Kentfield and Gail Greene of Novato; a son, Warren Davis of Lafayette; and five grandchildren.

ACKNOWLEDGMENTS
Some material was taken from an obituary in the *San Francisco Chronicle* on August 15, 2006, by John Wildermuth; an interview with Mr. Davis by Professor William Van Vorst, UCLA (2005); and Mr. Davis' biography provided to the National Academy of Engineering.

LESLIE C. DIRKS

1936–2001

Elected in 1980

*"For contributions to technology development of importance
to the national security of the United States."*

BY HANS MARK

I HAD THE PLEASURE AND privilege of working for a few years with Leslie Dirks, one of the most talented and accomplished scientists and engineers on the payroll of the U.S. government. I first met him in 1977 and worked closely with him for the next three years.

Les was born in 1936 in Minnesota, so we were almost contemporaries—I was older by seven years. We had in common that we were both graduates of Massachusetts Institute of Technology, which was a strong bond. He went on to be a Rhodes Scholar at Oxford University and to teach physics for a year at Phillips Academy. In 1961, he joined the Central Intelligence Agency (CIA), where he was quickly recognized as an extraordinary scientist-engineer and a talented leader. By the time I met him in the spring of 1977, Les was deputy director of science and technology. In that capacity, he headed one of the major units of the National Reconnaissance Office, which I headed at the time. We became very close friends in short order, and my wife and I frequently went out with the Dirks family. I often felt like Les' older brother.

Les Dirks had a fine mind; I know only two or three people who were his equal. His highly original technical innovations to our intelligence-gathering satellites contributed substantially to our national security. He was also a superb technical manager who knew how to inspire people to do their best. In spite of the highly classified nature of his work, he received a good deal of public recognition for his many accomplishments. In 1979, President Carter awarded him the National Security Medal, and, in 1980, at the age of 44, he was elected to the National Academy of Engineering.

What I remember most fondly about Les were the dinners his wife Eleanor prepared for us at his house and playing "Space Cadet" with the Dirks' children. Les and his wife raised three wonderful children, Anthony, Jason, and Elizabeth. Tragically, Eleanor lost her gallant battle with cancer in 1987.

In 1990, Les married Janet Church, who survives him. Janet recalls that he enjoyed having his children visit, and she remembers particularly his happiness in 1991 when his son Anthony and his wife Ann brought their one-month old son, his first grandchild to visit. Les was an avid reader, enjoyed all kinds of music, and was a frequent bicyclist and hiker.

Les retired from the CIA in 1980 and moved to California to join the Hughes Aircraft Communications Satellite Organization, headed at the time by his distinguished predecessor in the CIA, Dr. Albert C. Wheelon. In 1991, the CIA named one of its buildings the Dirks-Duckett Wing after Les and another of his predecessors, Carl Duckett. Les died on August 7, 2001. I miss him, and I mourn him.

HARRY GEORGE DRICKAMER

1918–2002

Elected in 1979

"For contributions in the development of high pressure techniques, and in the elucidation of new properties of solids, and of diffusion in liquids."

BY THOMAS J. HANRATTY

HARRY G. DRICKAMER played a unique role among chemical engineering educators by championing the role of modern chemistry and physics in engineering research. For example, long before quantum chemistry and physics gained their current acceptance in the graduate chemical engineering curricula, Drickamer insisted that his students master those disciplines at a level of proficiency equal to that of their peers in the basic sciences. In so doing, he helped produce an outstanding cadre of scholars who have gone on to universities and research laboratories to demonstrate the modern chemical engineering approach to the understanding and design of new materials. (From the presentation of the John Scott Award at the 1985 meeting of the Division of Chemical Physics of the American Chemical Society.)

During his long tenure at the University of Illinois (1946–2002), Harry Drickamer dominated the field of high-pressure research, and its present status in chemistry, physics, geology, and materials science is due largely to his efforts and those of his students. Their adaptation of virtually every kind of spectroscopy to high-pressure studies led to many discoveries and to the invention of pressure-tuning spectroscopy.

Harry Drickamer was born Harold George Wiedenthal to Louise and Harold Wiedenthal in Cleveland, Ohio. His father died when he was very young, and after his mother remarried, Harry's stepfather, George Drickamer, adopted him. Harry was active in sports and played in the farm system of the Cleveland Indians. He attended Vanderbilt University on a football scholarship, transferred to Indiana University, and, a short time later, to the University of Michigan, where he was elected president of his class in the Engineering College. He received B.S. and M.S. degrees in 1941 and 1942.

In 1942, he took a position at the Pan American Refinery in Texas City, Texas, where, in his "spare time," he carried out measurements on vapor-liquid equilibrium. The University of Michigan agreed to accept these studies and the results from a plant test on an extractive distillation tower (the first of its kind in the world) as a Ph.D. thesis. His publications on tray efficiency received considerable attention. With Harry Hummel, a colleague at Pan American, he published "Application of Vapor-Liquid Equilibria to an Analysis of a Commercial Unit for Toluene Purification," which was recognized with the Colburn Award of the American Institute of Chemical Engineers in 1947.

Harry returned to the University of Michigan in February 1946 to complete course work requirements for the Ph.D. degree. His growing interest in scientific issues in engineering was a factor in his accepting a position later that year at the University of Illinois as an assistant professor in the chemical engineering curriculum, which was then part of the Chemistry Department. Of the 105 doctoral theses he directed, 86 were on chemical engineering. His research is described in 478 publications.

Harry Drickamer recognized that the most interesting properties of matter are determined by the outer shell electrons of atoms ("valence" electrons), which form the bonds that hold atoms together in molecules and materials. They also give rise to a material's optical (e.g., color, phosphorescence, etc.), electrical, and magnetic properties. He understood that if one changed the distance between atoms by applying external pressure, interactions between the valence electrons of the constituent atoms in a molecule must change and that this would be manifested by alterations in physical and chemical properties.

He discovered that the application of pressure causes a change of insulators into conductors for six elements (e.g., iodine) and more than 30 compounds. He observed paramagnetic-to-diamagnetic and ferromagnetic-to-paramagnetic transitions in ferrous compounds and in iron. He discovered that radicals are formed in many electron donor-acceptor complexes (under pressure) and found that these radicals react to form new chemical bonds. He showed how the conduction band of metals (e.g., cesium, rubidium, and potassium) and of rare earth atoms exhibit a different character at high pressure; metals like calcium, strontium, and ytterbium become semiconductors. Starting in the 1980s, Harry's research expanded into studies of protein chemistry, the efficiency of luminescent devices, and organic photochemistry. Together with Professor Gregorio Weber, he demonstrated that one can reversibly change protein conformation and modify enzymatic activity, thus opening a new approach to protein folding.

In the process of making these discoveries, Harry provided tests of a number of important theories, including Bethe's ligand field theory, Van Vleck's theory of the high-spin to low-spin transition, the Förster-Dexter theory of energy transfer in phosphors, Mulliken's theory of electron-donor complexes, the Marcus theory of electron-transfer reactions, and the rigid-band model for deformation-potential analysis in semiconductors. Insights from these research studies have contributed to advances in the engineering of materials, such as lasers, phosphors, semiconductors, polymers, catalysts, and proteins. Harry's work led to discoveries of the first organic superconductor and of the chemical reactivity of charge-transfer complexes (the basis for the recognition of new types of bonds between molecules). He provided a new understanding of metallic hydrogen and the interior of the Jovian planets. His very early work on diffusion in liquids had an impact on the design of a thermal diffusion process that was used to separate hydrogen isotopes.

Harry Drickamer's contributions were recognized by his peers in his election to the National Academy of Engineering, National Academy of Sciences, American Academy of Arts and Sciences, and American Philosophical Society. He received the Robert A. Welch Prize from the Welch Foundation in 1987 and the National Medal of Science in 1989. He was awarded a Doctor of Chemical Science *honoris causa* from the Russian Academy of Sciences in 1994.

The breadth of Harry's research is reflected in the variety of honors he received: the Colburn (1947), William H. Walker (1972), and Alpha Chi Sigma (1967) research awards, and the Warren K. Lewis Teaching Award of the American Institute of Chemical Engineers (1986); the Bendix Research Prize of the American Society of Engineering Education (1968); the Ipatieff Prize (1956), the Irving Langmuir Award in Chemical Physics (1974), and the Peter Debye Award in Physical Chemistry (1987) from the American Chemical Society; the Buckley Solid State Physics Award of the American Physical Society (1967); the inaugural P.W. Bridgman Award of the International Association for the Advancement of High Pressure Science and Technology (1977); the Chemical Pioneers Award (1983) and the Gold Medal Award (1996) from the American Institute of Chemists; the Michelson-Morley Award of Case-Western Reserve University (1978); the John Scott Award for "Ingenious Inventions" from the city of Philadelphia (1984); the Elliot Cresson Medal from the Franklin Institute of Philadelphia (1988); Awards for Outstanding Materials Chemistry (1985) and for Outstanding Sustained Research (1989) from the U.S. Department of Energy; the Alexander van Humboldt Award from the Federal Republic of Germany (1986); and the Distinguished Professional Achievement Award from the University of Michigan (1987).

Professor Drickamer had a profound effect on the academic environment at the University of Illinois, where he collaborated with faculty in the departments of physics, electrical engineering, chemistry, and biochemistry. In addition to his appointment in chemical engineering, he held professorships in physical chemistry in the School of Chemistry and in chemical engineering, chemistry, and physics in the Center of Advanced Study of the University of Illinois.

His impact on the university went beyond his research, his service on numerous committees, and his role as head of chemical engineering (1955 to 1958). With his broad range of scientific knowledge, his extensive reading in Greek, Roman, and

English history, his love of humor, especially of Mark Twain, W.C. Fields, and the Marx brothers, and his penchant for quoting Shakespeare, he was a delightful companion and had a wide range of friendships. His wisdom and his ability to judge human character were reflected in his impact on the affairs of the university as a mentor and as an advisor. His own earthy humor and often repeated stories are part of the lore of the School of Chemical Sciences.

On the occasion of a symposium honoring Harry Drickamer on March 15, 2004, his colleagues at the University of Illinois had this to say:

> Complementing his greatness as a scientist, Drickamer's persona was noteworthy. He was fiercely dedicated to his scholarship and outspokenly suspicious of all things that might distract his students and colleagues from research. He had little patience for mere competence but an abiding admiration for the experiment well done and concisely described. His colleagues and students remain grateful for the years that he shared with us, years filled with great science, colorful anecdotes, and clear excellence.

Harry met Mae Elizabeth McFillen, a nursing student, while he was at the University of Michigan, and they were married in New Orleans on October 28, 1942. Mae Elizabeth, the first family-planning nurse practitioner in East Central Illinois, worked for many years at Planned Parenthood. The couple had two sons and three daughters. The oldest son, Lee, recently retired from the chairmanship of the Department of Biology at Northern Arizona University at Flagstaff. Kurt is a professor of biochemistry at The Imperial College in England. Lynn works in the Law Library at the University of Michigan and is active in training groups about tolerance and acceptance of gays. Margaret is an M.D. and associate professor of medicine (geriatrics) at the Yale University School of Medicine. Priscilla is a reference librarian and poet at Hope College in Holland, Michigan.

ROBERT C. DUNCAN

1923–2003

Elected in 1981

"For guiding two major technologically significant programs to successful application—Apollo's guidance and control and the SX-70 camera systems."

BY ROBERT C. SEAMANS JR.

ROBERT C. DUNCAN, nicknamed Cliff, naval officer, engineer, government official, and corporate officer, died in 2003 at the age of 79. Cliff was elected to the National Academy of Engineering in 1981. Born November 21, 1923, in Jonesville, Virginia, Cliff married Rosemary Flemming on March 18, 1949. They had four children: two girls, Babette (Wilson) and Melissa, and two boys, Robert and Scott.

Cliff received his B.S. from the U.S. Naval Academy in 1945 and was immediately assigned duty aboard the *USS Bremerton*. A year later, he was sent to Pensacola for flight training. While on flight status, he served in three squadrons, flying both fighters and heavy attack bombers. When he completed his flight duties in 1960, he was a Lt. Commander.

In 1952, Cliff commenced an intense educational program, first at the U.S. Naval Post Graduate School in Monterey, California, where he earned a second B.S. in 1953. He was then transferred directly to the Massachusetts Institute of Technology (MIT) for graduate studies. His academic work was conducted primarily in the Department of Aeronautical Engineering, now the Department of Aeronautics and Astronautics, from which he received degrees at the master's and doctoral levels. His masters and doctoral theses had a direct influence on his future activities.

Cliff's master's thesis was titled "Fundamental Design Princi-pals of an Attack Simulator for Airborne Fire Control Systems." During World War II, the performance of a fire-control system was tested by towing a target and counting the number of bullet holes. The speeds, altitudes, and target maneuvers were severely limited, and the effects of variations could not be determined. In his thesis, Cliff concluded that an airborne simulation that included a stabilized platform in the interceptor aircraft would solve the problem.

In his doctoral thesis, "Guidance Parameters and Constraints for Controlled Atmospheric Entry," Cliff's thinking advanced from test to design. Based on his experience as a pilot, he was a strong advocate for manned space flight. He said in his thesis, "the trained human being has the capacity to analyze problems never before encountered, and there is much expert opinion to substantiate the belief that he can exercise this function to a useful extent even at reentry velocities." He went on to discuss the operational phases of reentry and the guidance parameters for orbital flight, as well as the physical characteristics of the solar system, emphasizing the moon and nearby planets. This thesis proved to be an excellent introduction for his activities at the National Aeronautics and Space Administration (NASA), which soon followed.

Upon completion of his studies at MIT, Cliff served in the Pentagon from 1960 to 1964, first as chief of space programs for the chief of naval operations and then as staff assistant director for research and engineering. He retired from the Navy in 1965, by which time he had been assigned to NASA in Houston, Texas.

During his three years at the Manned Spacecraft Center (now the Johnson Spacecraft Center), Cliff was chief of the Guidance and Control Division. During this time, he held weekly sessions with Apollo contractors to ensure that the guidance systems in the capsule, produced by North American, and the lunar lander, produced by Grumman, would be compatible. Compatibility was desirable for crew operations, but was essential for keeping the systems synchronized throughout the mission. Without that com-patibility, the Apollo 13 astronauts might not have been brought home safely.

Prior to leaving NASA, Cliff spent a year back in Cambridge, Massachusetts, as assistant director of the Electronics Research Center. When he left government employment in 1968, he became a vice president of the Polaroid Corporation in nearby Waltham, Massachusetts. He spent seven years at Polaroid as program manager of the SX-70 camera, with responsibilities for its design, engineering, and production. In 1975, he was elected Polaroid vice president of engineering.

Cliff returned to the government from 1985 to 1993, serving in a number of key positions. He first became director of the Defense Advanced Research Projects Agency (DARPA) and then, a year later, was confirmed in a dual capacity, assistant secretary of defense (research and technology) and continuing head of DARPA.

His final role in the Pentagon was a four-year tour as director of operational test and evaluation, where he was principal advisor to both the secretary of defense and the under secretary of defense for acquisitions. His master's thesis proved to be useful background for serving in this capacity. Cliff retired from the government in 1993 to become a vice president at Hicks and Associates, national security consultants.

By the time he retired, at age 77, he had done it all—on the ground and in the air, as a civilian and in military service, as an engineer and a manager. During his government service, his outside professional activities were restricted. From 1974 to 1985, however, while he was at Polaroid, he was a member of the board of the Charles S. Draper Laboratory, a nonprofit organization involved primarily in national security projects. He was also a trustee of the Forsyth Dental Center (Boston), a member of the Industrial and Professional Advisory Council of Pennsylvania State University, and a member of the Air Force Science Advisory Board.

Cliff's awards include the Legion of Merit (1964), Norman P. Hays Award for outstanding contributions in the field of inertial guidance control (1967), NASA Exceptional Service Medal (1968), Distinguished Eagle Scout Award (1984) from the Boy Scouts of America, and the U.S. Department of Defense Distinguished Public Service Award (1987 and 1989). Cliff was the author of *Dynamics of Atmospheric Entry* (McGraw-Hill, 1962) and co-author of three other books; he also published a number of technical papers.

Cliff's passion for his career in engineering and public service was exceeded only by his love of his family. He was a devoted husband and father and is survived by his wife Rosemary of Pasadena, California, daughters Melissa of Sierra Madre, California, and Babette of Derry, New Hampshire, and sons Robert, Jr. of Austin, Texas, and Scott of Los Angeles, California. He was at his happiest when hiking and camping in the wilderness of New England, and was notorious for his delicious camp breakfasts and poor but enthusiastic campfire singing. Cliff had a positive influence on countless young men's lives as Scoutmaster of Boy Scout Troop 157 in Weston, Massachusetts. Himself an excellent shortstop up through his Naval Academy days, Cliff became an avid Red Sox fan during the Impossible Dream season of 1967. The sound of the Red Sox on the radio was ever-present at the Duncan house in the summer, and although Cliff had passed just a year before his team finally broke the Curse, Rosemary and the children are quite sure he had a front row seat for the whole thing.

CARROLL HILTON DUNN SR.

1916–2003

Elected in 1998

*"For engineering and research efforts in the construction industry
and national defense."*

BY RICHARD TUCKER AND STRETCH DUNN

CARROLL H. DUNN SR., former deputy chief of the U.S. Army
Corps of Engineers and senior vice president of Consolidated
Edison and head of the Business Rountable Construction In-
dustry Effectiveness Project, died at Fort Belvoir, Virginia, on
January 31, 2003, at the age of 86. He was interred at Arlington
National Cemetery on March 6, 2003.

Carroll was born in rural Arkansas, the second of three sur-
viving sons. While in grade school, his back was badly burned
and he was bedridden for several months. However, he perse-
vered, recovered, and completed his public school education.
He then enrolled at the University of Illinois on a ROTC scholarship and received a bachelor of science degree in mechanical
engineering in 1938. While a student at Illinois, he met Letha
Jontz; the couple was married immediately after Carroll's graduation, a union that lasted until his death in 2003.

Upon graduation from Illinois, Carroll was assigned to active
duty in Laredo, Texas, where he embarked on a distinguished
military career. He became a combat engineer battalion commander and served with the 30th Infantry Division in WWII, landing at Omaha Beach and participating in the final drive into
Germany. He was wounded by an enemy mine, but, after two
months in a hospital in England, he rejoined his unit. Carroll's
"Memoirs," which were written by the Historian for the U.S. Army
Office of the Chief of Engineers, include fascinating stories of

many engineering innovations during the European invasion.

During his postwar military career, he had many assignments, both domestic and overseas, in Japan, Greenland, Korea, and Vietnam. He wrote a book describing construction and logistics support for the U.S. and Free World Forces in Vietnam. His assignments included heading the Corps of Engineers Waterways Experiment Station in Vicksburg, Mississippi, directorship of construction of the Titan II Missile System in the early 1960s, and Southwest Division Engineer, which was responsible for construction of the Manned Spacecraft Center in Houston and many other projects. At one time, Carroll was responsible for military construction in the Army, Air Force, National Aeronautics and Space Administration (NASA), and other government agencies, as well as the Army Nuclear Power Program and specialized engineering support for the construction of fallout shelters for Civil Defense.

Carroll's final assignments in the Army were as deputy chief of engineers, director of the Defense Nuclear Agency, and chairman of the NASA Aerospace Safety Advisory Panel. He retired from military service as a lieutenant general in September 1973 after a remarkable 35-year career.

After retiring from the military, he launched into two new careers. In 1973, he joined Consolidated Edison Company of New York, where he was senior vice president for construction, engineering, and environmental affairs until 1981. Among his many accomplishments at Consolidated Edison were several pioneering environmental remediation projects. In his later years, he became active in the Business Roundtable Construction Industry Effectiveness (CICE) Project.

Carroll's leadership of the CICE Project resulted in a series of landmark reports that are still in distribution. The Project extended over a period of several years and involved more than 250 volunteer executives, in addition to many universities, and publication of 23 individual reports and a summary report. More than two million copies of these reports have been distributed to date.

One of the CICE Project's recommendations was the establishment of a continuing research program for the construction industry. Carroll was instrumental in establishing the Construction Industry Institute (CII), which satisfied that recommendation. Even after his retirement from the Roundtable in 1988, he remained an active supporter of CII. The institute named its most prestigious award the Carroll H. Dunn Award of Excellence, and Carroll himself was the first recipient in 1985.

Carroll Dunn received many other awards in recognition of his illustrious accomplishments. The long list of his military awards can best be summarized by the rare Chief of Engineers Award for Outstanding Public Service, which he was given by current and past Chief Engineers 20 years after his retirement from the military. Carroll was elected to the National Academy of Construction and the National Academy of Engineering. He held prominent positions in church and civic organizations, including presidency of the Board of Governors of Pinehurst Country Club, the former home of the Golf Hall of Fame.

Carroll Dunn always had an allegiance to higher education. Although his baccalaureate degree was in mechanical engineering, he received a master's degree in civil engineering from Iowa State University in 1947. The University of Texas at Austin established the Carroll H. Dunn Endowed Graduate Fellowship in 1992 in recognition of Carroll's contributions to higher education.

Carroll often cited his family and personal friendships as his most significant accomplishments. He and Letha worked together as a team raising their two children, five grandchildren, and seven great grandchildren. Letha, who died recently, assisted in editing all of the CICE reports; she was also an accomplished pianist who performed in numerous venues. Their daughter, Carolyn Dunn Dean, recently deceased, was the mother of three children (Robert, Mike, and Brian). Carroll H. Dunn Jr. (Stretch), followed in Carroll's footsteps; after retiring from the U.S. Army Corps of Engineers, he recently retired from private industry and is now a consultant in Birmingham, Alabama. Stretch has two children (Steve and Cheryl).

Carroll and Letha doted on their family. They had personalized license plates on their car composed of the initials of their grandchildren. They never missed family events and drove cross-country several times to watch their grandson play professional baseball. They could quote their grandchildren's grades and test scores.

Much has been said about the lasting benefits to our nation from the WWII generation, and Carroll Dunn was the epitome of that generation. His many titles and awards reflect his dedication and hard work driven by love of God, love of family, and love of country. This man of integrity and high principles will be missed by the engineering community.

ERNST R.G. ECKERT

1904–2004

Elected in 1970

"For contributions to the solution of basic problems in heat and mass transfer."

BY EMIL PFENDER

ERNST R.G. ECKERT, Regents' Professor Emeritus at the University of Minnesota, died on July 8, 2004, less than three months before his 100th birthday. On September 13, 2004, the date of his 100th birthday, his colleagues and friends at the University of Minnesota organized the Ernst R.G. Eckert 100th Anniversary Symposium on Heat Transfer: A Career That Changed a Field. The symposium was attended by national and international leaders in the field from academia and industry.

Ernst Eckert was born September 13, 1904, in Prague, Czechoslovakia, where he spent his youth and attended the German Institute of Technology, earning the degree of Diplom Ingenieur (bachelor of science) in 1927 and Doctor of Ingenieurwissenschaften (doctor of engineering science) in 1931. He stayed on as an assistant at the institute until 1935, when he moved to Danzig, where Ernst Schmidt, professor and director of the engine laboratory, was conducting research into thermal radiation from solids and gases. Dr. Eckert pursued his growing interest in this field and earned his Dr. Habil. (doctorate) in thermal radiation in 1938. Professor Schmidt moved to Braunschweig, Germany, in 1937, and, after finishing his degree, Eckert followed him. There he assumed the positions of docent (associate professor) at the Institute of Technology and section chief at the newly established Aeronautical Research Institute.

In 1943, Eckert left his academic post at the Institute of Technology in Braunschweig (but retained his position at the Aeronautical Research Institute) and returned to the German Institute of Technology in Prague as professor at the Institute of Thermodynamics. He continued to hold both positions until the end of World War II.

Eckert came to the United States in 1945 as part of Action Paperclip. Action Paperclip was initiated by the U.S. Armed Forces in 1945 in Germany after the end of the second World War. Leading German scientists and engineers in aeronautics and related fields were invited to come to the United States with their families and work under contract for the U.S. government. From 1945 to 1949, he was consultant to the Power Plant Laboratory at Wright-Patterson Air Force Base in Dayton, Ohio. In 1949, he moved to Cleveland as a consultant to the Compressor and Turbine Division, Lewis Flight Propulsion Laboratory, National Advisory Committee for Aeronautics. In 1951, he returned to the academic life of teaching, research, and writing as full professor of mechanical engineering at the University of Minnesota-Twin Cities, a position he chose from among several invitations across the United States. When he joined the faculty at Minnesota, he founded the Heat Transfer Laboratory, and, in 1955, he was named director of the laboratory and the Thermodynamics and Heat Transfer Division, positions he held until he retired in 1973.

A man of vision and imagination, Eckert inspired his colleagues and students, both graduate and undergraduate, to participate in an environment distinguished for its breadth, versatility, and excellence in heat-transfer research. During his time in Minnesota, he led outstanding research on a wide variety of topics, from the recovery-factor method of determining gas thermal conductivity coefficients to convective heat transfer in circular and noncircular passages, mass-transfer cooling, thermal radiation, film cooling, interferometric studies of free convection, mass transfer in flowing suspensions, transport-property measurements, mass transfer in bioengineering, heat and mass transfer in fires, and the heat-transfer aspects of solar energy and power systems. After his retirement, he continued to conduct research, consult, write, and advise graduate students.

Dr. Eckert had an enormous impact on the science of heat transfer and related areas of application for almost 50 years. He began his career with pioneering research in the field of radiation heat transfer and continued to pioneer numerous other aspects of heat transfer. His work was distinguished by the development of practical applications (to steam generators, turbines, re-entry and high-speed flight, and solar energy), as well as breakthrough contributions to the understanding of fundamental mechanisms of heat transfer.

In recognition of his contributions to heat transfer in high-velocity flows, the dimensionless quantity that measures the temperature increase from adiabatic compression was named the Eckert number. In 1970, he was elected to the National Academy of Engineering (NAE), and in 1995 he received the NAE Founders Award with the following citation: "The recognized international leader in the field of heat and mass transfer for over 50 years, he has led several generations of researchers and practitioners to advanced knowledge of fundamental physical processes and important applications through his teaching, his books, and his archival journal publications."

In 1965, in recognition of his outstanding teaching, he received the University of Minnesota Institute of Technology Distinguished Teaching Award and the Western Electric Fund Award for Excellence in Instruction of Engineering Students. In 1966, in honor of his many accomplishments, the University of Minnesota bestowed its highest honor on Dr. Eckert by appointing him Regents Professor of Mechanical Engineering. This title is conferred in recognition of academic distinction, judged on the basis of the scope and quality of scholarly contributions, quality of teaching, and contributions to the public good.

Eckert was the first recipient of the Max Jakob Medal and Award (1961) and the recipient of a gold medal from the French Institute for Energy and Fuel/Institute of Energy and Combustion in Paris. As a reflection of the esteem in which he was held by the international community of scientists in the field of heat transfer, he was awarded seven honorary doctorates from universities in the United States and Europe. These are only a few of the many honors he received over the years.

Dr. Eckert was appointed by President Richard M. Nixon to the National Fire Prevention and Control Commission in 1970, and he was technical director of the University of Minnesota/ Honeywell Solar Power Study for the National Science Foundation. He was the author of more than 500 scientific papers and two textbooks that have been translated into Russian, Iranian, and Chinese.

Dr. Eckert believed that cooperation not only advances the cause of science, but also contributes to international understanding, and he tirelessly promoted cooperation among heat-transfer scientists of all nations. He was a founder, and chairman, of the Editorial Advisory Board of the *International Journal of Heat and Mass Transfer; International Journal of Heat and Mass Transfer;* co-chair of the Editorial Advisory Board of *Heat Transfer–Soviet Research* and *Heat Transfer–Japanese Research;* co-editor of *Energy Developments in Japan;* and a member of the Editorial Board of *Wärme-und Stoffübertragung.*

Dr. Eckert set high standards and encouraged excellence, not only in technical and scientific matters, but also in personal conduct and relationships. He gave generously of his time to students and colleagues, and his gentle manners, quiet good humor, and friendliness called forth the best in everyone he knew. It was an honor and a privilege to have known and worked with him, and his memory is a continuing source of inspiration.

Dr. Eckert is survived by his four children, Christa Eckert-Kohler, Elke Eckert, Karin Winter, and Dieter Eckert.

RALPH E. FADUM

1912–2000

Elected in 1975

"For contributions as a civil engineer, educator, consultant, researcher and author, a pioneer in soil mechanics and foundation engineering."

BY PAUL ZIA

Rᴀʟᴘʜ E. FADUM, Emeritus Dean of Engineering at North Carolina State University, died of natural causes at Mayview Convalescent Center in Raleigh on July 12, 2000. He was 87 years old.

Ralph was born in Pittsburgh, Pennsylvania, on July 19, 1912, one of four children of Torgeir and Mimmi Fadum, who had immigrated to the United States from Norway. Around 1920, the family moved from Pittsburgh to Niagara Falls, New York, where Torgeir, an electrical engineer, joined Niagara-Hudson Power Corporation to work on a new generating station. Ralph, his two younger brothers, and an older sister were raised in Niagara Falls where they attended elementary and secondary school.

Inspired by a science teacher in high school, Ralph decided to study civil engineering at the University of Illinois, where an education cost less than at universities in the northeast. When Ralph graduated high school, the country was in the midst of the Great Depression, and he had to take on a variety of temporary jobs to meet his college expenses. These included working in the dining hall, tutoring fellow students, and painting steel transmission towers during the summer.

In 1935, after earning a B.S. in civil engineering from the University of Illinois, he was offered a fellowship to enter Harvard

University, where he became a member of the pioneering soil mechanics team headed by Karl Terzaghi and Arthur Casagrande. Under their tutelage, Ralph received his M.S. in 1937 and Sc.D. in 1941 in soil mechanics and foundation engineering. He remained at Harvard as a faculty instructor until 1943.

While at Harvard, he began his training in professional practice with full-time summer assignments at the Niagara-Hudson Power Corporation (1935); W.P. Creager Consulting Engineers, Buffalo, New York (1936); Chicago Bridge and Iron Company, Greenville, Pennsylvania (1937); Dry Dock Associates, Portsmouth, Virginia (1940); and Jackson and Moreland, Boston, Massachusetts (1942). In addition, he served as part-time assistant to both Casagrande and Terzaghi in their consulting engagements in dam and foundation investigations in many parts of the United States and Central and South America.

Ralph began his academic career in 1943 at Purdue University, where he assumed leadership of the university's soil mechanics program. He rose through the ranks quickly from assistant professor to professor of soil mechanics in a few years. In 1949, he accepted the position of professor and head of civil engineering at North Carolina State University in Raleigh, North Carolina. In 1962, he was appointed dean of engineering, and he served in that capacity for 16 years until his retirement in 1978.

His 29-year tenure as an engineering professor and administrator coincided with the great expansion of American engineering education in the 1960s and 1970s. Ralph provided leadership and guidance for the phenomenal growth of engineering programs at North Carolina State University, especially in enrollment, faculty, and graduate and research programs. He was instrumental in transforming a high-quality undergraduate engineering program into a first-class undergraduate and graduate program at a major research university.

As an engineering educator, Ralph believed that engineering is a practicing profession. He believed that everything practiced in the field should be brought into the classroom, and everything discovered in the laboratory should be brought into practice. He was a strong advocate for a dual-track graduate engineering education, one track oriented toward research and the other toward practice.

After his retirement in 1978, he continued to advise a group of civil engineering students and regularly presented special lectures on engineering ethics and professionalism to graduating students in civil engineering. He enjoyed his contacts with these young people, and the students valued his advice and insights.

During his active years at North Carolina State, Ralph maintained an intense schedule, serving as a consultant or advisor to many federal agencies and national laboratories, including the U.S. Department of Defense, U.S. Department of the Army, U.S. Air Force, National Science Foundation, and U.S. Department of Transportation. As a consultant, he was involved in solving many complex geotechnical problems, such as the construction of airfields in Greenland; the Alaska pipeline; launch facilities for the National Aeronautics and Space Administration Apollo Project; the development of the road test program of the American Association of State Highway and Transportation Officials; landslide stabilization for the Panama Canal; the construction of underground ICBM missile silos that could withstand nuclear blast effects; and the development of foundation requirements for radar stations in the North American Defense System.

A long-time member of the American Society of Civil Engineers (ASCE) and the American Society for Engineering Education (ASEE), Ralph served on numerous boards and committees of these professional societies. He was a founding member and chairman of the Executive Committee of the ASCE Engineering Mechanics Division, a member and chairman of the Executive Committee of the ASCE Geotechnical Division, and a member of the ASCE Research Committee. In addition, over a period of 32 years, he served on some two dozen ASEE committees, including the Board of Directors, and as vice president from 1972 to 1974. He was also called upon by three North Carolina governors to serve on a variety of state boards and commissions.

For his many contributions to engineering education and geotechnical engineering, he received many honors and awards, including various citations and medals from the U.S. Department of the Army, a Distinguished Civil Engineering Alumnus Award from the University of Illinois, an honorary doctorate in engineering from Purdue University, and an Outstanding Engineering Achievement Award from the North Carolina Society of Engineers. He was an ASEE fellow and was elected an honorary member of both ASCE and ASEE. In 1975, he was elected a member of the National Academy of Engineering for his pioneering work in soil mechanics and foundation engineering. In 1978, he was named a National Honor Member of Chi Epsilon, the honorary society of civil engineering. Shortly before his death, he was honored as a member of the charter class of fellows by the Professional Engineers of North Carolina.

Ralph enjoyed many sports activities, such as golf and fishing, and for many years he jogged regularly to maintain his physical fitness. He led the North Carolina State University Faculty Athletics Council for 12 years, served twice as president of the Atlantic Coast Conference, and served a four-year term as vice president of District 3 of the National Collegiate Athletic Association. Ralph was a caring and civic-minded person. For many years, he served as a commissioner of the Raleigh Housing Authority and was active with the Salvation Army.

Ralph is survived by his wife, Elaine; a daughter, Jane Fields Fadum of Raleigh; a brother, Torgeir B. Fadum Jr., and his wife, Mary, of Grand Island, New York; two stepdaughters, Cynthia Haverly of Valparaiso, Indiana, and Linda Eason of Canton, Michigan; and a stepgranddaughter, Kristen Eason.

A man of the highest integrity with a strong sense of loyalty to the institutions he served, his staff, and his friends, Ralph was an inspiring teacher and an outstanding leader. He will be greatly missed by his friends, colleagues, students, and all who knew him.

P. OLE FANGER

1934–2006

Elected in 2001

"For significant interdisciplinary research on the influence of indoor environment on human comfort, health, and productivity."

BY ARTHUR E. BERGLES

PAVEL OLE FANGER, widely considered the world's leading expert on the effects of indoor environments on human comfort, health, and productivity, died September 18, 2006, at the age of 72, during his second visit to Syracuse University in his new role as a University Professor. The cause of his sudden, premature death was an abdominal aortic aneurism.

Ole Fanger was born in Vejlby, Denmark, on July 16, 1934, attended local schools, including the Marselisborg Gymnasium in Arhus, and entered the Technical University of Denmark (DTU), then called Danmarks Tekniske Hoejskole. He received the Cand. Polyt. degree (M.S.) in civil engineering in 1957 and subsequently served in the military for two years. He then began a lifelong association with DTU, with an initial academic appointment as Adjunkt (Assistant Professor). Then, as Lektor (Associate Professor) from 1967 to 1977, he received his Dr.Techn. (D. Sc.) for a thesis entitled "Thermal Comfort," which became a best-seller among technical books. In 1977, he was promoted to Professor, and, after his retirement in 2004, he was active as Senior Professor. He guided more than 100 M.S. and Ph.D. students, published 12 books or book chapters, was author or co-author of more than 300 technical papers, and presented more than 300 invited lectures.

Not one to shy away from administrative responsibilities, Fanger established the International Centre for Indoor Environment and Energy (ICIEE) at DTU in 1998 and was director of the center until 2004. The facility, funded by a 10-year grant from the Danish government for 10 million euros, had unique environmental chambers that attracted numerous world-class researchers from many disciplines, including classical engineering disciplines, medicine, chemistry, and psychology. The personnel, from some 15 nations, now number more than 50, including 30 graduate students. In 2003, an international evaluation declared ICIEE to be the best facility in the world for studying indoor environment and energy.

Fanger first demonstrated his flair for international activities when he spent a year as a research associate at Kansas State University (1966–1967) at the new Institute of Environmental Research. Under the mentorship of icons Press McNall, Fred Rohles, and Ralph Nevins, he began his investigations of the human effects of thermal comfort. The construction of the environmental chamber at Kansas State was sponsored by the American Society for Heating, Refrigerating, and Air-Conditioning Engineers (ASHRAE), and Fanger became a member of that organization in 1968. For the next 40 years, he attended most of the biannual meetings, where he could frequently be seen with his many friends and colleagues in the networking lounge.

Fanger spent his second sabbatical year, 2000, at the National University of Singapore (NUS) as Distinguished Visiting Professor. During that year, he initiated collaborative research and development studies between NUS and ICIEE on the impact of indoor environments in different climates on human comfort, health, perceptions, and productivity.

Fanger's research, which was focused almost exclusively on people's responses to indoor environments, established the importance of indoor environments to the quality of life. In the 1960s, he introduced indices for quantifying thermal sensation and comfort. The thermal environment can be characterized by temperature (air and radiant surface), humidity, air velocity, and personal parameters (clothing and activity level). Subjective factors obviously influence satisfaction/dissatisfaction with certain

conditions (e.g., a draught and the associated turbulence inten-
sity). Discomfort can also be caused by radiant asymmetry and
vertical air-temperature gradients.

The index Fanger developed for measuring indoor environments is now used worldwide and is included in many national
and international standards for the design of buildings. The
specifications for thermal environmental-control systems (heating, ventilating, and air conditioning) are based on models he
developed. His work has been extremely useful for the establishment of energy requirements for buildings.

In the 1980s, digging even deeper into human physiology,
psychology, and subjective behavior, he introduced sensory units
for perceived air quality. In his puckish Danish way, these units
were designated the "olf" and "decipol." An olf is the emission
rate of air pollutants (bioeffluents) from a standard (sedentary)
person. A decipol is one olf ventilated at a rate of 20 cubic feet
per minute of unpolluted air. Based on extensive experimental
data, Fanger developed a curve that gives the percentage of dis-
satisfied persons as a function of ventilation rate per olf.

The olf concept can also be applied to other sensory sources,
such as building materials and even personal computers. Extensive field studies have shown that indoor air quality can be improved and the ventilation requirement decreased by reducing
superfluous sources of pollution. Fanger and his associates were
the first to identify the significant impact of indoor air quality
on productivity (office workers, factory workers, etc.) and on
the symptoms of sick-building syndrome.

Fanger was very active in professional societies. He was president of the Scandinavian HVAC Societies since 1984 and president of the International Academy of Indoor Air Sciences from
1996 to 2002. He was vice president of both the Federation of
European Heating, Ventilating and Air Conditioning Associations and the International Institute of Refrigeration. Between
1974 and 2006, he served on 18 ASHRAE committees and panels, often as the international representative.

Ole Fanger's outstanding accomplishments did not go un-
recognized. In fact, he was arguably the most "decorated" Dane
in scientific and technical affairs. He was elected to the Danish

Academy of Technical Sciences (member, 1975), International Academy of Indoor Air Sciences (founding member, 1990), Royal Academy of Engineering (foreign member, 1994), Russian Academy of Architecture and Building Science (foreign member, 1995), Royal Society of Health (fellow, 1997), International Academy of Refrigeration (member, 2001), and NAE (foreign associate, 2001). In addition, he was an honorary member of 17 engineering societies in Europe and Asia. He was the recipient of eight awards from ASHRAE, including the two highest awards given to living members. He was awarded nine honorary doctorates from universities in nine different countries and was honorary professor at six major Chinese universities. In addition, he was awarded 28 medals, plaques, and prizes by engineering societies throughout the world. A Festschrift was prepared in his honor on the occasion of his "retirement" from DTU.

From early on, Fanger promoted international collaboration and the dissemination of research results and publications to a wide audience. He attracted more than 100 international postdoctoral students and visiting professors to his research group at DTU, and he was recognized worldwide and in the English-speaking press as one of the top Danish researchers. In 2002, the Queen of Denmark made him Knight of the Order of Dannebrog, Premier Degree. After receiving this honor, accolades poured in from everywhere, and he felt very fortunate to be thought of so highly in his lifetime.

Fanger was married to Britt Eva Hellieson in April 1958, who predeceased him in April 2006. He is survived by two daughters, Bine (and two grandsons) of Copenhagen, and Tone of Frederiksberg.

ROBERT BRUCE FRIDLEY

1934–2006

Elected in 1985

*"For his managerial ability and research toward
the mechanization of tree harvests."*

BY BRUCE R. HARTSOUGH, JOHN R. GOSS, AND
WILLIAM J. CHANCELLOR

ROBERT FRIDLEY, Professor of Biological and Agricultural Engineering, Emeritus, University of California (UC), Davis, passed away at his home on March 19, 2006.

Born in Burns, Oregon, on June 6, 1934, Bob was raised in farming and lumbering communities in Oregon, Washington, and California, where his family was involved with farming and ranching on a part-time basis. To support his college education, he worked with livestock and in a fruit-packing shed and lumber mill, experiences that provided a strong foundation for his stellar career in engineering research focused on solving problems associated with biological systems.

Bob entered Sierra College in Auburn, California, in 1952 and graduated with an A.A. degree in 1954. He then entered the B.S. program in agricultural engineering at UC Davis. In 1955, he married Jean Griggs of Nevada City, California, and, just a year later, in 1956, he graduated with a degree in mechanical engineering (issued by the College of Engineering, UC Berkeley). He was then offered a position at UC Davis as an assistant specialist in the Department of Agricultural Engineering. After he completed his M.S. in agricultural engineering in 1960, he was appointed assistant professor in 1961 and rapidly advanced to professor in 1969. He received his Ph.D. from Michigan State University in 1973 and became chair of the Department of Agricultural Engineering at UC Davis in 1974.

127

With Paul Adrian (a U.S. Department of Agriculture agricultural engineer stationed at UC Davis), Bob initiated studies of mechanized harvesting of tree fruits and nuts. Although some mechanical harvesting had been done prior to this time, Bob identified the parameters that influence tree response to vibration and provided a basis for the rational design of shakers. He then studied the response of fruit to impact and determined the best design for collecting surfaces to minimize bruising. This work led to several patents and advanced mechanization in California, nationally, and around the world. Bob also collaborated with several other individuals at UC Davis, most notably Dr. Larry Claypool, a postharvest physiologist in the Department of Pomology, and James Mehlschau, a development engineer in the Department of Agricultural Engineering.

Bob's accomplishments included the development of the inertial tree shaker, the integrated shake-catch harvester, shaker clamps that minimize damage to tree bark, and criteria for the design of fruit-catching surfaces to minimize the bruising of fruit during harvesting and handling. Most tree-fruit harvesters today are designed based on principles developed by Bob, and most growers who produce fruit to be mechanically harvested follow the guidelines for tree shape and pruning that were identified during his research. In 1983, Bob co-authored, with Michael O'Brien, UC Davis, and Burton Cargill, Michigan State University, *Principles and Practices for Harvesting Fruits and Vegetables* (AVI Publishing Company, 1983).

Bob was known as much for his leadership and ability to foresee the future as for his creativity, problem solving, and productivity. In 1977, he left the university and put all of those capabilities to good use in pursuing his interest in forest engineering research with the Weyerhaeuser Company. He began as manager of silvicultural research and development (R&D) and advanced through multiple positions to manager of diversified technology R&D. In the latter role, he was responsible for all research related to silviculture, agriculture, and aquaculture. Bob's team at Weyerhaeuser developed technology for reforestation and methods of raising and releasing juvenile salmon for ocean ranching.

During his eight years in industry, Bob maintained close ties with UC Davis and provided many opportunities for internships, summer jobs, and permanent positions for UC Davis students. He returned to UC Davis in 1985 as director of the Aquaculture and Fisheries Program, which he expanded and strengthened.

In 1989, he headed the National Research Council Marine Board Committee on the Assessment of Technology and Opportunities for Marine Aquaculture in the United States; the results of this committee study were published in *Marine Aquaculture, Opportunities for Growth* (National Academy Press, 1989).

While directing the Aquaculture and Fisheries Program at UC Davis, Bob also chaired the UC Davis Project 2000 Strategic Planning Steering Committee for the College of Agricultural and Environmental Sciences. In recognition of his organizational skills and ability to bring together people with diverse backgrounds and interests to achieve meaningful results, the college appointed him executive associate dean in 1989. He retired in 1994 but remained a special assistant to the dean through 2000.

Bob was recognized nationally and internationally for his achievements. In 1966, he was co-recipient of the Charles G. Woodbury Award of the American Society for Horticultural Science, and in 1988 he was awarded a Doctor Honoris Causa by the Universidad Politecnica de Madrid. He was also a much sought-after consultant; he participated in research programs in Canada, China, Denmark, Finland, Germany, Honduras, Hungary, Italy, the Netherlands, Norway, the Philippines, Puerto Rico, Spain, Sweden, Thailand, the United Kingdom, and the former USSR.

The American Society of Agricultural Engineers (ASAE) bestowed numerous honors on Bob: five Outstanding Paper Awards (1966, 1968, 1969, 1976, and 1986), Outstanding Young Researcher Award for Engineering Achievement (1972), Pacific Coast Region Engineer of the Year (1974), Engineering Concept of the Year Award (1976), ASAE Fellow (1978), and three Presidential Distinguished Service Awards (the latest in 1988). He served as president of the ASAE Foundation (1993 to 1996) and president of ASAE (1997 to 1998).

In 1985, Bob was elected to the National Academy of Engineering "for his managerial ability and research toward the mechanization of tree harvests," becoming the fourth faculty member from UC Davis to be so honored. From 2000 to 2002, he served on the National Research Council Board on Agriculture and Natural Resources. The UC Davis Cal Aggie Alumni Association awarded him a Citation for Excellence Award (1990), and the College of Agricultural and Environmental Sciences honored him with an Award of Distinction (2005).

Bob was also a devoted family man and was able to balance his professional success with success at home. He and his wife of over 50 years were true partners in life. Together, they (quite literally) built their first home and raised three sons who eventually followed in their father's engineering footsteps. While the engineering community will remember Bob's many professional accomplishments, his family will remember "Papa Bob" with stories of backpacking and fishing trips, golf, and singing "Sneaky Snake" and other Tom T. Hall songs for his grandchildren. In his retirement, Bob and Jean enjoyed traveling the world, visiting family, and enjoying sunsets over Lake Tahoe together.

Bob is survived by his wife, Jean, three sons, James, Michael, and Kenneth (all of whom are in engineering positions), and eight grandchildren. Bob seemed to thrive on seemingly unresolvable problems, nearly impossible-to-achieve objectives, and high-responsibility positions. Bob Fridley never expressed any doubts that these difficult objectives could be achieved.

Bernard Gold

BERNARD GOLD

1923–2005

Elected in 1982

"For development of digital signal processing theory and processors and their applications to speech compression and pattern recognition."

BY WALTER E. MORROW JR.

BERNARD GOLD was born in New York City in 1923. After attending primary and secondary schools, he entered City College, from which he graduated with a Bachelor of Electrical Engineering in 1944. He went on to receive a Masters of Electrical Engineering from the Polytechnic Institute of Brooklyn (now called Polytechnic University). In 1948, he received a Doctorate of Electrical Engineering from that same institution.

After working briefly for a small Manhattan company (Avion Instrument) on the theory of radar range and angle tracking, he joined the Hughes Aircraft Company in Culver City, California, where he did research on statistical problems associated with missile guidance. In 1953, he became a staff member at the Lincoln Laboratory at Massachusetts Institute of Technology (MIT); his initial focus was on the application of probability theory to problems in communications.

In 1954, Ben received a Fulbright Fellowship to spend a year in Italy, where he lectured, in Italian, on the response of linear dynamic systems to random noise stimuli. Upon returning to Lincoln Laboratory in 1955, he began research on the development of an automatic recognition device that could translate hand-sent Morse code transmissions into text. In 1958, his research came to fruition. This was one of the first practical applications of what later became known as artificial intelligence.

Ben's success in translating Morse code led to an early effort in automatic machine recognition of speech using an early advanced digital computer (TX2) at Lincoln Laboratory. The focus of this early work was on the precision detection of speech pitch, an important component of early speech-compression devices, called Vocoders, as well as early speech-recognition systems.

In 1965, Ben was invited to work with MIT Professor Ken Stevens on the theory of digital-signal processing, which became a central capability in many subsequent applications, including speech recognition, radar, sonar, communications, seismology, and biologic systems. While on the MIT campus, Ben taught what is believed to be the first course on this subject. His pioneering research continues to have an enormous impact on modern electronic devices and systems. In 1969, he published (with Charles Rader) *Digital Processing of Signals*, the first treatise, and seminal text, on this topic. He then focused his attention on human-speech perception and related topics. In 1975, he published (with Lawrence Rabiner) a comprehensive textbook on digital-signal processing, *Theory and Applications of Digital Signal Processing*. Finally, in 2000, he published (with Nelson Morgan) *Speech and Audio Signal Processing*.

In his later career, Ben played a leading role at Lincoln Laboratory in the development of customized, very-high-speed digital-signal processors designed for specialized fast-Fourier transform operations, and digital filtering. These designs led to a number of important applications, including coherent Doppler radar processors, very-high-speed packet speech processors, and clutter rejection in air traffic control radar. These specialized computational processors achieved speeds far in excess of the speed of conventional, nonspecialized processors. Ben published more than 20 significant papers on applications of digital-signal processors.

In 1988, at the age of 65, he retired from research at MIT Lincoln Laboratory, although he continued to conduct research on the MIT campus on speech synthesis, speech recognition, human auditory systems, and related areas. He also taught courses on these topics at the University of California, Berkeley, for several years.

Ben was a member of the National Academy of Engineering, a fellow of the Acoustic Society of America, and a fellow of the Institute of Electrical and Electronic Engineers (IEEE). In addition to these honors, he received a Fullbright Fellowship in 1955. His numerous awards include IEEE Achievement Award (1986) and IEEE Society Award from the Acoustic, Speech, and Signal Processing Society (1985). In 1997, he and Rader shared the first Kilby Signal Processing Medal awarded by IEEE.

Ben Gold was one of a small group of creative individuals who laid the theoretical foundations for the electronic devices and systems we use today.

Ben spent many years creating collages, which have been exhibited at various venues; he also painted with oil. He was a voracious reader and walker.

Ben leaves his wife of 60 years, Sylvia; two daughters, Laura and Lisa and their partners Collette and Karen; two grandchildren, Matthew and Rebecca. He was predeceased by a son, Daniel.

William A. Golomski

WILLIAM A.J. GOLOMSKI

1924–2002

Elected in 1996

"For contributions in integrating
customer-centered quality and engineering design."

BY WILLIAM A.J. GOLOMSKI JR. AND WAY KUO

WILLIAM A.J. GOLOMSKI, president, W.A. Golomski and Associates, international technical and management consultants, passed away February 17, 2002, at the age of 77.

Born on October 14, 1924, in the small town of Custer, Wisconsin, Bill was the son of the late John and Margaret (Glisczinski) Golomski, who ran the local butcher shop and general store. Bill served during WWII in the Army Air Force with the 438th Troop Carrier Group. On June 19, 1960, he married Joan Hagen in a ceremony at Marquette University in Milwaukee.

Indicative of his lifelong passion for learning, Bill earned many academic degrees: a B.S. in mathematics, English, and history at the University of Wisconsin, Stevens Point (1948); an M.S. in mathematics and physics, Marquette University (1950); an M.S.E.M. in engineering management, Milwaukee School of Engineering (1969); an M.B.A. in accounting and finance, University of Chicago (1972); a B.A. in television and video production, Columbia College, Chicago (1987); and an M.A. in sociology, Roosevelt University (1990). His dedication to personal and professional development was reflected in his membership in a wide range of organizations, including the American Association for the Advancement of Science (AAAS), American Society for Quality (ASQ), American Statistical Association, Institute of Industrial Engineers (IIE), New York Academy of Sciences, Royal

Society of Health, World Association of Productivity Sciences, and the Philippine Society of Quality.

Bill worked as a consultant, speaker, writer, and educator in more than 60 countries and with more than 2,000 organizations, including Ford, Kodak, Del Monte, and GE. One of his many research interests was the development and application of concepts of quality and reliability in industry, government, education, and health care, blending quantitative and social and behavioral science methods. The impact of his accomplishments in engineering has been far-reaching and long-lasting.

Bill emphasized the need for customer focus long before it became popular. He developed an entirely new approach to measuring customer satisfaction and conducted the first ever conference in that field. He also designed programs for assessing the safety of products, such as safety helmets, bicycle helmets, firefighting helmets, safety spectacles, and chemical protective units.

He developed the use of linear programming theory and statistics to optimize the nutritional mix of processed foods from variable input stock, resulting in dramatic improvements in quality at significantly lower cost. His leadership in the measurement, control, and improvement in quality in the food, drug, and cosmetic industries led to a comprehensive quality system for the medical-device industry and earned him explicit recognition from the ASQ Food, Drug and Cosmetic Division, which named its premier award the William A. Golomski Research Award. He also developed successful optimization methods for blending both animal feeds and gasoline.

While at Ford Motor Company, before quality function deployment (QFD) and concurrent engineering became commonplace, he developed a methodology for explicitly including customer input in the engineering design process for the Taurus and Lincoln Town Car. Bill also designed the control system used for technical supervision of the building of the Sears Tower, the world's tallest building at the time.

Among his myriad professional accomplishments, Bill developed the criteria for the first certification program for a technical society, the Certified Quality Engineer (CQE) distinction. In the past 30 years, some 50,000 persons have been credentialed.

Invited by the U.S. Secretary of Commerce to serve on the initial Panel of Judges for the Malcolm Baldrige National Quality Award in 1988, and then on the Board of Overseers from 1989 to 1991, his ideas on management were instrumental in the development of the criteria known as the Malcolm Baldrige National Quality Award criteria, now the worldwide, de facto definition of Total Quality. He subsequently helped to establish similar awards in Florida, Illinois, and Wisconsin (the Forward Award).

In 1996, Bill was elected to the National Academy of Engineering (NAE) for his contributions to quality engineering. During his tenure at NAE, he served on the Section 8 Industrial, Manufacturing and Operational Systems Engineering Peer Committee, where he was a strong advocate and role model for the "quality profession." His talents were also recognized internationally. He was elected an academician and served as vice president of the prestigious International Academy of Quality, an organization whose membership is limited to 70 individuals worldwide.

From 1966 to 1967, Bill was president of ASQ, an organization with more than 130,000 members, and, in 1994, he was granted an Honorary Membership, only the fourteenth in 50 years. He co-founded the ASQ Food, Drug and Cosmetics Division, sponsored the Education Division, and was founding editor of the *Quality Management Journal.* He was also president of the Midwest Planning Association and the Wisconsin Mathematics Council, an association of elementary and high school teachers. From ASQ, he received the Edwards Medal for Management Innovation and the Eugene L. Grant Award for Educational Improvement.

Bill was honored by many organizations and received the American Deming Medal, the Frank and Lillian Gilbreth Industrial Engineering Award of the Institute of Industrial Engineers (the organization's highest honor and one not bestowed every year), and numerous other awards. He served as chair of ANSI Committee Z–16, and, at the time of his death, was chair of the American Association for the Advancement of Science (AAAS)

Section in Industrial Science and Technology and chair of the Quality Assurance Executive Committee of the Institute of Food Technologists. During his life, he came into contact with many cultures, globally and domestically. He was always very proud of his service to the Oklahoma Choctaws and Seminoles, who made him an Honorary Chief.

Bill passed on his knowledge in many ways. He taught accounting, marketing, and business strategy in graduate schools of business at the Illinois Institute of Technology, Roosevelt University, and Marquette University and was adjunct lecturer at the University of Chicago.

Bill is survived by his wife, Joan, of Algoma, Wisconsin; a daughter, Gretchen Wilson, of Algoma; a son, William Arthur Golomski Jr., of Green Bay; two grandchildren, William Zachary Wilson and Robert Troy Wilson; two sisters, Dorothy Golomski, of Milwaukee, and Arlene (Paul) Golomski-Zei of LaCrosse; a cousin Marcella (Robert) Kolacke of Edina, Minnesota; and a brother-in-law and sister-in-law, Kurt and Patsy Hagen of Grove, Oklahoma.

Bill Golomski was an admirable man, an extraordinary engineer, an outstanding role model, a devoted mentor, and a true friend to mankind, and his life's work has left an indelible imprint. He will be remembered not only for benefiting humanity, but also for inspiring future generations of engineers.

Donald RF Harleman

DONALD R. F. HARLEMAN

1922–2005

Elected in 1974

"For leadership in the development of theoretical and experimental techniques in the field of fluid mechanics."

BY RAFAEL L. BRAS, FRÉDÉRIC CHAGNON, ERIC E. ADAMS,
PETER S. EAGLESON, OLE MADSEN, SUSAN MURCOTT,
LEW THATCHER, AND PETER SHANAHAN

DONALD R.F. HARLEMAN, Ford Professor Emeritus of the Massachusetts Institute of Technology (MIT), died of cancer on September 28, 2005, on Nantucket, Massachusetts. He was 82 years old.

Born on December 5, 1922, in Palmerton, Pennsylvania, Don received a bachelor's degree in civil engineering from Pennsylvania State University in 1943 and then worked as a design engineer for the Curtis-Wright Corporation in Ohio during the last years of World War II. In October 1945, he arrived at MIT, a 22-year-old beginning graduate student in the Department of Civil and Sanitary Engineering with an interest in fluid flow. On that same October day, Dr. Arthur T. Ippen, a Caltech Ph.D. student of the renowned fluid dynamicist Theodore von Karman, also arrived in Cambridge to take up a new appointment as professor in charge of the department's hydrodynamics and hydraulic engineering program. Thus began a collaboration and friendship that continued until Ippen's death in 1973.

In 1947, Don Harleman completed his master's thesis, "The Characteristics of Density Currents," based on a problem Ippen encountered on one of his consulting jobs. A conclusion of that thesis paper reflects the principle of Don's subsequent research: "Any theory, in order that it may be accepted, must stand the

test of experimental confirmation.... Accordingly, any conclusions as to the accuracy of the entire theory must be postponed
until experimental results are available."

In his doctoral thesis, "Studies of the Validity of the Hydraulic Analogy to Supersonic Flow," Don investigated experimen-
tally the nature of pressure variations around airfoils at supersonic velocities from measurements of oblique hydraulic jump
characteristics resulting from airfoil-shaped obstacles in a
supercritical flow. Because there were no adequate high-speed
wind tunnels to test his thesis, Don designed and supervised the
construction of a unique high-velocity tilting-flume facility, a testimony to his prowess as an engineer.

Upon completion of his doctorate in 1950, Don accepted an
appointment as assistant professor of hydraulics at MIT. That
year was most significant, though, because he married his beloved companion, Martha Havens, who remained his life partner until his death. On May 2, 2006, Martha died of complications of respiratory disease. She was 82.

Don had an extraordinary career at MIT. His appointment in
1950 coincided with the dedication of a new hydrodynamics laboratory. In 1970, with funding from the founder of the Ralph M.
Parsons Company, the laboratory was doubled in size and re-
dedicated as the Ralph M. Parsons Laboratory for Water Resources and Hydrodynamics. Don Harleman followed Arthur
Ippen as director of the laboratory from 1973 to 1983.

Don was motivated to solve issues that would improve the
quality of life and protect the environment. In pursuit of those
goals, he changed research directions several times during his
long career. His early work on stratified saltwater systems afforded
a natural segue to thermally stratified freshwater systems (lakes
and reservoirs). In the mid-1950s, he investigated engineering
controls of stratified flow from freshwater reservoirs for the Tennessee Valley Authority. Don and his students established a fundamental model for predicting stratification based on meteoro-
logical conditions. The model relied on molecular diffusion for
vertical heat transport, a formulation that avoided calibrating
an eddy diffusion function to capture turbulent diffusion. As
part of a series of studies of stratified reservoirs, Don then worked

with other students to develop predictive techniques for water quality.

During a sabbatical at the International Institute for Applied Systems Analysis in Laxenburg, Austria, in 1977–1978, Don explored a topic related to his prior work on temperature—the trophic status of lakes and reservoirs. Algae grow in lakes and reservoirs in response to the availability of sunlight for photosynthesis and nutrients for the creation of cellular matter. Lakes enriched with nutrients are subject to eutrophication, the excessive growth of algae, which creates unaesthetic conditions. Don theorized that the physics of lakes and reservoirs could alter nutrient distribution, and hence eutrophication, just as temperature stratification affects dissolved oxygen.

Don's work on natural lakes and reservoirs led to related work on the heated lakes used to dissipate waste heat from the condensers of electric power plants. In places where cooling water is limited, closed-cycle cooling is used, most commonly wet cooling towers. But if sufficient land is available, cooling ponds (shallow bodies of water built by erecting perimeter dikes) or reservoirs (deeper bodies of water formed by damming streams) are useful alternatives. Because of their depth, cooling reservoirs provide greater thermal inertia than towers, helping to keep down peak temperatures caused by temporary extremes in weather. In addition, many cooling reservoirs also provide recreational opportunities. Fundamental studies by Don and his students were integrated into MITEMP, a computer program that contained a collection of hydrothermal modules applicable to ponds and reservoirs of varying thermal structure.

As a direct corollary of Don's leadership, MIT was arguably the leader in analyzing thermal discharges. Compared with wastewater outfalls, thermal discharges are characterized by generally larger flow rates, lower density differences, and shallower water depths; hence flow is dominated more by momentum than by buoyancy, and designs are strongly influenced by port velocity, elevation (surface vs. submerged), and orientation (in plan view). The results of these studies are incorporated in many popular computer models of initial mixing models.

Don's interest in estuary hydraulics and transport increased as graduate students became more adept at implementing computer solutions to the equations of fluid flow and fluid transport. Analyses of experimental and field data provided a relationship between the longitudinal salinity gradient and the effective 1-D dispersion coefficient, which made possible the numerical solution for studies of impacts of dredging, sea level rise, and other scenarios. Ultimately, Don's models represented the flow and transport of contaminants in estuaries, forming a basis for the more sophisticated, multidimensional models and tools used in environmental impact studies.

In the mid-1980s, when the city of Boston began planning the cleanup of Boston Harbor, Don's focus shifted from biogeochemical processes to wastewater treatment. The Boston Harbor cleanup was a hot topic, and he frequently took public positions, guided by his sense of civic responsibility and his conviction that scientists and engineers should take the lead in such debates.

It was widely accepted at the time that the problems in Boston Harbor were caused mainly by frequent discharges of untreated sewage combined with stormwater through combined sewer overflows (CSO). Don argued that conventional primary treatment followed by an activated sludge plant was not an optimal solution. Based on his knowledge of first principles and of the process known as "physical-chemical treatment," he recognized that making the first stage of wastewater treatment more efficient, prior to a biological step, made far more sense. He was also an early advocate of an ocean outfall, which ultimately became an integral part of the Boston Harbor cleanup.

During a visit to southern California in 1989, Don found evidence to support his case. In response to a California regulation requiring that 75 percent of solids be removed from effluents discharged into the Pacific Ocean, primary clarifiers at wastewater treatment plants serving more than 12 million people in the Los Angeles and San Diego areas had been retrofitted to accept chemical additives. The addition of low doses of primary coagulants plus polymers (an innovation not historically part of physical-chemical treatment with metal salts) increased the amount of solids and biochemical oxygen demand (BOD) removed.

Moreover, plant capacity was increased as a result of the shorter retention time in primary clarifiers and improved secondary efficiency and flow capacity (exemplified in the Los Angeles Hyperion Plant).

Don Harleman coined the term "chemically enhanced primary treatment" (CEPT) to describe the use of low doses of a primary coagulant, typically a metal salt, and potentially also a polymer, in the first stage of municipal wastewater treatment. He advocated the use of CEPT in the Boston Harbor cleanup, arguing that it would accomplish several sensible aims: it would halve the size of the proposed Deer Island plant and concurrently free financial resources for solving the "real" problem— CSO overflows. Despite his valiant efforts, however, Don lost the political battle to bring CEPT to Boston Harbor . . . an important lesson.

Don was convinced that water-related illnesses plagued developing countries, had huge impacts on human health and ecosystems, and impeded sustainable economic growth. The lack of municipal wastewater and sanitation infrastructure was the underlying reason for the spread of these illnesses, especially in densely populated urban areas, but also in rural areas. Don believed that Western-style treatment systems, particularly activated sludge systems, were not appropriate to address the problem because of their complexity, high cost, high-energy requirements, and complicated operation and maintenance requirements. He was especially upset that, in most cases, only a fraction of the wastewater in urban areas was being treated, typically in "showcase" activated-sludge plants. He believed it would be better to treat all wastewater to an adequate, initial level, thereby improving both public health and the environment.

Don's idea was for staged wastewater treatment for developing countries. The initial stage should provide only enough treatment for effective disinfection to meet immediate public health and environmental requirements. Only after all of the wastewater in an urban area had been treated to that level should more advanced treatment technologies be introduced to improve the effluent quality and meet higher environmental standards. The requirements for first-stage treatment technology were: (1) disinfection of the effluent; (2) frugal space requirements; (3) low cost; (4) simple operation; and (5) easy upgrades. He believed that CEPT was an excellent candidate for the first stage.

The 1989 Hong Kong Harbor cleanup plan called for a conventional primary treatment plant followed by a 30-km-long ocean outfall. This plan encountered strong opposition from local environmental groups and from Chinese authorities who opposed the export of pollution to Chinese waters. In 1994, the Hong Kong Environmental Protection Department asked Don Harleman to take part in an international review panel, which ultimately recommended using CEPT followed by ultraviolet disinfection and a shorter outfall whose location would be determined by a proposed model study. The Hong Kong government accepted these recommendations, and the Stone Cutters Island Sewage Treatment Works was inaugurated in 2001.

Don believed in good engineering to improve the quality of life and environment everywhere in the world. He loved traveling with his wife Martha and was a popular consultant throughout the United States and abroad. Besides Hong Kong, he worked in Hungary, Egypt, the Netherlands, Brazil, Puerto Rico, Australia, Portugal, Lebanon, China, Mexico, and Italy, where, beginning in the 1970s, he helped tackle the problems of the lagoon of Venice. In 1995, he joined a panel of experts to oversee the development of the environmental impact assessment of the system of tidal barriers proposed to protect the city and the lagoon from increasingly frequent, damaging floods. With typical conviction and aplomb, Don insisted on the highest standards, not only to protect the lagoon, but also to improve it. Don lived to see the project well into construction, and his beloved Venice was on his mind almost to the day of his death.

Don's signature approach was to find an analytical solution to problems using simple geometry, followed by meticulous experimental confirmation, often followed by application to actual situations. His many published studies, along with his textbook, *Fluid Dynamics,* written with Jim Daily in 1966, propelled him to the forefront of his field and led to his election to the National Academy of Engineering in 1974, among many other honors. He was an honorary member of the American Society of Civil Engineers and the Boston Society of Civil Engineers. In 1987, his alma mater, Penn State, named him Alumni Fellow.

Perhaps Don's greatest contributions to his profession were the students, colleagues, and friends he inspired. He and Martha opened their hearts and their home to students, colleagues, and friends in ways that cannot be described but that some of us were lucky enough to experience.

In March 2000, more than 300 friends, family, and colleagues gathered to honor Don and Martha by establishing the Donald and Martha Harleman Professorship of Civil and Environmental Engineering at MIT. This was a fitting recognition of an inseparable couple dedicated to improving the lives of students, faculty, staff, and partners. Nobody who ever met them will ever forget them. They are very much missed.

Don and Martha are survived by three children (Kathleen Harleman of Champaign, Illinois; Robert Harleman of Wilton, Connecticut; and Anne Krieger of New Cannan, Connecticut), six grandchildren, and innumerable friends around the world.

Willis M. Hawkins

WILLIS M. HAWKINS

1913–2004

Elected in 1966

"For design and development of aircraft, missile, and space systems."

BY SHERMAN N. MULLIN

WILLIS MOORE HAWKINS, retired senior vice president and director of Lockheed Corporation, died of natural causes at his home in Woodland Hills, California, on September 28, 2004. He was 90 years old.

Willis was born in Kansas City, Missouri, on December 1, 1913, but spent most of his early life in Michigan. He prepared for college at the Leelanau School in Glen Arbor, Michigan, a unique private academy, which he generously supported all his life. His love of airplanes started early and continued until the day he died. He received a Bachelor of Science degree in aeronautical engineering from the University of Michigan in 1937, which also awarded him an honorary Doctor of Engineering degree in 1965. Willis was an exceptional student, noted for his amazing memory and impeccable printing on papers and examinations. These became lifelong traits.

In June 1937, an uncle gave Willis a new Model A Ford, which he and a classmate, Jack Duffendack, drove from Ann Arbor to Burbank, California, to start work at Lockheed Aircraft Corporation. Willis began as a draftsman on July 1, 1937, initiating an association that lasted 67 years. He advanced rapidly, becoming manager of an engineering department in 1944, when Lockheed employment reached a World War II high of 94,000. He was involved in the design of many propeller-driven airplanes, including the four-engine Constellation transport, which was flown by many airlines worldwide for two decades after the war. His exceptional competence was evident to Lockheed management, including Robert E. Gross, chairman of the board from 1932 to 1961.

Besides designing airplanes, Willis was an eager flying student. After instruction in several small airplanes, he received his pilot's license in 1939. Over the years, he owned a long series of airplanes, his favorite being a Bonanza. He flew often for more than 50 years.

In 1949, Willis became chief preliminary design engineer, a position of enormous responsibility and influence. In this position, he led the design of the C-130 Hercules four-engine turboprop transport aircraft, which became one of the most versatile, successful, widely used aircraft of the century. In 2004, it was still in production and being operated in many countries. He also led the development of supersonic jet aircraft and pioneering hypersonic test vehicles. During his long career, he nurtured a group of notable engineers.

In 1954, Lockheed formed a Missile Systems Division, later Lockheed Missiles and Space Company, with Willis as director of engineering; he became vice president in 1960. For his major contributions to the development of the Polaris fleet ballistic missile system, which went into operation aboard U.S. Navy submarines in 1960, he was awarded the Navy Distinguished Service Medal in 1961.

From 1963 to 1966, Willis served as assistant secretary of the Army for research and development. He liked the Army, and the Army liked him, particularly the senior generals. Willis developed a close relationship with General Creighton (Abe) Abrams (1914–1974), the legendary World War II tank commander. After Abrams returned from Europe in 1964 to become vice chief of staff, he and Willis made many productive field trips together, neither being content to carry out endless bureaucratic work in the Pentagon. Willis was involved in many major projects, including the development of a new main battle tank, later known as the Abrams tank, which became the most capable tank in the world and was still operational in 2004. Willis received the Army's Distinguished Civilian Service Award in both 1965 and 1966.

Also in 1966, Willis was elected a member of the National Academy of Engineering for "design and development of aircraft, missile, and space systems." In that same year, he returned to Lockheed. In 1969, as senior vice president of science and engineering, he was the senior technical officer of a very large, diversified aerospace corporation involved in a wide variety of technology and major product-development programs, including the research and development programs of Lockheed's many divisions covering advanced aircraft, missiles, satellites, and electronic systems.

Willis operated informally and directly with engineers and scientists. A master of incisive questioning with little interest in academic credentials, he judged people by their creative technical contributions and ability to achieve practical results. He had even less enthusiasm for formal administrative procedures, big meetings, or a large supporting staff, and he kept his own file of meticulously printed notes.

Willis was a member of the Lockheed board of directors from 1972 to 1980. He briefly took early retirement in 1974 but was recalled in 1976 to become president of Lockheed California Company, a position he held until 1979. As company president, he traveled extensively, seeking new sales of the L-1011 Tristar wide-body aircraft, considered by many to be one of the best commercial aircraft of the era. He then became Lockheed senior vice president for aircraft until he retired in 1980. After retirement, he continued to be an active senior advisor to Lockheed and, after 1995, to the merged Lockheed Martin Corporation. From 1977 to 1996, three of his former subordinates— Roy A. Anderson, Lawrence O. Kitchen, and Daniel M. Tellep— served sequentially as Lockheed chief executive officer. They all respected Willis's frank advice, solicited or unsolicited. In effect, he never fully retired.

Willis had a long record of distinguished public service from 1957 to 1992 with the National Aeronautics and Space Administration (NASA), the Army, the Navy, and the National Research Council, where he served on 10 major boards and panels. He was awarded the NASA Distinguished Public Service Medal and was a longtime member, then fellow, then honorary fellow of the American Institute of Aeronautics and Astronautics (AIAA). In 1974, he was the recipient of the AIAA Reed Aeronautics Award. Willis was also a fellow of the Royal Aeronautical Society.

In 1982, Willis received the Wright Brothers Memorial Trophy Award for "significant public service of enduring value to aviation in the United States." In 1985, he was selected by the National Academy of Engineering to give the Founders Lecture. His talk, "Risk and Technical Health," reflected his deep concern that the government's unwillingness to take technical risks was undermining the technical health of the country. In 1988, he was awarded the National Medal of Science by President Ronald Reagan, which he said "made me mighty happy." He was posthumously inducted into the National Management Association Hall of Fame in 2004.

In his quiet way, Willis was a dedicated American patriot, deeply concerned about the future of science and technology in the United States. He was an egalitarian and privately had little respect for people who were not. Daniel M. Tellep, Lockheed chief executive officer from 1989 to 1995, was associated with Willis from 1955 to 2004. At a celebration of Willis's life, Tellep said, "He represented to many of us engineers a template for what a good and decent and skilled and dedicated professional engineer should be. He was and always remained my engineering hero." Willis was deeply respected by a broad range of people in many walks of life. Very few people can match his accomplishments.

Willis's wife Anita predeceased him. He is survived by his sons, Willis Jr. and James, a daughter, Nancy Gay Bostick, and grandchildren, William L. Hawkins and Elena V.S. Hawkins.

EDWARD GRAHAM JEFFERSON

1921–2006

Elected in 1986

"For outstanding research leadership and exceptional contributions to university-industry cooperation in science and engineering, and for creative direction of one of the world's largest industrial organizations."

WRITTEN BY CHARLES O. HOLLIDAY JR.
SUBMITTED BY THE NAE HOME SECRETARY

EDWARD GRAHAM JEFFERSON, retired chairman and chief executive officer of DuPont, died on February 9, 2006.

Born July 15, 1921, in London, Ed served in the British Royal Artillery during World War II and took part in the Normandy invasion in 1944. While in Normandy, he was involved in operations of the 30th Corps and the 43rd Wessex Division, including Operation Epsom and Operation Goodwood. Later, in Holland, Captain Jefferson participated in Operation Market Garden, during which American and British forces attacked across the Meuse-Escant Canal toward Eindhoven, Nijmegen, and Arnhem. In recognition of his service, Ed was awarded several campaign medals and stars and has the distinction of "Mentioned in Dispatches" by King George VI.

Ed graduated from King's College, University of London, with first-class honors in chemistry and was awarded the Samuel Smiles Prize for Chemistry. He received a doctoral degree at King's College. He later became a Fellow of King's College and served as president and treasurer of Friends of King's College. He became a citizen of the United States in 1957. He was a member of the American Philosophical Society and the American Academy of Arts and Sciences and a trustee of the Academy of Natural Sciences. In 1986, he was elected to the National Academy of Engineering.

Recruited by DuPont in 1951, Ed joined the company at the Belle Works in West Virginia and worked in a variety of locations until 1958 when he settled in Wilmington, Delaware. In 1973, he was appointed a director, senior vice president, and member of the Executive Committee. In 1978, he was given responsibility for the direction and coordination of all research and development activities for the company. On January 1, 1980, he was named president and chief operating officer, and, on May 1, 1981, he became chairman and chief executive officer. That same year, he led the DuPont acquisition of Conoco. He served on the DuPont Board of Directors from 1973 to 1992.

During his long career, Ed was co-chair of the Business Roundtable; a member of the American Section of the Society of Chemical Industry, of which he was formerly chair; vice chair of the Conference Board; a member of the President's Export Council; and a member of the U.S. Council for International Business. He was an honorary member of the Business Council and a member of the American Institute of Chemical Engineers, American Chemical Society, and Directors of Industrial Research. He was a director of the Chemical Banking Corporation and its subsidiary, Chemical Bank, and a director of the American Telephone and Telegraph Company. He also served on the boards of the Diamond State Telephone Company and Seagram Company Ltd.

Ed was also vice chair of the Board of Trustees of the University of Delaware, which the Jefferson family held in special regard. The family made many contributions to the school, including the donation of a pipe organ to the Edward G. and Naomi L. Jefferson Music Gallery and the establishment of a music scholarship. A chair in the Biotechnology Institute was established in Dr. Jefferson's name. Ed also contributed to higher education in a number of other ways. He was chair of the Advisory Board, School of International and Public Affairs, Columbia University, and a member of the Board of Trustees of the University of Pennsylvania and of Tuskegee University. Dr. Jefferson was awarded the Chemical Industry Medal by the Society of the Chemical Industry and received a number of honorary degrees.

He was a trustee of the Dole Foundation for the Handicapped

and an honorary trustee of Winterthur Museum and Gardens, of which he had been chairman of the board. He also served as a member of the Business Committee for the Arts and the Delaware State Arts Council. He was a Senior Warden of Trinity Episcopal Church and president and Trustee Emeritus of the Delaware Art Museum.

Ed personified DuPont's emphasis on science, and his leadership and insights throughout his career helped shape the direction of the company. He was a strong supporter of research and development and provided personal leadership in biochemical and bioengineering. His accomplishments at DuPont were numerous, but he will be long remembered for recognizing the importance of biotechnology to the growth of the company and setting the company on a path toward realizing the potential of biotechnology.

On the occasion of the dedication of a life-sciences laboratory at the DuPont Experimental Station in 1984, Ed said that the company's products "in the next decade and beyond will come not just from chemistry and polymer science, but increasingly from electronics and plant and health sciences." It was his good fortune to see his prediction come true on a scale that would have startled him and his peers at the time, but which confirmed his intuitive understanding of the importance of biotechnology to DuPont in the 21st century.

Ed Jefferson will also be remembered for preserving the company's history for the benefit of future business leaders at DuPont and other companies. He was instrumental in the decision to engage academic historians of business to produce a history of DuPont research (Cambridge University Press, 1988). He gave the authors, historians David A. Hounshell and John Kenly Smith, access to all relevant company records and complete academic freedom. The result was a substantial volume that remains the essential publication about DuPont.

In a speech at the Center for the History of Chemistry—now the Chemical Heritage Foundation—in 1985, Ed said, "Without the study of corporate histories, the story of science and technology in our century will be told inadequately or not at all.... If by neglect we imply that our histories are unimportant or if we subject them to unscholarly treatment, we then have no defense against those who would seek to diminish our achievements."

Ed Jefferson held the achievements of his industry and his company in high regard. Everyone who knew and worked with him was greatly enriched by the experience, and the impact of his leadership will be felt at DuPont for years to come.

Dr. Jefferson is survived by his wife of 52 years, the former Naomi Nale Love of Charleston, West Virginia; son Charles David Jefferson of Charlottesville, Virginia; son Andrew McKinley Jefferson (wife, Heather D. Jefferson) of Greenville, Delaware; and four grandchildren, Peter Marion Jefferson, Charles David Jefferson Jr., Marshall Edward Jefferson, and Edward Graham Jefferson, III. Dr. Jefferson is also survived by his brother David Jefferson, and sisters-in-law Barbara, Delphine, and Bettine all of the United Kingdom. Dr. Jefferson was predeceased by his sons Edward G. Jefferson Jr., and Peter L. Jefferson.

Howard S. Jones, Jr.

HOWARD ST. CLAIRE JONES JR.

1921–2005

Elected in 1999

*"For the invention and development of antennas and
microwave components for missiles and spacecraft."*

BY JOHN BROOKS SLAUGHTER

HOWARD S. JONES JR., an engineer, scientist, and inventor
who was renowned for his work on radar and communications
antennas and systems, died on February 26, 2005, at the age of
83. At the time of his death, he was an independent consultant
in microwave electronics, a field in which he had made significant technical contributions.

Howard Jones was born on August 18, 1921, in Richmond,
Virginia. He received his education in that city culminating with
a B.S. in mathematics and physics from Virginia Union University in 1943. He received a Certificate in Engineering from
Howard University in 1944 and an M.S. in electrical engineering from Bucknell University, Lewisburg, Pennsylvania, in 1973.
In a career that spanned more than 60 years, Howard served in
the military, in academe, in the corporate world, and in government. An internationally recognized expert on microwaves and
radar antenna systems, Howard was elected to the National Academy of Engineering in 1999.

After two years in the army during World War II, Howard went
to work as an electronics physicist with the National Bureau of
Standards, later the Harry Diamond Research Laboratories of
the U.S. Army Laboratory Command, in Adelphi, Maryland.
During his 34-year tenure there, he was a prolific inventor who
received 31 patents for microwave antennas, electronic compo-

nents, and test equipment for missile fuses and radar systems, as well as instruments for military and space applications. During his last 12 years at the Harry Diamond Laboratories, Howard was a supervisory physical scientist and chief of the microwave and research development branch. He retired in 1980.

Howard's first patent was for an "antenna testing shield," a device still used today to test the fusing system for missiles under conditions similar to those encountered in operation. His most important patents were for small, lightweight, reliable conformal array antennas that could be enclosed within a missile. Today, conformal antenna arrays are used in nearly every modern U.S. missile, and the technology developed for them laid the foundation for the development of aircraft and missiles that are difficult, if not impossible, to detect by radar. In addition to these inventions, Howard designed and developed state-of-the-art microwave antennas, electronic components, and devices that could be used in a wide range of weapons and communications systems. Although much of his work was done under the auspices of the U.S. Army, he was a strong believer in technology transfer and looked for opportunities to use his inventions and developments in the commercial arena.

Although Howard Jones was an advisor and consultant to the U.S. armed services for more than 20 years, he also participated with university and industry researchers working on many facets of microwave and antenna technology. He published more than 40 technical articles in the scientific and technical literature, made many presentations at national and international conferences, and was an invited speaker at many universities and meetings of professional societies.

Among his many awards were honorary doctorates from Virginia Union University and Trinity College. He was a fellow of the American Association for the Advancement of Science and Institute of Electrical and Electronics Engineers (IEEE), which bestowed upon him the prestigious Harry Diamond Memorial Award (1985), fitting recognition for his years of dedicated service to the safety of our nation.

Howard Jones loved working with young people, and he encouraged them to study math and science so that they could pursue careers in engineering. He loved what he did and took great pleasure in sharing the joys and opportunities of engineering with students. He was particularly interested in helping minority young people to study engineering, and he spent many hours mentoring and tutoring them for that purpose. He was a kind and generous person who took great pride in his achievements and had a strong desire to see others be as accomplished and happy in their careers as he was in his. Howard resided in Washington, D.C., with his beloved wife, Evelyn.

J. Erik Jonsson

J. ERIK JONSSON

1901–1995

Elected in 1971

"For contributions as an engineer, industrialist, public servant, and philanthropist, to effective management and the broad-scale application of engineering concepts to urban problems."

BY ROLAND W. SCHMITT

J. ERIK JONSSON, a pioneer of the semiconductor industry, visionary political leader of his home city of Dallas, and generous philanthropist, died at the age of 93 at his home on September 1, 1995. In 1971, he was elected to the National Academy of Engineering, and in 1974 the academy awarded him the prestigious Founders Medal.

Erik Jonsson was born in 1901 in Brooklyn, New York, the only child of Swedish immigrants. His father, who owned a small grocery store, wanted Erik to cut school short and join him in the business, but his mother encouraged him to get a good education. She prevailed, and after completing four years of high school in three years, Erik entered Rensselaer Polytechnic Institute (RPI), from which he graduated in 1922 with a degree in mechanical engineering. Thus, began his lifelong association with RPI. He eventually became the largest benefactor of that institution in its history.

After graduation, Erik Jonsson took the best job offer he could get—$125 a month—as a rolling mill apprentice with the Aluminum Company of America (ALCOA). He made a brief but unsuccessful try as a Pontiac dealer but soon returned to ALCOA. He met his future wife, Margaret Fonde, at a Halloween party on a business trip to Tennessee and proposed the next day on their first date. They were married in 1923 and remained joined for 61 years until Margaret's death in 1984. The couple had three children, Kenneth, Philip, and Margaret.

In 1929, Erik began conducting business with J. Clarence Karcher, the husband of his wife's cousin. Karcher and Eugene McDermott were using reflection seismology to search for oil. Erik joined their company in 1930 as head of their laboratory in Newark, New Jersey. He later said he thought Karcher and McDermott were "crazy" for starting a business during the Depression, but he admired them and wanted to be part of the venture.

The company, Geophysical Service Inc. (GSI), manufactured equipment to locate oil. Because of the nature of the business, in 1934 the firm moved to Dallas, closer to the oil fields. After the company had made a few significant oil discoveries of its own, Stanoline Oil (later Standard Oil of New Jersey) decided to buy the company in 1941. However, the new owners did not want the oil exploration part of the business, so Jonsson, Eugene McDermott, Cecil Green, and H. Bates Peacock bought it. The deal was closed on December 6, 1941, the day before Pearl Harbor.

Because of their experience making seismometers, GSI soon had a contract making magnetic detectors as antisubmarine devices. Erik Jonsson became the sales representative in Washington, and the business grew into sonar, radar, and other military equipment. At the end of the war, the military business was bigger than the geophysical business, so they changed the name to Texas Instruments (TI), and Erik Jonsson became president of the company in 1951.

In 1952, at the urging of Pat Haggerty who had joined the company in 1945, Erik persuaded a reluctant Western Electric to sell TI a license to manufacture transistors; Western Electric had thought TI was too young and inexperienced a company to succeed. Nevertheless, TI got the license in May and produced its first transistor by Christmas. By 1954, the first pocket-sized transistor radio, using TI's mass-produced transistors, appeared on the market. TI subsequently introduced a number of pioneering innovations in semiconductors, including breakthrough production of silicon transistors and the integrated circuit. Erik became chairman of the board in 1958, a position he held for eight years; he was honorary chairman for another 11 years.

During his tenure at TI, Erik was also heavily involved in civic affairs. He was president of the Dallas Chamber of Commerce from 1957–1958, president of the United Way of Dallas from 1961–1962, and president of the Dallas Citizens' Council in 1963. In the latter capacity, he hosted a luncheon on November 22, 1963, at which he had to inform the 2,600 guests that crowded the room that the speaker they were awaiting, President John F. Kennedy, had been shot. In 1964, the mayor of Dallas, Earle Cabell, resigned to run for Congress. Other civic leaders turned to Erik Jonsson at this gloomy period following Kennedy's assassination and asked him to become mayor. He was elected to the vacancy by the City Council and was subsequently re-elected three times by popular vote. He held the post from February 1964 to May 1971.

As mayor of Dallas, Erik Jonsson launched a pioneering program, Goals for Dallas, to define the future course of growth and development for the city. His vision was essential to the development of the Dallas/Fort Worth International Airport, the Dallas city hall, the Dallas convention center, and the Dallas central library, which was named for him.

Erik Jonsson was a wide-ranging, generous philanthropist whose contributions were focused largely on education. He was a large contributor to Skidmore College and to his alma mater, RPI. He and his cofounders at TI, Eugene McDermott and Cecil Green, also founded the Southwest Center for Advanced Studies, which grew into the University of Texas at Dallas. He gave generously to many institutions of higher education: a hospital at Baylor University Medical Center; a cancer research center at UCLA; and general donations to Massachusetts Institute of Technology, Tulane University, Carnegie Mellon University, Bishop College, and Austin College. His support of pre-college education included significant contributions to the Hockaday School and the Lamplighter School. He made his philanthropic contributions with as much perception and foresight as he devoted to his endeavors in industry and politics. To honor in perpetuity Erik's many contributions to science, technology, and policy, in

1991 Kenneth A. Jonsson, the honoree's son, The Jonsson Foundation, and an anonymous donor provided funds to name the National Academy of Sciences' conference facility in Woods Hole, Massachusetts, the J. Erik Jonsson Center.

During my tenure as president of RPI (1988–1993), I often visited Erik in Dallas and was struck by the regard and affection the citizens of that city showed for him as we moved about the town. He also visited the campus in Troy, New York, occasionally. After every encounter with him, I came away with a new idea or challenge; his energy and insight remained strong until the end.

Erik Jonsson's life, filled with achievements and generosity, inspired many around him. He constantly urged others to reach for more challenging goals and visionary plans than they might otherwise have considered.

Erik Jonsson is survived by his sons Kenneth Jonsson of Santa Monica, California, and Philip Jonsson of Dallas, Texas, and a daughter, Margaret Jonsson Rogers of Dallas, Texas.

RICHARD C. JORDAN

1909–2002

Elected in 1975

"For pioneering in research on energy conservation through climate control, on solar energy, and national and international leadership in engineering education."

BY RICHARD J. GOLDSTEIN, BENJAMIN Y.H. LIU, AND DEANE MORRISON

RICHARD C. JORDAN, former head of the University of Minnesota Department of Mechanical Engineering, died of natural causes in Rio Verde, Arizona, on June 14, 2002, at the age of 93.

Jordan was born in Minneapolis on April 16, 1909. As a youngster interested in mechanics and electricity, he was the first in his Minneapolis neighborhood to build a radio and receive transmissions from across the country. Fascinated by advances in the mechanical sciences at the beginning of the century, he decided at an early age to become an engineer. He attended West High School in Minneapolis and continued his education at the University of Minnesota, where he received a bachelor's degree in aeronautical engineering in 1931 and a master's degree in mechanical engineering in 1933. In 1940, as a specialist in the science of heating and refrigeration, with minors in mathematics and physical metallurgy, he earned the first doctorate in mechanical engineering at the University of Minnesota.

The university was also the beneficiary of Jordan's teaching talents. He began his career at the university Engineering Experiment Station and rose to become a full professor and, in 1949, head of the Mechanical Engineering Department. He continued to hold that post until his retirement in 1977.

In his capacity as professor and department head, Jordan modernized the experimental laboratories and broadened the curriculum to include studies focused on new technologies. He encouraged engineering innovation and recruited faculty members with worldwide reputations in engineering science. Under his leadership, the department became a center of excellence in a number of areas, including heat-transfer studies, particularly the generation of solar power through the use of solar collectors, and rose in the rankings to fourth in the country. He also oversaw the creation of a particle-transfer laboratory and took part in its research projects.

Jordan, whose work in heating and refrigeration was internationally recognized, wrote more than 200 technical publications, including *Refrigeration and Air-Conditioning*, with G.B. Priester, (Prentice-Hall, 1949, revised 1956), a key textbook in the field for many years.

Aware of diminishing world-energy resources, Jordan advocated solar energy as an alternative to fossil fuels. "Any home in the United States may be heated entirely by a solar energy heat pump system," he wrote, "if a sufficiently large collector, heat pump, and heat storage facilities are provided." He established a solar-energy research program at the University of Minnesota in the mid-1950s; it focused on solar energy as a way to control energy consumption in buildings. He and his students made pioneering contributions to fundamental research on solar radiation that are still widely regarded.

Jordan began studying sustainable, cost-effective ways of collecting solar energy early in his career. His papers "Solar-Energy Heating" (1954), "Heat Pumps and Solar Energy" (1955), and "Solar Energy Utilization" (1956) are as relevant today as they were when they were published. "Direct Solar Radiation Available on Clear Days" (1958) and "The Interrelationship and Characteristic Distribution of Direct, Diffuse and Total Solar Radiation" (1960) provided fundamental data on solar radiation that have remained substantially unchanged over the years.

Recognizing the importance of air quality in the building sciences and the need for energy conservation, Jordan began a program of study on air filtration and building insulation.

Through a series of publications, which included Air Filtration Studies (University of Minnesota Department of Mechanical Engineering, ASHRAE, and U.S. Public Health Service Cooperative Research Project Progress Reports 2, 3, 5, 6, and 7), Size Distribution and Concentration of Air Borne Dust (American Society of Heating and Air-Conditioning Engineers, 1956), and Photometer for Dust Measurement (University of Minnesota Department of Mechanical Engineering, ASHRAE, and U.S. Public Health Service Cooperative Research Project, 1955), he laid the groundwork for the study of air quality in buildings and for using filtration to reduce airborne dust.

In the 1950s, long before the global exchange of scientific research results was common, Jordan was vice president of the Technical Board of the International Institute of Refrigeration, headquartered in Paris; he later served on the institute's Scientific Council. In the 1960s, he participated in four U.S. State Department missions to promote engineering education in developing countries in the Middle East, South America, and the Far East.

Jordan was much in demand as a consultant, and the U.S. State Department, World Bank, U.S. Agency for International Development, U.S. Army Corps of Engineers, U.S. Department of Education, and California and Florida were among his clients. His industrial clients included Control Data, Reynolds Metals, DuPont, Goodyear Aircraft Corporation, Owens Corning Corporation, and Emerson Electric Company. He served on the boards of directors of several companies, including 10 years on the board of Onan Corporation, a division of Studebaker Worthington.

Jordan's numerous awards include the Outstanding Achievement Award of the University of Minnesota (the highest honor for an alumnus) in 1979 and the Wolverine Award for outstanding publication and research from the American Society of Heating, Refrigerating and Air-Conditioning Engineers (ASHRAE) in 1949. In 1966, he won two ASHRAE awards: the E.K. Campbell Award for outstanding contributions to education and the F. Paul Anderson Medal for "outstanding contributions in all phases of heating, refrigerating and air-conditioning."

In 1972, Jordan was named Engineer of the Year by the Minnesota Society of Professional Engineers, and in 1980, he was named to the Solar Hall of Fame. He was a fellow of the American Society of Mechanical Engineers, a fellow and president of ASHRAE, and a fellow of the American Association for the Advancement of Science. Jordan was elected to the National Academy of Engineering in 1975. After his retirement, he became an associate dean of the University of Minnesota Institute of Technology, a post he held until 1985.

Jordan enjoyed vacationing with his family at an island cabin on Lake Kabetogama in northern Minnesota. While on the island, informally know as Retreat from Reason, he fished and went boating and put his talents to use installing water and electrical systems. His love of travel began with trips to Montana in his childhood and to Mexico in the 1930s, and he and his wife, Freda, visited more than 67 countries. Jordan led an active social life with colleagues and friends at the University of Minnesota. He also took a keen interest in his daughters' and grandchildren's educations.

Benjamin Liu, a retired Regents Professor of Mechanical Engineering, called Jordan a visionary and pioneer who had the ability to recognize talent. Liu said that, at a time when science and engineering were considered separate disciplines—with science focusing on nature and engineering on mechanics—Jordan worked to combine the two fields. He was also a terrific fundraiser.

Jordan's wife of 66 years, Freda Laudon Jordan died in January 2006. He is survived by his daughters Mary Ann Jordan and her husband David Johnson, Carol (Wolfgang) Wawersik, and Linda (John) Cogdill; four grandchildren Andrea Lommen, Kate Lommen, Matthew Wawersik, and Stefan Wawersik; and five great grandchildren.

Jordan was a legend in the field of mechanical engineering whose legacy will last for a very long time.

Thomas J. Kelly

THOMAS J. KELLY

1929–2002

Elected in 1991

"For leadership in designing, developing, and
supervising the construction of the Apollo Lunar Module."

BY J.G. GAVIN JR.
WITH CONTRIBUTIONS BY JOAN KELLY

WHEN THE PRESS REPORTED the death of Thomas J. Kelly on March 23, 2002, the nation learned that it had lost a true space pioneer. Kelly played a major role in validating the advantages of lunar orbit rendezvous as the preferred strategy for sending humans to the Moon. He was instrumental in the development of Grumman's proposal that resulted in the selection of Grumman Aerospace to design and build the Lunar Module for Apollo. As chief engineer, manager of spacecraft assembly and testing, and engineering manager, he was the engineering leader in the development of the Lunar Module, and, based on his accomplishments, he earned the unofficial title, "Father of the Lunar Module."

The Lunar Module was successful in every mission and was the "lifeboat" for the aborted Apollo 13 mission. This was the result of an extraordinary team effort, and Thomas J. Kelly deserves a great deal of the credit for forming, leading, and motivating the engineering team. Considering the unknowns at the beginning of the Apollo Program, his team's accomplishments provide a classic example of inspired systems design. At the time, one of the founders of Grumman commented, "I hope you young fellows understand what you have committed the company to do!"

Kelly was not only a competent, practical engineer, but also a visionary. He worked well with people on a demanding schedule and in a tense environment; the Lunar Module Program was initiated less than a year after the Command and Service Module Program began. People liked to work with or for Kelly. He "told it like it was" and refused to be discouraged by setbacks.

Thomas J. Kelly spent most of his professional career which began right after he graduated from Cornell, at Grumman. Kelly was born June 14, 1929, in Brooklyn, New York, spent his formative years on Long Island, and his undergraduate education was supported by a Grumman scholarship. A number of early assignments at Grumman prepared him for his later responsibilities. He designed the air inlets for the first Grumman aircraft to exceed twice the speed of sound. He was a prime mover in the well regarded but unsuccessful proposal for Project Mercury. He was a key player in a Grumman team that supported General Electric's unsuccessful bid for the Apollo Command and Service Module contract.

As mentioned earlier, Kelly led the Grumman-funded study that validated the Lunar Orbit Rendezvous strategy for going to the Moon. John Houbolt of the National Aeronautics and Space Administration (NASA) had argued that this approach was clearly more efficient than the Earth Orbit Rendezvous plan. An intense debate in NASA ensued, and Kelly's briefing based on Grumman's study was a major contributor to the acceptance of the Lunar Orbit Rendezvous plan.

The competition for the Lunar Module contract was unique. Instead of the usual proposed design, NASA asked bidders to answer 20 questions to show their understanding of the design challenge. Kelly led the group that assembled Grumman's winning response. In the early days of the Grumman effort, it became apparent that NASA, North American (later Rockwell), and Grumman needed a common, standard mission on which to base design efforts. Kelly proposed a joint undertaking, which led to the formation of the Apollo Mission Planning Task Force to work on this vital problem.

During Apollo Missions 9, 10, 11, and 12, Kelly led the Grumman support team at Mission Control at the Manned Space Flight Center in Houston. Grumman then sent Kelly to the Sloan School of Management at the Massachusetts Institute of Technology, but he returned to Houston without finishing his assignment to join the Grumman support team coping with the aftermath of the explosion in the Apollo Service Module during the Apollo 13 mission. The Lunar Module became a cold but successful "lifeboat," and the astronauts were saved. In the post-Apollo, post-Sloan days, Kelly made a major contribution to Grumman's bid for the Space Shuttle contract.

Kelly was appointed to the Board of Directors of the New York State Science and Technology Foundation by Governor Hugh Carey in 1979. The organization helped state businesses and universities with useful encouragement for notable start up projects, and Tom served on the board until he retired.

He was elected to the National Academy of Engineering in 1991. He received the NASA Certificate of Appreciation, 1969, and the NASA Distinguished Public Service Medal, 1973. In 1972 he was awarded the AIAA Spacecraft Design Award and the Cornell Engineering Award.

He was a member of the following societies: American Astronautical Society (AAS); American Institute of Aeronautics (AIAA) (Board of Directors member 1974–1980); American Society of Mechanical Engineers (ASME); Cornell Society of Engineers; and Columbia Engineering Council.

Tom Kelly was a multi-talented musician. He had a wonderful baritone singing voice and sang with the Huntington Choral Society and then with the North Fork Chorale when the family moved to Cutchogue.

Even though he never really gained weight as he became older Tom decided he needed something else to keep him healthy. That was running. He was usually up at 5:30 a.m. to run before work, and he felt it cleared his head and made him feel good. He ran, when he was home, away, or even on vacation and enjoyed every minute of it. It was precious time for him.

Tom Kelly is survived by his wife and life partner, Joan Tantum Kelly, and two generations of younger Kellys. His sons are David, Thomas Jr., Edward, Christopher, and Peter and his daughter, Jennifer, the only one who has pursued a career in engineering so far. His 11 grandchildren are Shannon, Rachel, Kevin, Christopher, Cuchulain, Finn, Cormac, Oonagh, Savanna (all Kellys), and Ryan and Katchen Lachmayr.

JACK ST. CLAIR KILBY

1923–2005

Elected in 1967

"For inventions basic to integrated circuits."

BY TOM ENGIBOUS

JACK ST. CLAIR KILBY, inventor of the integrated circuit and pioneer in the semiconductor industry, died of cancer on June 20, 2005, at his home in Dallas at the age of 81. First and foremost an engineer, he took satisfaction and pleasure in finding practical solutions to vexing problems.

Jack was born on November 8, 1923, in Jefferson City, Missouri, to Hubert and Vina Freitag Kilby. When he was still young, the family moved to Great Bend, Kansas, where he and his sister, Jane, were reared. He considered Great Bend his hometown.

His father was president of a small power company with customers scattered across rural western Kansas. In 1937, a severe ice storm hit the region, downing telephone and power lines. Although he was just a teenager at the time, Jack accompanied his father as he worked with amateur radio operators to communicate with isolated customers. That experience triggered Jack's lifelong interest in electronics. Following the storm, he got his own radio license, built a transmitter, learned all he could from older ham radio operators, and began to operate radios himself. These events influenced his decision to study electrical engineering.

Jack applied to MIT but narrowly missed passing the math portion of his entrance exam. Instead, in 1941, he ended up at his father's alma mater, the University of Illinois. Like many in his generation, his education was interrupted by World War II.

Jack joined the U.S. Army where, after taking radio operator training, he was transferred to the Office of Strategic Services. He spent the war as a radio operator and repairman in the India-China-Burma theatre.

After the war, he returned to the university to resume his studies and received his bachelor's degree in electrical engineering in 1947. During this period, he also met his wife, Barbara Annegers Kilby. They were married on June 27, 1947, and were together for 34 years until she died in 1981.

After graduation, Jack went to work for the Centralab Division of Globe-Union Inc. (now part of Johnson Controls) in Milwaukee, where he designed and developed ceramic-base silkscreen circuits for consumer electronics products. In spring 1952, he was Centralab's representative at an eight-day symposium hosted by Bell Labs, where he learned about Western Electric's new technology, transistors. Jack remained at Centralab for 11 years, immersing himself in the nascent field of semiconductors. During this time, he also earned a master's degree in electrical engineering from the University of Wisconsin.

In May 1958, Jack moved to Dallas to work for Texas Instruments (TI) in the general area of microminiaturization—a key issue facing the young semiconductor industry. At the time, semiconductors required hand soldering of thousands of discrete components, which was a gating factor in the development of more elaborate, reliable, cost-effective electronic circuits. TI, and the industry as a whole, was struggling to resolve the dilemma posed by this "tyranny of numbers."

TI made resistors, capacitors, transistors, and diodes, and Jack's first solution was repackaging. But a detailed cost analysis showed that this would be impractical, because the overhead at a semiconductor house like TI was two to three times what it was at Centralab. Fearing he would be assigned to work on a proposal for the micro-module program, a miniaturization initiative sponsored by the U.S. Army Signal Corps that Jack didn't believe would work, he threw himself into finding a viable alternative quickly. Coincidentally, TI was readying itself for the mass vacation that was customary for employees at the time. As a new employee, Jack didn't have any vacation time stored up, so he had some relatively quiet time on the TI campus to ponder the issue.

Ever the practical engineer, Jack came to the conclusion that the only thing a semiconductor firm could make cost effectively was a semiconductor. Then, in the course of a day, he came to the conclusion that resistors and capacitors could be made from the same material as the active devices, and that they could be made in situ, that is, interconnected to form a complete circuit. This was a simple, elegant solution to a problem that had stymied the best and brightest minds for several years.

When his supervisor returned from vacation, Jack showed him his sketches and was challenged to prove that circuits made entirely of semiconductors would work. Jack did so and then set out to build an integrated structure as he had originally planned. On September 12, 1958, he put the monolithic integrated circuit to the test—and it worked! He had conceived and built the first integrated circuit. Little did he know that his invention would change the world.

Jack's achievement was publicly announced in March 1959, but, like many breakthrough technologies, it wasn't widely accepted at first. The industry was still wedded to transistor technology, design, and manufacturing, and so did not initially embrace the integrated circuit.

However, the U.S. Air Force was very interested in a technology that could reduce the size and cost of its computers. In 1962, TI won its first major integrated circuit contract to design and build a family of 22 special circuits for the Minuteman missile. The success with the Minuteman slowly opened the doors to customer acceptance, and computer manufacturers began to adopt integrated circuits as well.

Still, the chip had yet to cross over to consumer applications. Hoping to jump-start the market, TI management challenged Jack to design a calculator powerful enough to perform the math functions of the large, electromechanical desktop models of the day but small enough to fit in a coat pocket. Jack led a team comprised of Jerry Merryman, Jim Van Tassel, and himself that successfully delivered a working model by December 1966.

Jack went on to pioneer military, industrial, and commercial applications of his invention, manage projects, and pursue concepts for new generations of integrated circuits. He was instrumental in the continuing development of integrated circuit technology during those years, as he worked "hands on" on various aspects of design, packaging, and process technology tools.

In 1970, he took a leave of absence from TI to become an independent consultant, focusing his energies on integrated circuits, primarily in consumer-related applications. He explored, among other subjects, the use of silicon technology for generating electrical power from sunlight. From 1978 to 1984, he served as Distinguished Professor of Electrical Engineering at Texas A&M University. He officially retired from TI in 1983 but continued to do consulting work with the company and maintained a significant relationship with TI until his death. In later years, Jack was director of a few corporate boards and a member of advisory committees for selected organizations.

Jack's work laid the foundation for the field of modern microelectronics and moved the industry toward the miniaturization and integration that continues today. As a pioneer in the industry, he received innumerable honors and awards recognizing his contributions to the field and their impact on the world at large.

Jack was awarded the Nobel Prize in Physics (2000) for his role in the invention of the integrated circuit. He was one of only 13 Americans to receive both the National Medal of Science and the National Medal of Technology, the highest technical awards given by the U.S. government. He was awarded the Kyoto Prize in Advanced Technology, Japan's highest private award for lifetime achievement. He was also the recipient of the first international Charles Stark Draper Prize, the world's top engineering award, from the National Academy of Engineering.

Jack was elected a member of the National Academy of Engineering in 1967, was an IEEE Fellow, and held more than 60 patents for a variety of electronics inventions. In addition to the integrated circuit, these included the handheld electronic calculator and the thermal printer, both of which he co-invented.

Jack received honorary degrees from several institutions of higher learning, including the University of Miami, Rochester Institute of Technology, University of Illinois, Southern Methodist University, Texas A&M University, and Georgia Institute of Technology.

Any biography of Jack would be incomplete without describing the quality of the man. Jack was a unique and special individual. Quiet and thoughtful with a generous spirit, he took the time to encourage young engineers and frequently allowed grade-school students to interview him for class papers. He was a man of few words, yet his well-thought-out comments were often peppered with quiet humor. Jack was quick to credit the thousands of engineers who followed him for growing the semiconductor industry. Quoting an earlier Nobel Prize winner in the introductory remarks of his Nobel Lecture, Jack compared his feelings about the tremendous strides the industry had made with those of a beaver looking at Hoover Dam—"It's based on an idea of mine."

Jack was a gentle man and a gentleman, and at 6 feet 6 inches, he was occasionally called a "gentle giant" by the media. Low-key and practical, Jack was a man who had earned the right to boast but never did. Above all, he was an engineer who enjoyed both the craft and art of his profession. Jack shaped an industry, but even more, he touched our souls. He will be remembered both for what he accomplished and for who he was.

It would be an incomplete portrait of Jack not to mention how important his family was to him. He is survived by two daughters, Janet Kilby Cameron and Ann Kilby; five granddaughters, Caitlan, Marcy, and Gwen Cameron, and Erica and Katrina Venhuizen; and a son-in-law, Thomas Cameron. His wife, Barbara, and sister, Jane, preceded him in death.

R. PETER KING

1938–2006

Elected in 2003

*"For the development of techniques for quantifying mineral liberation
and for leadership in Internet education about mineral processing."*

BY JOHN A. HERBST

THE WORLD LOST an outstanding scholar and human being on September 11, 2006, when R. Peter King died at the age
of 68. At the time of his death, Dr. King was a professor of metallurgical engineering at the University of Utah in Salt Lake City.
His accomplishments over his lifetime were truly remarkable.

Peter was born in Springs, South Africa, on March 12, 1938,
and spent his youth in the goldfields of South Africa. His formal
education began at Witwatersrand University in 1954. In 1956,
he met Ellen Courtenay, who became his constant companion,
loving wife, and partner for all the years that followed. Peter
graduated with a B.Sc. Chem. Eng. (cum laude) from Wits in
1958 and received an M.Sc. in 1962. Upon graduation, he received a scholarship from Shell Oil to pursue his doctoral studies at Manchester University; Peter and Ellen were married while
living in Manchester. In 1963, after receiving a Ph.D. from the
University of Manchester, the couple returned to South Africa,
where they started their family, which soon included Jeremy,
Andrew, and Janet.

From 1963 to 1990, Peter taught at Wits and led a research
group at the National Institute of Metallurgy. He was the recipient of many honors during this period, including election as
president, and later a life fellow, of the South African Institute
of Mining Metallurgy (SAIMM). He was also a member of the

Scientific Advisory Committee of the Prime Minister. In 1991, Peter was awarded the Gold Medal by SAIMM.

In 1990, Peter was appointed professor of metallurgy and director of the Generic Mineral Processing Center in Comminution at the University of Utah. On December 19, 1995, he became a U.S. citizen, and in 1999, he was appointed chairman of the Department of Metallurgical Engineering at the University of Utah. Between 1999 and 2006, he received many additional honors. He was appointed editor-in-chief of one of the most respected journals in his field, the *International Journal of Mineral Processing*. In 2002, he received the Antoine M. Gaudin Award of the Society of Mining Engineers for his "seminal research in mineral liberation." In 2003, at the zenith of his career, he was elected to the National Academy of Engineering in "recognition of the development of useful techniques to quantify mineral liberation and his leadership in Internet education of mineral processing." That same year, he was recognized with the prestigious International Mineral Processing Douglas W. Fuerstenau Lifetime Achievement Award.

Professor King excelled in both research and education. His research on the modeling and simulation of mineral processing operations led to the highly successful MODSIM computer software system for the simulation of plant operations. In addition, his pioneering research in mineral liberation represented a quantum leap forward in the accurate, quantitative description of multiphase particles. In fact, his research in mineral liberation provided a basis for collaboration that eventually led to a state-of-the-art micro-CT laboratory in the Department of Metallurgy at the University of Utah. Subsequently, these advances were integrated into detailed comminution models for quantifying the breakage of multiphase particles in complex grinding circuits. Dr. King's recent research was focused on the fundamental analysis of particle fracture and the aspects of this phenomenon that limit efficient energy utilization during comminution.

Professor King was truly a "distinguished teacher" in every sense, and he gave other educators in the field a model to emulate. In recognition of his contributions, he received the University of Utah Departmental Teaching Excellence Award in 1987 (as a visiting professor), 1996, 2000, and 2001 (as a regular faculty member). Peter's career was dedicated to education. He was a pioneer in the use of modern engineering methods in the classroom. Students were taught computer-based methodologies, and software was integrated not only into classroom work, but also into traditional lectures so students came away with a confident understanding of advanced engineering procedures. He not only challenged his students, but also provided them with a vision, or goal, and his students usually achieved academic excellence.

With the advent of the World Wide Web, new dimensions in engineering education became a reality. Professor King's leadership in this new arena of education was exemplified by his highly successful Internet course, "Modeling and Simulation of Mineral Processing Plants." In the first year, 44 students enrolled in the course from all over the world (Sweden, Brazil, Turkey, Peru, Australia, and South Africa), ranging from currently enrolled undergraduate/graduate students to university faculty, industrial researchers, and plant engineers.

Another online course, "The Virtual Laboratory," was created and enhanced under Peter's leadership. By simulating metallurgical equipment, processes, and reactions, the Virtual Laboratory environment made it possible for students to perform laboratory experiments easily, quickly, conveniently, and accurately.

Dr. King published more than 150 scholarly papers on fundamental aspects of mineral processing. He authored or co-authored five books, the most recent of which are *Introduction to Practical Fluid Flow* (Elsevier, 2002) and *Modeling and Simulation of Mineral Process Systems* (Butterworth-Heinemann, 2001).

Admired by colleagues and students around the world, Peter was always willing to mentor people who asked for his help, no matter their age or professional level. He and his wife Ellen contributed to the tuition of many engineering students both in South Africa and the United States

On a more personal level, Ellen says that Peter was a dedicated father and grandfather who took time with the family to visit the national parks and to ski. Peter very much enjoyed being with his seven grandchildren, and he recently told Ellen he regretted that he hadn't had an opportunity to teach his grand-sons how to make and fly model airplanes. He also told her he longed to return to the South African game parks. Peter en-joyed listening to classical music and opera, which he was able to do up until the day of his passing.

Peter is survived by his wife, Ellen; sons Jeremy and Andrew; daughter Janet; grandchildren Ryan, Ashley, Michael, Anthony, Robert, Lucy, and Nicholas; son-in-law Richard; and daughters-in-law Sylvia and Angela.

LEON K. KIRCHMAYER

1924–1995

Elected in 1979

"For contributions in the fields of electric power system control, economic simulation, and planning and dispatch."

BY FREDERICK J. ELLERT
WITH CONTRIBUTIONS BY OLGA T. KIRCHMAYER

LEON K. KIRCHMAYER, a world renowned expert in power-system simulation, planning, operation, and control, died on November 12, 1995, at the Ellis Hospital in Schenectady, New York, at the age of 71. Prior to his retirement from the General Electric (GE) Company in 1984, Kirch (as he was known to his many friends around the world) was the manager of advanced system technology and planning in the Electric Utility Systems Engineering Department of GE. He and his wife, Olga, lived in Rexford, New York.

Born on July 24, 1924, Kirch was the eldest of three children born to Henry and Clara Kirchmayer in Milwaukee, Wisconsin. His father was a mechanic, and his grandparents were immigrants from Bavaria, Germany. Kirch and his wife, Olga, have two children. Their son, Kenneth, has a degree in industrial and management engineering and is employed as a manager at GE's jet engine plant in Ohio. Their daughter, Karen, has a bachelor's degree in accounting and an MBA, with an emphasis on management information systems.

Kirch and his wife were avid sailors, skiers, hikers, swimmers, and dancers throughout their married life until 1984, when Kirch had an attack of severe arrhythmia that left him comatose. He and Olga then embarked on an intensive 12-year program that led to a remarkable recovery. Kirch responded to the arduous demands of rehabilitation with a strong, positive attitude, great determination, a sense of humor, cooperation, and a determination to meet the difficult challenges facing him.

Kirch graduated from Marquette University with a bachelor's degree in electrical engineering in 1945; he received the Engineering Professional Achievement Award from Marquette in 1991. He pursued graduate studies at the University of Wisconsin at Madison and received a master's degree in electrical engineering in 1947 and a doctorate in electrical engineering in 1950. He received a Distinguished Service Citation from the University of Wisconsin in 1972.

In 1948, he joined the Analytical Engineering Section of GE in Schenectady, New York, and for the next eight years he did pioneering work on the economical operation, planning, and control of large electric utility power systems. His work is still the basis for contemporary methods of operation. He also led the development of analytical methods of predicting power system responses and was instrumental in the development of techniques for calculating losses in large interconnected power systems. He published more than 20 technical papers dealing with these important matters.

In 1956, Kirch was promoted to the position of manager of investigations into power systems operation. In that position, he developed advanced mathematical and computer techniques for improving electric utility system operations. In 1958, he became the manager of the System Generation Analytical Engineering Operation, and, from 1963 to 1977, manager of the System Planning and Control Section. Over that 21-year period, he published 72 technical papers and two books dealing with the economical operation of power systems. In 1977, he became the manager of the Advanced System Technology and Planning Section, a position he held until he retired from GE. He published another five technical papers in the last phase of his career, bringing the total to more than 100, a truly astounding accomplishment. He also held four patents dealing with the computer control of power systems.

Kirch was elected to several honor societies, including Sigma Xi, Tau Beta Pi, Eta Kappa Nu, and Pi Mu Epsilon. In 1954 he received the Eta Kappa Nu Recognition for Outstanding Young Engineer Award. In 1966 he received the Engineer of the Year Award presented by the Schenectady Professional Engineering Society. Most important, he was elected to membership in the prestigious National Academy of Engineering in 1979.

Throughout his outstanding career, Kirch was actively involved in the work of many committees in various technical societies, including Institute of Electrical and Electronic Engineers (IEEE), American Society of Mechanical Engineers (ASME), National Society of Professional Engineers, Operations Research Society of America, and International Council on Large Electric Systems (CIGRE). He was also active in the formation of the IEEE Systems, Man, and Cybernetics Society. His many contributions to these organizations were recognized by his election to the grade of fellow of both IEEE and ASME, the IEEE and ASME Centennial Awards in 1984, and the prestigious IEEE Lamme Medal in 1988. The IEEE Leon K. Kirchmayer Award was established in 1997 in recognition of his many accomplishments. In 2003 it was replaced by the IEEE Leon K. Kirchmayer Graduate Teaching Award.

Kirch's work was also recognized internationally. He received the Bernard Price Memorial Award from the South African Institute of Electrical Engineers, was a guest speaker at the India Institute of Electrical Engineers in 1979, and was a member of the IEEE Power Engineering Society delegation to China in 1978.

Dr. Kirchmayer is survived by his wife, Olga Temoshok Kirchmayer, whom he married on December 2, 1950; a son, Kenneth L. Kirchmayer of Cincinnati, Ohio; a daughter, Karen C. Demuth of Dayton, Ohio; a sister, Carol Kirchmayer Destland of West Bend, Wisconsin; and five grandchildren.

Jerome Lederer

JEROME FOX LEDERER

1902–2004

Elected in 1967

"For air safety research."

BY DENNIS M. BUSHNELL

JEROME F. LEDERER, President Emeritus of the Flight Safety Foundation, died of congestive heart failure at Saddleback Memorial Medical Center in Laguna Hills, California, on February 6, 2004. He was 101 years old.

Born in New York City on September 26, 1902, Jerry became interested in aviation at an early age, stimulated by his attendance at the second aviation tournament in the United States in 1910 at Belmont Park, where one of the participants was the renowned Glenn Curtiss. Jerry graduated from the newly instituted aviation curriculum at New York University (NYU) in 1924 with a B.S. in mechanical engineering with aeronautical option. He received a master's degree in mechanical engineering from NYU in 1925 and was subsequently assistant to the director of the NYU Guggenheim School of Aeronautics. Jerry was responsible for building, calibrating, and operating NYU's 40-mph wind tunnel.

After a brief stint as a surveyor for the West Shore Railroad, Jerry began his career in aviation as the only aeronautical engineer working for the U.S. Airmail Service in 1926 and 1927. His job was to develop specifications, test parts, and examine wreckages to determine their "repairability." His experiences in this, his first nonacademic professional position, started him in the direction of aviation safety (and eventually industrial safety), the subjects of his entire career. Many people, in many generations worldwide, are alive today thanks to the creativity and continuous efforts of Jerry Lederer.

Jerry was proud that his career made it possible for professional pilots to obtain life insurance at the same rates as clergymen. In 1926, about one in four Airmail Service pilots was killed, usually in a fire consequent to a crash. An early example of Jerry's creative, hands-on approach to problem solving was an experiment in which an Airline Service airplane (a de Havilland 4 biplane) was accelerated at full power down a ramp and crashed into a concrete wall. Photography indicated that the crash caused fuel to spill out of the tank onto the hot exhaust manifold, which then ignited, causing a fire that often incinerated the pilot. Having identified this major problem, he proceeded to redesign the aircraft, reduce pilot morbidity, and, in the process, publish his first flight-safety bulletin. Around this time, he became friends with Charles Lindbergh, one of the airmail pilots, and, at Lindbergh's request, he inspected the Spirit of St. Louis the day before Lindy's historic transatlantic flight. Jerry's oft-quoted comment after the inspection was, "I did not have too much hope that he would make it."

In 1927, Jerry became a consultant to airplane manufacturers and an insurer, and in 1929, he became chief engineer of Aero Insurance Underwriters in charge of loss prevention and safety. He remained in that position until 1940, evaluating aviation risks, reducing losses through safety audits and educational programs, and disseminating safety bulletins and newsletters on how to improve safety.

From 1940 to 1942, he was a member of the Civil Aeronautics Board (predecessor of the Federal Aviation Administration [FAA]) and director of the Bureau of Flight Safety (a predecessor of the National Transportation Safety Board), where he was responsible for rule-making and accident investigation. He developed the accident investigation procedures that are still followed by government and military safety investigation groups. Several of his decisions during this time had lasting impacts, including requirements that aircraft be equipped with flight data recorders and blinking anti-collision lights.

During World War II, Jerry was named director of training and head of the administrative section of the Airlines War Training Institute, where he developed a program that trained some

10,000 pilots and 35,000 maintenance technicians for the Air Transport Command. Later in the war, he was operations analyst for the Second Air Force and was appointed to the U.S. Strategic Bombing Survey in Europe.

In 1947, at the request of airline engineers and executives, he initiated, and directed for some 20 years thereafter, an aviation safety information service, Engineering for Safety, that later became the Flight Safety Foundation. This nonprofit organization disseminated information on operational problems that transcended competing commercial interests and national borders and conducted research in several areas. He also instituted the worldwide exchange of safety and prevention information and experiences. In 1950, in addition to his responsibilities with the Flight Safety Foundation, he became the director of the Cornell Guggenheim Aviation Safety Center.

In 1956, Jerry was appointed to President Eisenhower's seven-person Aviation Facilities Investigation Group, which modernized the air traffic control system and paved the way for the formation of the FAA. He also served on the International Civil Aviation Organization (ICAO) panel that integrated jet aircraft into the worldwide air transportation system. Jerry retired from the Flight Safety Foundation in 1967, and that same year, following the fire on the Apollo space capsule that killed three astronauts, was asked to establish and direct an office for the safety of manned space flight for the National Aeronautics and Space Administration (NASA). He later became director of safety for all NASA activities.

During his tenure at NASA, Jerry advocated changing the focus from safety per se to risk management and "systems safety engineering." He argued that safety/risk management should be "designed into" the product initially, with input from engineering, operations, and management personnel. He instituted a policy of rewarding, rather than punishing, those who admitted mistakes.

After retiring from NASA in 1972, his second retirement, Jerry remained active in the safety/risk management community. He served on numerous boards and panels and taught at the Institute of Safety and Systems Management at the University of

Southern California. In 1984, at the age of 81, he published two papers ("Past and Present in Air Safety" and "The Psychology of Copilot Assertiveness"). Starting in 1979, he served two three-year terms on the Advisory Council for the Institute of Nuclear Power Operations in the wake of the Three Mile Island accident, where he advocated applying aerospace risk management techniques to the nuclear power industry. He also served on government investigative panels for train and ship collisions.

During his remarkable career, Jerry became known as Mr. Aviation Safety and the Father of Aviation Safety, the "go-to" person first for aviation safety and later for industrial safety writ large. Jerry fulfilled this function with wit and creativity. He was acutely aware of the prevalence of human error, both in design and operation. "The alleviation of human error," he said, "whether design or intrinsically human, continues to be the most important problem facing aerospace safety."

In his later years, Jerry researched, spoke, and wrote about personnel safety problems, such as substance abuse, subtle cognitive incapacitation, cockpit boredom in an age of automatic systems, and the importance of interpersonal communications. Jerry was evidently of the opinion that automatic systems could be safer than human-operated systems, but he was also a consummate realist. "Of the major incentives to improve safety, by far the most compelling is that of economics," he said. "The moral incentive, which is most evident following an accident, is more intense but relatively short lived." In the course of his long career, he came to know not only Charles Lindbergh, but also many other brilliant individuals, such as Neil Armstrong and Werner von Braun.

Jerome Fox Lederer wrote a book, *Safety in the Operation of Air Transport*, in 1938, wrote and delivered hundreds of articles and presentations, and received about 100 honors and awards. He was elected to the National Academy of Engineering in 1967 for "air safety research." His awards included selection as a "Laurel Legend" by *Aviation Week*, the Wright Brothers Memorial Trophy, Edward Warner Award from the ICAO, National Aeronautic Association Cliff Henderson Award, NASA Exceptional Service Medal, FAA Distinguished Service Medal, Daniel

Guggenheim Medal, Amelia Earhart Medal, Von Baumhauer Medal of the Royal Dutch Aeronautical Society, Airline Medical Directors Award, Aerospace Lifetime Achievement Award of the American Institute of Aeronautics and Astronautics (AIAA), American Society of Mechanical Engineers (ASME) Triodyne Safety Award, and K.E. Tsiolkovsky Medal from the Soviet Federation of Cosmonauts. He was awarded an honorary doctorate from Embry-Riddle University and was an honorary member of numerous organizations and societies, including the Airline Pilots Association and the Air Traffic Controllers Association.

The International Society of Air Safety Investigators established the Jerome F. Lederer Award for outstanding contributions to technical excellence in aircraft accident investigation in his honor. *Air Safety Magazine* named him the "aviation man of the century," and he was inducted into the International Space Hall of Fame and the Safety and Health Hall of Fame. The Guggenheim Medal Citation sums up his contributions: "For his lifelong dedication to the cause of flight safety and his constant and untiring efforts to reduce the hazards of aviation." In his "spare time," Jerry was an avid canoeist, purportedly logging some 30,000 miles on canoeing trips in the northeast.

He is survived by Sarah, his wife of 68 years, of Santa Rosa, California; two daughters, Nancy Cain of Oklahoma City and Susan Lederer of Santa Rosa; and two grandchildren. Jerry Lederer often acknowledged the vital contributions of his wife to the success of the Flight Safety Foundation, which honored Sarah Lederer with a citation for her role in the initiation and nurturing of the foundation. The citation reads in part: "Sarah has always been at Jerry's side or with him in spirit, sharing the difficulties and the victories."

PLATO MALOZEMOFF

1909–1997

Elected in 1969

"For application of traditional and new metallurgical techniques in mining."

BY ROBERT R. BEEBE

ON FRIDAY, August 8, 1997, the mining industry lost a leader, this academy lost a distinguished member, and engineers lost a respected colleague. Plato Malozemoff's career in mining spanned more than five decades, but he is best remembered for his time with Newmont Mining Corporation, where he worked from the end of World War II until he retired, as chairman, in 1985. As he built Newmont into a leading mining house with global reach, his name became associated with many of the world's great mines and companies.

Plato was born in St. Petersburg, Russia, on August 28, 1909. At that time, his father, a mining engineer, was a political exile in Siberia, but under the terms of his sentence he was allowed to work, raise a family, and build a rather enviable career with appropriate compensation and savings. Eventually, however, he fell victim to the Russian Revolution, the Civil War, onerous inflation, and financial turmoil, which forced the family to emigrate to the United States in 1920. Plato finished high school in Oakland, California, became a naturalized citizen in 1926, and graduated *magna cum laude* from the University of California, Berkeley, in 1930, with a B.S. in metallurgical engineering. He was then 21 years of age.

Prospects for young engineers in the 1930s were bleak, but Plato decided to enter graduate school at the Montana School of Mines, attracted by the opportunity to study under Professor Antoine Marc Gaudin, then the leading teacher of mineral beneficiation in the United States, and, years later, a founding member of NAE. Plato received his M.S. in 1932 and was invited to stay on as Gaudin's assistant for an additional year. While in Butte, Plato made a number of close friends, some of whom later played significant roles in his career. In fact, lasting friendships were a salient feature of his personality throughout his life.

Despite his academic background, Plato chose to follow in his father's footsteps and work his way up in the mining industry. After a short stint at the famous Alaska Juneau gold mine, he became a laboratory and field engineer for Pan American Engineering Company, headquartered in the San Francisco Bay area. His salary was only $120.00 per month, but the experience he gained testing ores from all over the world proved invaluable. He was also a consultant for Pan American customers, which required extensive travel throughout the western United States.

Along the way, Plato was learning, not just about technology, but, more important, about how mining enterprises were financed and managed. For Pan American, he did field work for the Placer Development Company and Phelps Dodge, which was testing the latest equipment for a large copper mine in Arizona (the Morenci project).

By that time, Plato's father, who was established as a mining consultant in New York, encouraged him to get out of what he called "the peddling business" and concentrate on production. Through his father's contacts, Plato went to Argentina to investigate several prospects, one of which was a copper-gold deposit. While his father was arranging financing for the mine, Plato returned to Pan American, where he had been on leave. But when the mine in Argentina encountered difficulties, Plato returned to take over its management. Soon, he and his staff had solved the problems, and the El Oro mine achieved its rated capacity. Even though this was his first managerial post, Plato felt that what he had learned up to that point, based firmly on his own observations, qualified him to organize a mining operation on a sensible, economical basis. He never looked back!

The outbreak of World War II did not immediately put an end to El Oro, but various financial and supply problems forced the Malozemoffs out. In 1942, father and son moved to Costa Rica to investigate a small gold mine owned by United Fruit Company. This would have been an unhappy episode, had it not been that Plato and Alexandra, his wife and lifelong companion, were married in Costa Rica. A year later, Plato was stricken with a very painful benign tumor on his leg that eventually required surgery. Alexandra had already returned to California to await the birth of their first child, and he joined her and underwent medical treatment. By 1944, Plato, still on crutches and almost broke, was working for the Office of Price Administration (OPA). Ironically, during this time he first became known to several Newmont executives. With the end of the war in sight, Plato began to look around for a peacetime job. Philip Kraft, a Newmont vice president whom Plato had met during his stint at OPA, told him Newmont might have a job for him.

When Plato joined Newmont in October 1945, he found a relatively small company headed by Fred Searls, a legendary explorationist. Searls was rather cool to the idea of hiring him, but Plato was determined to have a place in the company's New York headquarters, so much so that he was willing to take a cut in pay to get it. Once hired, Plato was the only staff engineer in a group of men who had been together for more than a decade and had solid reputations in mining. He later described the situation as "all chiefs and one Indian—me." Among his assignments was management of Newmont's stock portfolio, a job the old-timers called, "working the Wall Street stope." The portfolio was worth $40 million when he took on the job, but eight years later, he had built it up to $125 million, plus another $75 million in unquoted assets. Nevertheless, he embarked on a rigorous program of self-study to redress his lack of formal training in finance, law, and corporate management.

The stage was then set for his rapid rise. He was elected a vice president in 1952, became a director of Newmont in 1953, president and CEO in 1954, and chairman and CEO in 1966. Throughout those years, he was already reshaping Newmont,

from an opportunistic company driven by exploration and acquisition to a diversified organization able to recognize new
opportunities and emerging technologies. Rather than being
diminished, exploration was actually strengthened, and the
search for acquisition targets was intensified. From its foundation in gold, copper, and base metals, Newmont diversified its
interests to include lithium, ferroalloys, nickel, cobalt, and ura-
nium. Not surprisingly, Newmont soon became known as "Plato's
company."

And Newmont really was his company! Beyond his titles, and
the power they conveyed, Plato was an engineer, an executive,
and a financier capable of dreaming great dreams and finding
the money to carry them out. Even these skills, however, may
have been less important to Newmont's growth than his personal skills, his amazing ability to find, hire, and motivate the
best people in mining. Contrary to a widely held belief that he
was a difficult and distant person to work for, Plato was so confident of his own intellectual powers that he could allow his subordinates to argue and disagree, but only directly with him, not
with each other. And when his people were right, he generously
told them they were right!

It was well known in the mining industry that it was difficult
to get a job in Newmont's headquarters, which was kept deliber-
ately small. It was less well known that it was even more difficult
to get fired! Plato was the epitome of forbearance and caring
when it came to employees who encountered problems, even in
their private lives. As a manager and leader, he believed that a
company had obligations to its employees that could not be dis-
posed of easily. In a way, his philosophy foreshadowed the
downsizing phenomenon, except that he believed the best way
to downsize was to avoid getting too big in the first place!

To appreciate Plato Malozemoff merely as an engineer, an
executive, and a builder of mines and companies would be to
misunderstand his true character. He was a cultured gentleman,
perhaps a Renaissance man in the best sense of the term. Some
knew him as a chess master, a highly proficient violinist, and a
patron of the arts, ballet, and music. All of these things were
true, and they would have been true if he had never seen a mine!

Plato was a philanthropist and an active fundraiser for causes as various as the American Museum of Natural History, the Boys and Girls Clubs of America, and the Tolstoy Foundation. He did these things not because they were expected of someone in his position but because he sincerely believed that all men and women have obligations to themselves and to society that cannot be discharged by mere business success. The most fortunate of the many people he came into contact with during his long and busy career are the ones who came away with a little bit of his philosophy of life.

Plato Malozemoff was a great engineer, a great builder, and a great human being. How fitting that another man of art and intellect, Leonardo da Vinci, perhaps the greatest engineer of all, wrote in his *Notebook* some 500 years ago:

> As a well-spent day brings happy sleep, so
> Life well used brings happy death.

Plato Malozemoff is survived by his wife, Alexandra; his son, Dr. Alexis P. Malozemoff; and his daughter, Dr. Irene K. Malozemoff, now Mrs. Lynn B. Weigel.

I. HARRY MANDIL

1919–2006

Elected in 1998

*"For engineering design and development of materials for
naval and commercial nuclear reactors."*

BY THEODORE ROCKWELL

THE BIOGRAPHICAL FACTS OF Harry Mandil's life are listed
in his obituary. Born December 11, 1919, in Istanbul to an American father and a French mother, he earned a bachelor of science degree from the University of London in 1939 and a master of science degree from the Massachusetts Institute of Technology in 1941. He received an Honorary Doctor of Science
degree from Thiel College in 1960 for his pioneering work in
the field of nuclear power. He also graduated from the legendary Oak Ridge School of Reactor Technology in 1950.

As an officer during World War II in the Navy Bureau of Ships
in Washington, D.C., Harry worked under Commander H.G.
Rickover on electrical power distribution systems for naval ships.
After the war, he went to work for an engineering company in
Newton, Massachusetts, but in 1949, then-Captain Rickover called
him back to Washington to participate in the Naval Reactors
Program, where he worked for both the U.S. Navy and U.S.
Atomic Energy Commission (AEC). Harry was director of the
Reactor Engineering Division, Bureau of Ships, and chief of the
Reactor Engineering Branch, Naval Reactors, AEC.

Harry was involved from the very beginning in all aspects of
the development, design, and application of nuclear reactor cores
and associated equipment for the propulsion of naval ships, from
the first nuclear submarine, *Nautilus*, to the aircraft carrier, *En-
terprise* (more than 75 ships and about 100 nuclear reactors). He
was also project manager for the development and design of the

Shippingport Atomic Power Station, the first commercial nuclear plant in the world for the generation of electricity, a demonstration of President Eisenhower's Atoms for Peace Program.

In 1964, Harry left the Naval Reactors Program with two colleagues (I was one of them) to found MPR Associates Inc., a company that provided engineering services to industry and government, with an emphasis on the generation of electricity from nuclear and fossil fuels. He retired as principal officer of the company in 1985; he died of brain cancer in Naples, Florida, on April 27, 2006.

Harry received numerous awards, including the Naval Letter of Commendation (1946) and Meritorious Civilian Service Award (1952); and the American Society of Mechanical Engineers (ASME) Prime Movers Award (1956) and Distinguished Civilian Service Award (1959). He was elected to the National Academy of Engineering in 1998, was a registered Professional Engineer in the District of Columbia, a member of ASME and the American Nuclear Society, and author or co-author of numerous technical papers. He is listed in *Who's Who in the World, Who's Who in America,* and *Who's Who in Engineering.* He was a member of the Secretary of Energy's Advisory Board (1995–1999) and a member of the Visiting Committee for the Nuclear Engineering Department of the Massachusetts Institute of Technology (1984–1993). He was also a Paul Harris Fellow of Rotary International.

But the biographical facts in the obituary don't really give a picture of the man. It's the personal anecdotes that begin to show who he was. For example, Admiral Rickover said Harry Mandil was the best engineer he had ever met—and he'd met some of the world's best. No one else can make that claim.

One of Harry's early responsibilities in the Naval Reactors Program was to find a company capable of fabricating a large pressure vessel to hold the nuclear reactor core. One of his technical specialties was mechanical design and properties of materials, and he knew that the vessel would be subject to pressure, temperatures, corrosion, and radiation that would require an unprecedented degree of quality assurance. When manufacturing officials assured him, "We've been making special pressure vessels, large and small, since long before you were born, Sonny.

We know what we're doing. Just leave it to us. We don't need your fancy QA systems," Harry didn't buy it. He noticed that vessels were being built in a roped-off section of the plant behind "Keep Out" signs. Something special was going on there. When he inquired, he was told it would not interest him. But he dug in his heels and was finally told that the vessels were being built for the Germans, and "You know how fussy those guys are." Harry did indeed. His response was, "You're going to have to get some more rope."

The obituary says Harry "worked in" and "was involved in" various projects, but that doesn't indicate the nature or importance of his personal contributions. Let me describe one remarkable task that isn't even mentioned in the obituary—the transfer of nuclear power technology to the British navy. In 1958, Admiral Rickover took Harry to Europe with him to survey the state of British nuclear and manufacturing technology and measure progress toward the British goal of building a U.K. version of a nuclear power plant for a submarine. After several days, Harry reported that the British were hopelessly bogged down, and the final product was nowhere in sight. At that point, Rickover made a startling decision—he would give the Brits an American nuclear submarine power plant, with all of the technological background necessary to install, operate, and maintain it. Subsequent plants could then be built without further U.S. aid.

Knowing that endless complications would ensue if the normal naval and atomic people and organizations on both sides were involved, Rickover decided his plan could only work as a commercial contract between Westinghouse and Rolls-Royce, with neither government involved. The arrangement was worked out on a personal basis among Rickover, Harry, Admiral Mountbatten, and Lord Hives, chairman of Rolls-Royce Ltd. The deal worked only because of the mutual respect, integrity, and competence of the four participants. Dr. Francis Duncan, AEC historian, later wrote that, without this unique personal arrangement, the British "would never have gotten their first nuclear submarine to sea [in 1963]."

The early years of MPR Associates Inc., were very revealing of

Harry Mandil's character. The three partners had very different technical specialties, personalities, and histories. Yet we were unquestioningly confident of each other's adherence to the highest technical and ethical standards. We did no advertising or promotional work for the new company, and once we had a place to sit down, we simply waited for the phone to ring. One of the first calls came to Harry. From our side of the conversation, it was clear that he was being offered a large contract. But then he said, "It sounds as if you don't want an objective technical evaluation of your project; you just want our endorsement of it. I'm sorry, but that's not what we do." And he hung up. He hadn't looked at either of us, and we hadn't even bothered to nod "Yes." We didn't have a single contract yet, but there was no question in Harry's mind that if we couldn't get quality work, we'd "just have to shine shoes."

Incredibly, the issue came up twice more, before we got our first real contract. And each time, there was no question about the decision. Only later did we learn that such an attitude was also good business.

None of this comes through in an obituary, but that's who Harry was. That's how he thought, and that's how he acted. He didn't ask us to agree because the issue was not negotiable. He was an excellent role model for his children and for his profession. What more could anyone ask of a person? Particularly, of an engineer.

He is survived by his wife of 60 years, Beverly, of Naples, Florida; his daughter, Jean Brolund, of Ellicott City, Maryland; his son Eric of Denver, Colorado; and three grandchildren, Matt, Beth, and Jon Brolund.

JOHN S. McNOWN

1916–1998

Elected in 1987

*"For outstanding contributions to the application of fluid mechanics,
and for exceptional professional leadership in advancing
engineering education in Africa."*

BY ROSS E. McKINNEY

JOHN S. McNOWN, former dean of engineering and Emeritus Professor of Civil Engineering at the University of Kansas (KU), died on February 19, 1998.

John was born on January 15, 1916, in Lawrence, Kansas, a short walk from the KU campus. His father, W.C. McNown, was a professor of civil engineering, and John grew up in an academic engineering environment. After graduating from Lawrence High School, John entered the School of Engineering at KU, where he developed an interest in hydraulic engineering. After receiving his B.S. in civil engineering in 1936, he continued his studies at the University of Iowa and received his M.S. in hydraulic engineering in 1937. He then moved to the University of Minnesota, where he was an instructor and doctoral student. He received his Ph.D. in hydraulic engineering from the University of Minnesota in 1942.

After working for a year as a research associate at the University of California on war-related projects, he joined the faculty of the University of Iowa as an assistant professor of mechanics and hydraulics and associate director of the Institute of Hydraulic Research. While at Iowa, he worked with Hunter Rouse. In 1950, on a Fulbright Fellowship, John studied and conducted research in Grenoble, France. After a very productive year there, he received a D.Sc. from the University of Grenoble. During that year, he also refined and modified his approach to engineering education.

John then returned to the University of Iowa, where he remained until 1954, when he left to become a professor of engineering mechanics at the University of Michigan. In 1957, after only three years at Michigan, he was asked to become dean of engineering at KU by Chancellor Franklin Murphy, whose ideas for modernizing engineering education dovetailed with John's. Unfortunately, because of differences of opinion between Chancellor Murphy and Kansas Governor George Docking, Murphy resigned in 1960, just as progress was beginning to show. The new chancellor, Clarke Wescoe, did not have the same vision for the School of Engineering.

John wanted to create a first-class engineering research facility at KU that would not be hampered by bureaucratic red tape. In 1962, he was instrumental in the creation of the Center for Research in Engineering Sciences (CRES) in the Center for Research, Incorporated. However, frustrated with the rate of development of engineering research and change in engineering education, he resigned as dean of engineering in 1965 and rejoined the faculty as the Albert P. Learned Professor of Civil Engineering.

Based on his experience as an administrator, John then turned his attention to international engineering education, especially in Africa, where he recognized that well-educated engineers could help raise the standard of living for millions of people. In 1973, John married a Swedish national, Eva Fernqvist, and began to split his time between the United States and Sweden. He became an expert in international engineering education, and, in 1983, he retired from KU and moved to Sweden.

Hydraulic research was John's passion, and teaching was his family heritage. The American Society of Civil Engineers recognized the value of John's research by awarding him the J.C. Stevens Prize in 1946, Walter L. Huber Engineering Research Prize in 1949, and J. James R. Croes Medal in 1955. As a dean of engineering, John was asked to serve on an advisory panel for the National Science Foundation (1957–1960) and the Engineers Council for Professional Development (1960–1965). In 1967, he became a member of the Overseas Liaison Committee for the American Council on Education in both Nairobi and Washington, D.C. In 1972, the World Bank retained John as a technical education specialist. He was a consultant on hydraulic engineering to the Swaziland Ministry of Agriculture in 1981 and a resident consultant for the Tunisia Ministry of Higher Education and Scientific Research in 1982. The next year, John became a visiting professor at the Royal Institute of Technology in Stockholm, Sweden.

John's ideas about university administration at all levels were influenced by his growing up in an engineering faculty family during the 1920s and 1930s. Eventually, he took his ideas for reforming engineering education, and engineering as a whole, to Washington, where he convinced many government agencies to incorporate them into plans to improve engineering education in Africa to meet the needs of the peoples of Africa.

In recognition of John McNown's contributions to fluid mechanics and international engineering education in Africa, he was elected a member of the National Academy of Engineering in 1987. In 1989, KU honored him with the Distinguished Engineering Service Award in recognition of his lifetime contributions to engineering education and research.

M. Eugene Merchant

M. EUGENE MERCHANT

1913–2006

Elected in 1975

"For contributions in machine tool research and development."

PROVIDED BY TECHSOLVE
SUBMITTED BY THE NAE HOME SECRETARY

M. EUGENE MERCHANT was honored and respected all over the world. Tireless travelers, Dr. Merchant and Helen, his wife of 69 years, were welcomed and given VIP treatment by universities, organizations, and friends worldwide.

Gene Merchant attended high school in Essex Junction, Vermont, and then the University of Vermont. He received a graduate fellowship from the Cincinnati Milling Machine Company (CMMC) to study at the University of Cincinnati, where he received his Sc.D. degree. In 1936, Gene began a long and illustrious career in engineering research at CMMC (later Milacron). His early research was focused on analyzing the nature of friction between the cutting tool and the chip. As a young engineer, he developed an innovative mathematical model of the metal-cutting process that continues to be taught and used. This was just the beginning of years of creative research, for which his name was recognized and respected all over the world.

As director of physical research at CMMC, Dr. Merchant created a world-class department to study manufacturing processes. He and his staff facilitated the growth of industry by building up the knowledge base of manufacturing engineers. Later, as Milacron's principal scientist for manufacturing research, he took a creative leap into the future. When computers were still in their infancy and software was extremely difficult to produce, he recognized the possibilities for computers in manufacturing.

In a series of far-reaching papers, he outlined his vision of computer-integrated manufacturing systems. His brilliant thinking influenced the development of computer-aided design/computer-aided manufacturing (CAD/CAM) and other software now used by manufacturing organizations throughout the world. He also helped introduce innovative concepts for eliminating waste in batch production, which is critical to lean manufacturing.

When he retired from Milacron at age 70, Dr. Merchant continued his work at Metcut Research Associates. Then, from 1995 to 2005, he was a senior consultant at TechSolve, a Cincinnati-based, nonprofit, engineering consulting firm. In his honor, TechSolve named its research laboratory for him and established the Dr. M. Eugene Merchant Scholarship Fund through the University of Cincinnati College of Engineering. TechSolve also published Dr. Merchant's recent book, *An Interpretive Review of 20ᵗʰ Century U.S. Manufacturing and Grinding Research.*

Dr. Merchant was a leader in many organizations, including the Society of Manufacturing Engineers (SME), American Society of Lubrication Engineers, Federation of Materials Societies, and International Institution for Production Engineering Research (CIRP), a prestigious organization with a limited international membership. Throughout his career of more than six decades, he received numerous honors and awards. In 1955, he was named Cincinnati's Engineer of the Year by the Technical and Scientific Societies Council of Cincinnati. In 1968, he was awarded the SME Frederick W. Taylor Research Medal. In 1986, he was the first to receive an honor named for him, the M. Eugene Merchant Manufacturing Medal, sponsored jointly by the American Society of Mechanical Engineers (ASME) and SME. He was also the recipient of the Award of *American Machinist Magazine*, the National Award of the American Society of Lubrication Engineers, and the Research Medal and Richards Memorial Award of ASME.

Dr. Merchant was held in high esteem by colleagues worldwide, and he received many international honors, including the 1980 Tribology Gold Medal of the Institution of Mechanical Engineers (Great Britain), the Otto Benedikt Prize of the Computer and Automation Institute of Hungary, and the Medal of the Polish Institute of Metal Cutting. Universities also recognized Dr. Merchant for his outstanding achievements. He held honorary doctorates from the University of Vermont (1973) and the University of Salford, England (1980), as well as an honorary doctor of engineering degree from GMI Engineering and Management Institute (1994).

Dr. Merchant always had time for friends and colleagues, as well as for young people. In March 2006, he was honored with the Spirits of Scouting Award for his 80-year affiliation with the Boy Scouts of America. His soft-spoken manner and courtly ways were appreciated by young engineers, who were in awe of his monumental reputation and his important accomplishments.

"He was a visionary," said grandson, George Alexander, of Taylor Mill. "He had a lifelong commitment to learning. He was never not learning something."

"It was always a charmingly surreal time to visit my 90-something grandfather and have him show me new tricks on his computer," said another grandson, John Jacobson of Milwaukee, a self-described techie. "It got to the point where I started taking along a notepad and pen whenever I'd sit with him in his home office."

His daughter, Leslie Alexander, died in 2004, and his son, M. David Merchant, also died earlier. Survivors include his wife of 69 years, Helen Merchant; daughter, Frances Sue Jacobson of Pontiac, Illinois; brother, Robert Prescott Merchant of Lynchburg, Virginia; six other grandchildren and four great grandchildren.

Arthur B. Metzner

ARTHUR B. METZNER

1927–2006

Elected in 1979

"For research in the fluid mechanics of viscoelastic and polymeric materials."

WRITTEN BY T.W. FRASER RUSSELL
SUBMITTED BY THE NAE HOME SECRETARY

ARTHUR B. METZNER, H. Fletcher Brown Professor Emeritus of Chemical Engineering, University of Delaware, died suddenly on May 4, 2006, while attending a meeting in Washington, D.C.

Born in Gravelbourg, Saskatchewan, Canada, in 1927, Arthur grew up and studied in Alberta, graduating from the University of Alberta in 1948 with a B.Sc. in chemical engineering. He received his Sc.D. in chemical engineering from Massachusetts Institute of Technology (MIT) in 1951. Although he spent nearly his entire professional career as a member of the faculty at the University of Delaware, his teaching career began with instructorships at MIT and Brooklyn Polytechnic Institute. Retiring in 1996, he continued to be active in the Department of Chemical Engineering until his death. He was a humorous, warm, yet demanding and exacting teacher; a world-renowned researcher; an editor of the *Journal of Rheology*; and a consultant to industry.

After two years at Colgate-Palmolive Company, in 1953 Art joined Allan P. Colburn, Robert L. Pigford, and others of the faculty at Delaware, bringing the department to six members. The group was very active in teaching, authoring textbooks, and conducting research all with the goal of improving the stature of the department and Art thrived in such an environment. He became a full professor in 1961 and the H. Fletcher Brown Professor in 1962. While he was department chairman from 1970 to 1978, six faculty members were added, five books were published, and the Center for Catalytic Science and Technology was established.

Art understood that chemical engineering education was both about teaching content, and equally, if not more importantly, about teaching student skills and giving them the confidence to solve a wide range of problems. His classes were interactive, and students knew it was dangerous to come to class unprepared. Students were encouraged to participate in a variety of ways, especially by explaining their solutions to the infamously many problems he assigned. Art wanted students to gain the confidence that they could solve problems on their own and in collaboration with others. His mentoring of students in their classroom and laboratory activities continued beyond their university days, and he had a major influence on many careers, several of whom have become leaders in academia and industry.

Art's research contributions to rheology and the mechanics of non-Newtonian fluids were developed through critical experiments and innovative analysis. The papers he and his students produced were used extensively by many engineers' throughout industry and academia to solve significant problems in fluid mechanics and heat transfer in tubular and in tank-type systems.

Recognition of his contributions included his election to the National Academy of Engineering in 1979, several national awards from the American Institute of Chemical Engineers, and designation as an Eminent Member of the profession in 1983. He also received awards from the Society of Rheology (the Bingham Medal and the Distinguished Service Award), the American Chemical Society, the American Society for Engineering Education, and the University of Delaware (Francis P. Alison Award). In addition, both the Katholieke Universiteit Leuven and the University of Delaware awarded him honorary doctorates.

Professor Metzner is survived by his wife of 58 years, Elisabeth "Betty" Krüger Metzner; daughter, Elisabeth Faulkner of Charlottesville, Virginia; son, Arthur P., daughter-in-law, Yemisrach, and grandson Samuel Metzner of Fort Washington, Maryland; and daughter, Rebecca Metzner, and son-in-law, R. Jeremy Clark, of Rome, Italy.

RUSSELL G. MEYERAND JR.

1933–2003

Elected in 1978

"For pioneering in gas breakdown at optical frequencies and developments of high-power gas lasers."

BY ANTHONY J. DEMARIA

RUSSELL G. MEYERAND JR., retired vice president of technology, United Technologies Corporation (UTC), died suddenly in West Palm Beach, Florida, on November 23, 2003. He was 69 years old.

Russell (or Russ as he was known to his colleagues) was born on December 2, 1933, in Kirkwood, Missouri, one of two children. Even as a child, he exhibited a notable interest and abilities in science, which continued to grow throughout his life, even after his retirement. He undertook formal training at Massachusetts Institute of Technology (MIT), where he earned a B.S. in electrical engineering in 1955, an M.S. in nuclear engineering in 1956, and a Ph.D. in plasma physics, under Professor "Sandy" C. Brown, in 1959. Russ's Ph.D. thesis on plasma sources led to advances in ion-propulsion research.

While at MIT, Russ met Mary Grace, the daughter of one of his professors of electrical engineering. They were married in 1956 when Russ was 23 years old; at the time of his death, they had been married for 47 years. The couple had one child, Mary Elizabeth, now a tenured associate professor of medical physics at the University of Wisconsin, Madison. Russ is also survived by two grandchildren, Elsa Dorothy born in 2004 and Henry Russell born in 2006.

From 1955 to 1956, while studying for his master's degree, Russ was a consultant to General Electric Company in Schenectady, New York. In 1958, he joined United Aircraft Research Laboratories (UARL), East Hartford, Connecticut, as principal scientist in plasma physics. When the name of the company was later changed to UTC, UARL became United Technologies Research Center (UTRC), as it is still known today.

When Russ joined UARL, the research laboratories were beginning a major effort to expand basic research activities in the physical sciences while continuing strong programs in applied engineering research focused on propulsion and aerodynamic technologies. With his wide range of technical interests, outstanding talent, and contagious enthusiasm for being on the cutting edge of science and technologies, Russ soon became a "bright star" in the research center, and his responsibilities were steadily increased. He was promoted to chief research scientist in 1964, director of research in 1967, vice president of research and development of UTC (while also serving as director of research of UTRC) in 1980, and vice president of technology in 1982, a position he held until 1989 when he retired at the age of 56.

Russ was instrumental in assembling a research staff capable of conducting an expanded, long-term research program. Under his direction, the program prospered and made notable advances in plasma physics, high-energy lasers, electro-optics, fiber-optics, adoptive optics, integrated optics, and new propulsion concepts. His major research contribution (published in 1963 and 1964) was in explaining the physics of gas breakdown at optical frequencies and how optical-energy absorption from laser radiation could yield high-density plasmas. This research was cited in his election to membership in the National Academy of Engineering (NAE).

Under Russ's leadership, UTRC's staff grew to 1,500, including a high-power optics group in West Palm Beach, Florida, initially intended to support UTC's expansion into aerospace technologies. Later, in the 1970s, the group supported the UTC companies-acquisition program, under the leadership of Harry Gray. Russ was the impetus for a strategy for obtaining funding for the research center from three sources: one-third from other divisions of UTC to ensure that research addressed problems relevant to the company's short-term needs; one-third from the corporation for research directed toward medium-term goals; and one-third from government contracts relevant to the long-term needs of UTC.

As corporate vice president of research and development and finally vice president of technology, Russ provided guidance for all technology matters, ranging from propulsion, helicopters, and avionic-type aerospace technologies to heating/ventilating/air conditioning systems, elevators/escalators, and automotive industrial/commercial technologies associated with new acquisitions.

In addition to NAE, Russ was a member of the Institute of Electrical and Electronic Engineers, American Physical Society, Scientific Research Society of America, Sigma Xi, National Bureau of Standards Visiting Committee, the board of directors of the Industrial Research Association, the board of directors of the Newington Children's Hospital in Newington, Connecticut, and a Fellow of the American Institute of Aeronautics and Astronautics. He served on the Scientific Advisory Board for the U.S. Air Force and the U.S. Army and was a member of the National Aeronautics and Space Administration Space Program Advisory Council.

In spite of heavy administrative duties throughout most of his career, Russ published 16 papers and was the owner of 19 patents, ranging from magneto-hydrodynamic generators, ion-acceleration propulsion devices, a laser radar system, and high-power lasers to thermionic converter batteries and hydrogen-generating devices.

Russ was also active in many volunteer activities. He was moderator of the Shady Harbor Fire District in Charlestown, Rhode Island, where he and Mary Grace owned a summer home; treasurer of the Nopes Island Conservation Association, an organization dedicated to the conservation of fragile barrier beach land on the south coast of Rhode Island; and a member of the board of directors and chairman of the Building Committee of Lake Point Tower in North Palm Beach, Florida, where the couple had a winter home.

In addition to his strong interest in preserving the environment, Russ was also very active in the Connecticut State Science Fair, acting as a judge for more than 15 years and spearheading the successful effort for a special award at the fair sponsored by UTC. As a father he could not have been more supportive and enthusiastic of his daughter's interest in science and engineering. Despite all of the responsibilities that came with his career at United Technologies, he made it clear that his role as father and husband always came first. In his daughter's words, while his professional accomplishments were many and of the highest quality, they could not even compare to who he was as a father.

He is survived by his wife, Mary Grace Meyerand; his daughter, Beth Meyerand, and her husband, Chad Moritz; his grandchildren, Elsa Dorothy and Henry Russell; and a sister, Kate; her husband, Larry Jacobs, and two nieces, Pam and Karen.

RENE HARCOURT MILLER

1916–2003

Elected in 1968

"For aircraft engineering, especially helicopters, other vertical flight vehicles, and supersonic transports."

BY JACK L. KERREBROCK

RENE HARCOURT MILLER died on January 28, 2003, at the age of 86. A consummate practicing aerospace engineer, Miller was also an enthusiastic educator dedicated to introducing young people to the joys of creation in aerospace engineering. Boundlessly enthusiastic, he transmitted his love of the process of creation of new aerospace systems to his students and to his peers.

Miller was born in Tenafly, New Jersey, in 1916, but attended grammar school and high school in France, where he lived with his mother and stepfather. He entered Cambridge University at 16 and received a B.A. in 1937 and an M.A. in 1956. Over his lifetime, he was successful in a wide range of increasingly responsible roles, beginning at the Glenn L. Martin Company and McDonnell Aircraft Corporation, where he participated in the design of some of the first jet-powered fighters for the U.S. Navy. He then did pioneering work on the design of helicopters at Kaman Aircraft, where, while on leave from the Massachusetts Institute of Technology (MIT), he became vice president of engineering.

When he returned to MIT, he dedicated himself to transmitting his knowledge and his attitudes to generations of students. He advanced through the academic ranks from assistant professor in 1944 to head of the Department of Aeronautics and Astronautics in 1968 and H.N. Slater Professor of Flight Transportation. Miller founded the MIT Flight Transportation Laboratory, which did research on the operations of the airline industry; for example, the laboratory undertook to determine optimum route structures and methodologies for setting airline ticket prices, although, at the time, both were set by government regulators. The laboratory and the work were unique in academia. Miller also conducted research on the aerodynamics and vibration of helicopter rotors and enthusiastically advocated the wider use of rotorcraft for short-haul transport.

In 1978, after a decade as department head, he returned to teaching, focusing on the development, with a colleague, James W. Mar, of a new academic organization, the MIT Space Systems Laboratory, which would introduce new generations of MIT students to the creative methodologies of design and the development of new artifacts for the exploration of space. At the time, such work was considered the exclusive province of mature professionals in large professional organizations. Miller and Mar made it possible for students in their early years, as undergraduates, to participate in such work. A key factor in their success was Miller's enthusiasm and confidence in students' abilities and his willingness to use his professional connections with highly placed people in government and the space industry on the students' behalf. This laboratory has continued to evolve and still fulfills the role Miller envisioned for it.

In his professional work and his teaching, Miller always emphasized the engineering of complete systems for aeronautical and space activities. He always focused on the most important questions, rather than those that admitted of elegant research approaches. At the same time, Miller believed that every engineer, especially professors, should also be an expert in at least one specific discipline (e.g., aerodynamics, propulsion, structures, control, etc.). He espoused the engineering of complete systems to show the interrelation of aerodynamics, propulsion, structures, control, etc., in the design of aerospace vehicles, emphasizing that a design, even if created by the world's best aerodynamicist, would not fulfill its function if the aerodynamics did not mesh with other components of the system.

Miller's holistic approach led to a revolutionary change in the undergraduate curriculum of the Department of Aeronautics. He authorized the introduction of a new subject, called unified engineering, that replaced four disciplinary subjects taught in the sophomore year. The unified engineering course covered the same technical material, but in an interrelated, systems context. The course was taught by a small group of senior faculty who took joint responsibility for the entire curriculum, rather than just material from their own disciplines. The sophomore core of the Department of Aeronautics and Astronautics at MIT is still taught this way.

Miller was also an active participant in the aerospace professional community. He held a number of leadership positions and received many awards in recognition of his technical achievements and his service to the community and the nation. Among these were membership in the National Academy of Engineering, honorary fellowships in the American Institute of Aeronautics and Astronautics (AIAA) and American Helicopter Society, fellow of the Royal Aeronautical Society, and fellow of the American Academy of Arts and Sciences. He was president of the AIAA in 1977. He was also a corresponding member of the International Academy of Astronautics. In 1976, he was awarded the I.B. Laskowitz Award of the New York Academy of Sciences for Research in Aerospace Engineering Science, Support Systems and Components. He received the Klemin Award of the American Helicopter Society, the Sylvanus Albert Reed Award of the AIAA, and Decorations for Meritorious Civilian Service to the U.S. Army in 1967 and 1970.

Throughout his career at MIT, Miller resided in a townhouse in Boston's Back Bay. He also owned a cottage on White's Pond in Concord, Massachusetts, and an Island (Scrag) in Maine, where he spent major portions of each summer, frequently in the company of his students.

Miller is survived by his wife, Maureen, who resides in Penzance, England, and by his daughter, Christal.

Herbert L. Misch

HERBERT LOUIS MISCH

1917–2003

Elected in 1976

"For contributions to the formation of a rational societal policy on matters of America's environmental and vehicle safety."

BY HAREN S. GANDHI

HERBERT LOUIS MISCH, born December 7, 1917, in Sandusky, Ohio, grew up in Port Clinton, Ohio. He attended Miami University of Ohio, then moved in 1939 to attend the University of Michigan. He graduated in 1941 with a Bachelor of Science in engineering.

Herb Misch made his mark first at Packard Motor Company, where he started his employment as a detail draftsman to the chief engineer. Although he had extremely limited resources and staff, he played a pivotal role in the development of Packard's Ultramatic (automatic) transmission. Misch recalled, with considerable amusement, that, after the transmission had proven successful, Packard marketing people bragged that the company had spent $7 million on its development. According to Misch, "We had to scrape up everything to even get close to that."

Misch was employed by Packard from 1941 to 1956, during which time Packard applied for nine U.S. patents on his transmission inventions. When the company folded in 1956, Herb had attained the level of chief engineer. His next career move was to the Cadillac Division of General Motors as director of advanced product planning during 1956–1957.

In May 1957, Misch began his career at Ford as an assistant chief engineer for the Mercury Division. He quickly moved through various areas of the company, achieving the rank of executive engineer in production engineering, chief engineer in the Metal-Stamping Division, and executive director of the engineering staff before being named vice president of engineering in February 1962.

Herb Misch, along with product planner Roy Lunn and stylist Gene Bordinat, led the T5 project team in developing and producing a prototype—a 1,200-pound, two-seat vehicle with a low, sloping nose and a racing style windshield sporting a V-4 mid-engine cooled by two radiators located at air vents just ahead of the rear wheels. While working with Gene Bordinat in 1960 on the redesign and performance upgrade of the Ford Falcon, the idea of a "sports car for the masses" was suggested to meet the anticipated demand of the baby boomers approaching car-buying age. The team established targets of $2,500, 2,500 pounds, 180 inches maximum length, a floor shift, and a host of options to allow buyers to customize the car.

The racing community received the Mustang I enthusiastically when, in October 1962, Dan Gurney and Stirling Moss drove demonstration laps at Watkins Glen to introduce the concept car at the Grand Prix. Based on these successes, the T5 was given the go-ahead for production. In April 1964, just 18 months after the unveiling at Watkins Glen, Mustangs were in showrooms across the country. A prototype Mustang is still on view at the Henry Ford Museum in Dearborn, Michigan.

Herb Misch's next major accomplishment at Ford was in the area of automotive emissions and safety. He became vice president of environmental and safety engineering in 1972, a challenging time for the automotive industry because the industry did not have the technology to meet newly enacted emission standards; they were considered overly stringent, perhaps even impossible, to achieve. Through the lens of time, these standards seem inconsequential, but, in fact, they could not be met with available technology.

Those early challenges propelled the automotive industry into massive research and development efforts that led to the sophisticated engine- and vehicle-emission control systems in cars today. These systems, and their attendant emission reductions, had not even been envisioned in the early 1970s. On behalf of Ford Motor Company and the automotive industry, Misch testified before the Environmental Protection Agency (EPA) that premature action could be counterproductive to air-quality improvement and that a reasoned, cautious approach would be better for the country as a whole. Confronted with hostile questions during the intense political debate on curbing pollution, Misch remained collegial and non-confrontational. He described the state of the technology and explained why the automotive industry needed time to develop new systems. From 1972 until his retirement in 1982, under Herb Misch's leadership, Ford technology improved from crude, carbureted control of engines to computer-controlled fuel-injection coupled with three-way catalysts.

Bruce Simpson, who worked for Misch, recalls his unwavering integrity. Some of the managers in charge of certifying vehicles tampered with them during the certification process. When Herb Misch learned that adjustments had been made on some of the test vehicles, he immediately contacted Henry Ford II, and then the responsible government office, telling them what had happened and promising that Ford would repeat all of the tests. He then led a massive effort to recruit a new team of engineers to re-run the certification program in a fraction of the normal time to avoid plant shutdowns. Thanks in large part to Herb Misch's guidance, the program was successful and led to the formation of a new organizational structure and rigorous procedures for future programs.

Bruce Simpson also recalls that during a review of durability test results on a new model car, Misch was disappointed with the brake life tests, even though they were similar to competitors' results. He decided to change to a larger, longer life brake design, regardless of the higher cost.

Kelly Brown, retired director of vehicle environmental engineering at Ford, commented that, "Herb was a true engineer. He always sought the facts, frequently complaining that 'we too often thrive on misinformation.' "

David Kulp, assistant director, Certification Programs, said he admired Herb Misch for his ability to see and appreciate both sides of an issue and to shape a proposal that addressed both. That characteristic was crucial to his success.

Wayne Brehob, who accompanied Misch on several trips to Washington, D.C., to testify before the EPA, recalls Mr. Misch as "a down-to-earth man who dined at the local burger restaurant with the troops rather than eat at a more posh restaurant that his travel budget authorization could accommodate." Herb Misch enjoyed helping others in the profession and always graciously accepted requests for nomination letters for former employees.

Misch received many honors for his contributions to the engineering profession. He was a fellow of the Society of Automotive Engineers, Society of Engineers International, and Engineering Society of Detroit. He was also a life member of the Society of Body Engineers, a member of the National Academy of Engineering (1976), and an honorary member of the Packard Club.

For the last 30 years of his life, Misch was an avid sailor. He raced his boat, Tiki II, in 23 Port Huron to Mackinac races in the PHRF-A Big Boat category. He had four sailboats, the last two of which were 45-foot racing sailboats. All were named Tiki II in honor of the Kon-Tiki raft that had crossed the Pacific. According to his daughter, Suzanne Wells, "He was far younger than his 85 years because he had to keep up with young people on the boat."

Herb Misch belonged to the Grosse Pointe Yacht Club and the North Star Sail Club of Harrison Township. He was a member of the Detroit Athletic Club and a longtime member of the Drayton Avenue Presbyterian Church, in Ferndale, Michigan.

Herb Misch died June 23, 2003, from complications from cancer. He is survived by his daughter, Suzanne Wells; grandchildren, Bradley and Jennifer Wells; a niece, Judith Misch Crosser; and a nephew, James R. Misch. He was preceded in death by his wife, Caroline, in 1990, and his son, Thomas, in 1988.

Rocco A Petrone

ROCCO A. PETRONE

1926–2006

Elected in 1975

"For pioneering accomplishments in the design, development, and implementation of space launching capabilities for the Apollo program."

BY WILLIAM R. LUCAS

ROCCO A. PETRONE, a pioneer in rocketry and space flight, died on August 24, 2006, at his home in Palos Verdes Estates, California. From humble beginnings, and with an uncommon intellect and unexcelled work ethic, he became one of the most important contributors to space technology of the 20th century. Among the many thousands of people who were involved in landing men on the moon and returning them safely to Earth, Rocco was one of a very small group of leaders whose contributions were critical to that effort. He was elected to the National Academy of Engineering in 1975.

Rocco was born on March 31, 1926, to Italian immigrant parents in Amsterdam, New York. In 1946, he graduated from the U.S. Military Academy, where, in addition to his academic leadership, he played tackle on the great Army football teams of the 1940s. After graduation, he served in the U.S. Army in Europe from 1947 to 1950. Upon his return to the United States, he studied at Massachusetts Institute of Technology (MIT) and earned a master's degree in 1951 and a professional degree in 1952, both in mechanical engineering.

Rocco's career in rocketry began in the early 1950s at Redstone Arsenal in Huntsville, Alabama, where, as an army officer, he joined the team headed by Wernher von Braun. He was assigned to the Missile Firing Laboratory, which was responsible for the development of hardware and techniques for the launch of ballistic missiles. In 1953, he participated in the launch of the Redstone missile, the first U.S. ballistic missile. He participated in subsequent launches of the Redstone missile, Jupiter missile, Pershing missile, and Jupiter C and Juno space launch vehicles.

In 1960, still on active duty in the U.S. Army, he was appointed manager of that part of the National Aeronautics and Space Administration (NASA) Saturn Program assigned to the Kennedy Space Center. When the Apollo Lunar Landing Program was established with the goal of landing men on the moon and returning them safely to Earth, Rocco was responsible for the planning, development, and activation of all launch facilities, including Launch Complex 39, where the Apollo/Saturn V vehicles were launched. The complex included the Vehicle Assembly Building, the launch towers, and the 3,000-ton Saturn V Crawler-Transporter, which transported the stacked Saturn V from the Assembly Building to the launch pad about three miles away.

In 1966, Rocco retired from the army and was employed immediately by NASA as director of launch operations, Kennedy Space Center, where he was responsible for the management and technical direction of pre-flight operations and systems integration, testing, checkout, and launch of all space vehicles. He personally directed the launches of the first five crewed Apollo vehicles, culminating with Apollo 11, which landed two crew members on the moon.

In 1969, Rocco was named Apollo program director, NASA Headquarters, Washington, D.C. He served in that capacity until 1973 when he was appointed director of the Marshall Space Flight Center (MSFC), where he presided over the participation of MSFC in the three Skylab missions, America's first space station. He directed a remarkable recovery after the critical loss of the Skylab heat shield on its first mission. He also oversaw the downsizing of MSFC in preparation for MSFC's changing roles in the late 1970s. In 1974, Rocco was appointed associate administrator of NASA and technical director of all of NASA's aeronautical and space programs. He also had overall responsibility for the Apollo-Soyuz Test Program, a joint venture by the United States and the Soviet Union.

In 1975, Rocco retired from NASA and accepted a position as president and chief executive officer of the National Center for Resource Recovery, a joint industry/labor effort to develop technologies for recovering materials and energy from solid waste. He considered this a challenge of national importance.

In 1981, he was appointed president of the Space Transportation Systems Group of Rockwell International Corporation, where he was responsible for the production of hardware for the Space Shuttle Orbiter and other space hardware. In 1987, he was appointed vice president of corporate development, Rockwell International, and he retired from that position in 1989. During his retirement, he pursued his hobbies, including civil war history and attending sporting events, with characteristic vigor.

Throughout his long professional career, Rocco demonstrated impeccable integrity. He was a shining example of the motto he had learned at the military academy, "Duty, Honor, Country." Rarely does one encounter a more committed or effective manager than Rocco Petrone. He always focused on the objective, was well informed of technical details, and was rigidly disciplined. Some called him a tough manager because he required the same discipline from those who reported to him as he demonstrated himself.

Rocco Petrone left a legacy of excellence in the art and science of managing massive technical programs involving people from different cultures with a wide range of talents and skills. Guided by extraordinary engineering insight, he had an uncanny ability to ask the right questions when assessing the integrity of a design or the readiness of hardware for flight. He also had the courage to do what seemed right, often under great stress. The successful launches of all of the Saturn V rockets are testimony to his excellence.

Rocco is survived by his wife of more than 50 years, Ruth Holley Petrone, and four adult children, Michael Petrone, Kathy Petrone Posey, Terry Petrone, and Nancy Petrone.

FREDERICK GEORGE POHLAND

1931–2004

Elected in 1993

"For advancing the theory of anaerobic treatment processes and applications to solid waste management."

BY RICHARD A. CONWAY

FREDERICK GEORGE POHLAND was born in Oconomowoc, Wisconsin, on May 3, 1931. The middle child of five, he had a rather strict Lutheran upbringing and spent summers on the Upper Peninsula of Michigan. His family later moved to Charlotte, North Carolina, where he attended his final year of high school. He received his B.S. in civil engineering from Valparaiso University (1953) and, after working as an engineer driving spikes with the Erie Lackawanna Railroad Company (one of many jobs that helped pay for his education), he completed service with the U.S. Army and then earned an M.S. (1958) and Ph.D. (1961) in environmental engineering at Purdue University. He was awarded the prestigious Harrison Prescott Eddy Medal by the Water Environment Federation (WEF) in 1964 for his excellent dissertation and research.

After working his way though college, and assisting his younger brother through the same institutions, Fred demonstrated his discipline and responsibility, which was reflected in all of his later endeavors. He received an Sc.D. (*honoris causa*) from Valparaiso University in 1996 for "excellence in service to the human family" as an engineer, student, explorer, teacher, professor, and writer interested in "the ways in which humans use and misuse that most vital of all elements—water."

Fred devoted most of his professional career to engineering education, research, practice, and service. He led the environmental engineering programs at the Georgia Institute of Technology (1961–1988) and then at the University of Pittsburgh (1989–2004). He was also Visiting Scholar at the University of Michigan (1967–1968) and a Guest Professor at the Delft University of Technology in the Netherlands (1976–1977). At the time of his death, Fred was Professor and Edward R. Weidlein Chair of Environmental Engineering at the University of Pittsburgh; after his death, he was awarded an Emeritus Professorship, the first time the university conferred this honor posthumously.

Fred's research led to fundamental advances in anaerobic processes. His concept of a landfill as a bioreactor through controlled leachate recycling was adopted by the Delaware Solid Waste Authority, among many others. Fred originated and chaired the International Water Association (IWA) Specialist Groups on Anaerobic Digestion (1985–1992) and Landfill Management (1995–1999), which brought together practitioners, researchers, and educators from all over the world.

In keeping with his commitment to applying research to practice and disseminating vital information, he served as regional editor of *Water Research* and *Water Science and Technology* (both 1993–2002) and as honorary executive editor of *Water Research* (1994–2000). Fred could often be found on weekends in his office working on manuscripts, and thanks to his expertise, these publications became the exceptional journals they are today. From 1991 to 1998, he chaired the American Academy of Environmental Engineers (AAEE) WASTECH Program, which developed two series of books for practitioners in remediation. A writer himself, Fred was the author of more than 150 technical and scientific publications. His clear, precise, insightful prose was praised by even the most rigorous critics.

As chair of the WEF Program Committee (1989–1992), he worked to ensure that all professionals in the water-quality field were supplied with the latest science and technology. In 1989, WEF honored him with the Gordon Maskew Fair Medal for "exemplary demonstration of proficient accomplishment in the training and development of engineers in the environmental engineering field." Fred served on the Environmental Protection Administration Science Advisory Board (1989–1997), where he worked hard to ensure that science and technology were used in the regulatory process.

Fred's ability to unite education, research, and practice was recognized in many ways, including his election to the National Academy of Engineering (1993), honorary memberships in WEF (1993) and IWA (2000) and the bestowal of the Gordon Maskew Fair Award (2000), the presidency of AAEE (1992–1993), selection as the American Society of Civil Engineers (ASCE) Simon Freeze Memorial Lecturer (2001), and bestowal of the Association of Environmental Engineering and Science Professors Frontier Award (2003).

Fred served on many National Research Council committees addressing research on water resources, innovative technologies, landfills, subsurface contamination, environmental remediation at Navy facilities, biosolids, and advanced technology for human support in space.

Fred was also an active member of his community. In Atlanta and Pittsburgh, he was a member of Rotary Club International (and president of his local club), and he hosted international students through the organization's exchange program. He was always a willing volunteer for Junior Achievement, Special Olympics, and state certifying and examining boards.

After his untimely death in 2004, the Association of Environmental Engineering and Science Professors, in conjunction with the American Academy of Environmental Engineers, established the Frederick George Pohland Medal and honorarium to recognize his outstanding, sustained efforts to bridge environmental engineering research, education, and practice. Fred's family, colleagues, and friends hope his example will encourage others to work toward combining these three elements of engineering and science.

When I reflect on Fred's life and accomplishments, I am reminded that he was fascinated by the achievements of Abraham Lincoln and other great statesmen like George Washington and John Adams. He was also inspired by great environmental engineers like Thomas Camp, Gerald Rohlich, Donald O'Connor, and Gordon Maskew Fair. What did Fred have in common with these men? A lot—especially courage and resolve. Here's an example.

At my invitation, Fred was one of four adventurous engineers who took a whitewater rafting trip down the Gauley River in West Virginia, the most difficult rafting river in the East. At high water, the Gauley River has Class V rapids. At the start of the trip, our guide cautioned us that our success in navigating the big rapids would depend on hard paddling to build up the velocity we would need to steer the raft. We made it through the first dozen or so scary rapids and then reached a Class V rapid, where photographers were waiting to record the event. Unlike many rafts before and after us, we did not capsize or lose anyone.

Looking at the photographs later, we saw that most of the self-proclaimed adventurers were hanging onto the raft for dear life. Fred was the only passenger with a paddle in the water. Commenting later, he said, "That is what we were supposed to do." His statement was simple but profound. Fred remained focused on accomplishing a goal—in this case paddling—although he thought he was just doing his duty. In the same way, his commitment to his professional life established him as one of the eminent engineers of his era. Fred's sense of responsibility was apparent in his career and in his commitments to his community, family, and friends. Such is a measure of his eminence.

His professional goals included helping his academic institutions become the best they could be. As a professor dedicated to excellence, he taught a full load of courses, brought in numerous research grants, mentored his students, and assisted his colleagues. He reached beyond his institutions to facilitate the practice of engineering on a broad scale, to assist government agencies in making environmentally sound decisions, all the while honing his own skills and expertise. He felt he had a responsibility to excel in his profession so he could have a greater impact. Finally, he felt he had a responsibility to maintain high personal standards, to live up to a professional code of conduct. As a result, prestigious professional societies awarded him their highest honors. Fred's guidance and leadership will be missed by his family, friends, colleagues, and students.

I had the good fortune of working with Fred on technical-society leadership, government advisory boards, and National Academy committees. We became close friends, and I got to know his family, his beloved wife, Ruth, and daughter, Elizabeth, very well. It was an honor for me to write this memorial tribute.

A. Alan B. Pritsker

A. ALAN B. PRITSKER

1933–2000

Elected in 1985

"For the design and development of simulation languages and network techniques and their applications in improving industrial productivity."

BY RALPH L. DISNEY AND JAMES R. WILSON

SOMETIME IN THE EARLY 1960s, I heard from a young professor at Arizona State University (ASU) about a not very sophisticated article I had written on congestion theory and materials handling. Alan Pritsker, my correspondent, had just begun work on the modeling of queuing networks and wanted to share ideas. I, of course, was happy to comply. Thus began an association I treasured for nearly 40 years. When I heard of his untimely death on August 24, 2000, at the age of 67, I was shocked.

A. Alan B. Pritsker was born in Philadelphia, Pennsylvania, on February 5, 1933, and lived there until he left for college. He attended Central High School, where he starred in basketball and soccer and received the school's student-athlete award in 1950. He entered Columbia University as a student-athlete until, as he said, he grew weary of sitting on the bench and decided to become exclusively a student. He received his B.S. in electrical engineering in 1955 and his M.S. in industrial engineering in 1956, both from Columbia. After graduation, he was hired at Battelle Memorial Institute (now Battelle Institute) in Columbus, Ohio; at the same time, he started a part-time Ph.D. program at Ohio State University under Jack Mitten. In 1961, he graduated with a Ph.D. in industrial engineering and operations research. His dissertation was titled "The Optimal Control of Discrete Stochastic Processes."

After graduation, Alan moved to ASU as assistant professor of industrial engineering; he was also a consultant to the RAND Corporation. He remained at ASU until 1969, when he became a professor of industrial and systems engineering at Virginia Polytechnic Institute and State University. In 1970, he moved to Purdue University, where he held professorships in the School of Industrial Engineering and the School of Aeronautical, Astronautical, and Engineering Science. He was also director of the Center for Large-Scale Systems (LSS), an interdisciplinary academic program involving eight departments. The goal of LSS was to reform engineering education to address societal needs directly; the role of engineering in service to society was a recurrent theme throughout the rest of Alan's career.

In 1973, still a professor of industrial engineering at Purdue, Alan and two graduate students established Pritsker and Associates, Inc., a major focus of his energy for the rest of his life. Alan became adjunct professor in 1981 but continued to teach courses at Purdue until he retired in 1998. Over a period of three decades, Pritsker and Associates developed at least 10 well-known commercial software packages, such as GASP, Q-GERT, SLAM, TESS, FACTOR/AIM, and AweSim, which are legendary in the field of discrete and combined discrete-continuous simulation. An extensive discussion of significant applications of these simulation packages can be found in Alan's professional autobiography, *Papers, Experiences, Perspectives* (Systems Publishing Corporation, 1990), and two excellent reviews of his work co-authored by James R. Wilson (one of Alan's many former students) and David Goldsman ("Alan Pritsker's Multifaceted Career: Theory, Practice, Education, Entrepreneurship, and Service," *IIE Transactions* 33(3) 139–147; and "In Memoriam: A. Alan B. Pritsker (1933–2000)" *OR/MS Today* 27(5), available online at: http://www.lionhrtpub.com/orms/orms-10-00/pritsker.html).

Alan was president of Pritsker and Associates from 1973 to 1986 and chairman of the board and CEO from 1987 to 1989. Beginning in 1986, he was also chairman of the board of FACTROL, Inc. When the two companies merged in 1989 to form Pritsker Corporation, Alan was chair and CEO until his retirement in 1998.

During the 1990s, Alan and Pritsker Corporation worked on a federally mandated study with the United Network for Organ Sharing (UNOS) to evaluate the allocation of liver transplants based on a national waiting list ranked by sickest-patients first. The results of this study showed that an allocation procedure based on a national waiting list would result in many more deaths than an improved version of the existing procedure, as revealed by comprehensive experimentation with the UNOS Liver Allocation Model (ULAM). In June 1998, Alan presented the results of the study in congressional hearings; the ULAM-based transplant-allocation procedure was subsequently adopted by UNOS.

When Alan was elected to the National Academy of Engineering (NAE) in 1985, he was only the second industrial engineer to be so honored. He served NAE as chair of the Peer Review Committee for Section 8, Industrial, Manufacturing and Operational Systems Engineering (IMOS); member of the Committee on Membership; chair of the IMOS Section; and various other committees, boards, and panels.

Alan was a member of the board of directors of the Winter Simulation Conference (1970–1973 and 1981–1987) and a cofounder of the Operations Research Division (1968) and Systems Engineering Conference (1973) of the Institute of Industrial Engineers (IIE). For service to IIE and for contributions to the welfare of mankind, Alan was elected Fellow in 1978 and was awarded the Frank and Lillian Gilbreth Industrial Engineering Award in 1991, the highest honor awarded by that institute. He was an active member of the Institute for Operations Research and the Management Sciences Simulation Society, which presented him with the Distinguished Service Award (1991) and the Lifetime Professional Achievement Award (1999), the highest award given by that organization.

In addition, Alan served on many advisory panels for commercial, government, and professional organizations, including the National Science Foundation, National Research Council, and colleges of engineering at several major universities. In fact, his many contributions to the engineering profession over a period of more than four decades can only be suggested in this brief summary.

Alan wrote 12 books on systems engineering and computer modeling and simulation and 15 chapters in handbooks of industrial engineering, production systems, and scheduling of manufacturing operations. He also published more than 90 research papers in prestigious journals in his field. He was awarded honorary doctor of science degrees from ASU in 1992 and Purdue University in 1998.

Alan is survived by his wife, Anne Pritsker; his children, Caryl DuBrock, Pamela Poteet, Kenneth Pritsker, and Jeffrey Pritsker; and five grandchildren.

ACKNOWLEDGMENT
Professor Jim Wilson, head of the Edward P. Fitts Department of Industrial and Systems Engineering at North Carolina State University, not only helped me with the writing of this tribute, but also shared his copy of Alan's professional autobiography, *Papers, Experiences, Perspectives,* and the two reviews of Alan's life that are referenced herein. I am grateful for his assistance.

Alvin Radkowsky

ALVIN RADKOWSKY

1915–2002

Elected in 1991

"For seminal contributions and innovations in the engineering development of nuclear power."

BY MILTON LEVENSON

ALVIN RADKOWSKY, professor of nuclear engineering at Tel Aviv University and Ben-Gurion University of the Negev, both in Israel, died of pneumonia on February 17, 2002. Before retiring to Israel, Dr. Radkowsky had been chief scientist of the U.S. Navy Nuclear Propulsion Program for more than 20 years.

Alvin was born on June 30, 1915, in Elizabeth, New Jersey, the same town where his mother was born; his father was an immigrant from Lithuania. Alvin attended City College of New York (CCNY) and, at age 20, received a B.S.E. in electrical engineering. His first job was as a troubleshooter for the Singer Sewing Machine Company. In 1938, he went to work as an electrical engineer at the U.S. Navy Bureau of Ships in the interior communications and fire-control section. While employed there, he continued his education and received an M.A. in physics from George Washington University in Washington, D.C., where his thesis advisor was Edward Teller, perhaps an indication of things to come.

In 1947, still working for the Bureau of Ships, Alvin earned a Ph.D. in physics from the Catholic University of America. His dissertation, "Temperature Dependence of Electron Energy Levels," written under the guidance of Karl P. Herzfeld, described a phenomenon now called "the Radkowsky effect."

Admiral, then Captain, Rickover started organizing his working group for the possibility of creating a navy based on nuclear propulsion sometime in 1947. He recruited Alvin to be his physicist and arranged for him to go to the Argonne National Laboratory in 1948 to attain proficiency in reactor physics. The appointment at the laboratory was for three years, but Rickover decided to have Alvin come back after two years since his group had already started to function in Washington and he was anxious for quick action. Alvin became then the chief scientist of the program. When Adm. Rickover's section became Naval Reactors in 1954, both as part of the Navy Department and the Atomic Energy Commission (AEC), Alvin became a joint civilian employee of both the Navy and AEC.

Alvin was responsible for originating and assisting in the development of two reactor concepts for which he was awarded the Navy's Distinguished Civilian Award (the highest non-military award) in 1954 and the AEC Citation (1963). One concept was "burnable poison," for which he also received a cash award of $25,000. This concept is important to all nuclear power plants, but it is especially important for navy vessels, because it enables them to operate for years without refueling, even in time of war. The other concept was the "seed blanket" reactor structure, which consists of a highly enriched fuel seed surrounded by a blanket of natural uranium. The blanket generates more than half of the reactor power and has a very long life necessitating only a relatively more frequent change of the seed providing thus for a large reduction in fuel cost.

In addition to his primary field of interest, Alvin had a long-standing interest in the use of thorium in nuclear reactors. He published a number of papers on this subject and owned several patents in the field, which he assigned to the company he helped found, Thorium Power, which is now publicly traded. The thorium fuel technology is designed to stop the reactors from producing weapons-suitable plutonium and reduce the toxicity and volume of spent fuel. The thorium fuel can also be used to dispose of existing stockpiles of plutonium while generating electricity. Alvin worked with Thorium Power to establish a program at the Kurchatov Institute in Moscow, Russia. That program continues and is testing the thorium fuel for use in commercial reactors.

Alvin was elected to the National Academy of Engineering in 1991. He also received many awards, including the Alvin M. Weinberg Medal of the American Nuclear Society for "seminal contributions and innovations in the engineering development of nuclear science and technology"; the Meritorious Civilian Service Award from the U.S. Department of the Navy for "outstanding service to the Navy during World War II"; the Alumni Outstanding Achievement Award in Science from Catholic University and the university's first Karl F. Herzfeld Medal for outstanding accomplishments in physics; and the Townsend Harris Medal from CCNY. He was also a fellow of the American Physical Society and American Nuclear Society.

One aspect of Alvin's life set him apart from most of his colleagues—he was both an outstanding physicist and a religious Jew. He saw no conflict between Orthodox Judaism and his vocation as a scientist. On the contrary, he felt strongly that there was a synergistic relationship between the two. He found that the rigors of logical Talmudic study and the meticulous observance of commandments regulating his religious life prepared him well for the mental discipline needed in inducing scientific theories from experimental data. He was convinced that a fundamental relationship exists between the concepts of Bohr's Complementarity and Heisenberg's Uncertainty Principle and the spiritual as well as the physical side of the existence of man. Moreover, he found the ever-increasing revelations of the wonders in the life sciences to be awe-inspiring. Professor Eugene P. Wigner had provided in a formal demonstration and discussed with Alvin that, according to quantum mechanics, the probability of the existence of a self-replicating unit is zero, thus questioning the emergence of even the simplest life form from the primeval "soup."

Alvin is survived by his wife, Annette Eisenberg Radkowsky, a daughter, Gilah Chukat, both currently living in Israel, and a brother, Lawrence, living in Silver Spring, Maryland.

Alvin took to fatherhood with gusto, although he reached that status rather late in life. He poured into his daughter, a most receptive imbiber, much of his knowledge and wonder of our world. He had the joy of being surrounded by six grandchildren but missed the birth of the last grandson by a little more than two years.

After Alvin's retirement from the U.S. government in 1972, the Radkowsky family moved to Israel, where Alvin became associated with Tel Aviv and Ben-Gurion Universities where he found, especially in the latter, an excellent nucleus of reactor physicists. His first Ph.D. student became a most proficient associate in the theoretical research that led to the development of the thorium-based reactor. During his years of research in Israel, Alvin continued his long-term relationship with Professors Teller, Bethe, and Wigner. Living in Israel also gave him the opportunity to seek out the luminaries of Orthodox Judaism who were appreciative of his mental powers and deep insights in Talmudic learning.

Although he devoted his time to physics, mathematics, and Talmud, he was dubbed by many of his acquaintances as the quintessential Renaissance man because of his deep knowledge of literature and his love of poetry, though not of avant-garde poetry. He always felt that the opportunities that life offered him were too exquisitely timed to have been fortuitous, giving him the sense that the strong Hand of Providential Guidance was directing him toward his accomplishments. He had a zest for living and one can almost say that Alvin never regarded himself as old. While the advancing years were awesome to him, his *raison d'être* was to complete old projects and start work on new ones. His wry sense of humor never left him, and his smile said it all.

WILLIAM C. REYNOLDS

1933–2004

Elected in 1979

"For development of theoretical bases for convective heat transfer analysis and contributions to fluid mechanics."

BY PARVIZ MOIN

WILLIAM CRAIG REYNOLDS died of a malignant brain tumor at his home in Los Altos, California, on January 3, 2004, after 53 years at Stanford. He was 70 years old.

Born in 1933 in Berkeley, Bill entered Stanford as an undergraduate and chose to remain there for the rest of his career. He completed his bachelor's (1954), master's (1955), and doctoral (1957) degrees at Stanford and then joined the faculty. He chaired the Department of Mechanical Engineering from 1972 to 1982 and from 1989 to 1992.

As a scientist, Bill was the ultimate independent thinker, a self-starter, perhaps even a maverick. While following his muse, he might have repeatedly reinvented the proverbial wheel, but he also found novel and exciting ideas and designs that enriched the field of engineering and inspired the people around him. He was a true believer in the familiar maxim, "If you want something done right, you had better do it yourself." Not a natural delegator and an advocate of hands-on problem solving, he usually found himself immersed in a variety of projects. Fortunately, he was blessed with boundless energy and indefatigable enthusiasm.

Bill's main research interest was in turbulent flow, but he worked in nearly all branches and extensions of fluid mechanics, using experimental, theoretical, and computational methods with equal facility. The list of research areas in which he participated includes: blow-down thermodynamics, ignition of metals, non-isothermal heat transfer, zero-g fluid mechanics, turbulent boundary-layer flow structure, turbulence-wall interactions, stability of gas films, hydrodynamic stability, boundary-layer calculation methods, surface-tension-driven flows, organized waves in turbulent shear flows, turbulence computation, unsteady turbulent boundary layers, internal combustion-engine-cylinder flows, unsteady jets and separating flows, turbulence modeling, flow control, microelectromechanical systems (MEMS), and large eddy simulation (LES) of turbulent flows.

Bill was one of the first to embrace the computer, and he authored programs for his own work, many of which were subsequently used by others worldwide in teaching and research. His program for chemical equilibrium analysis, STANJAN, for example, is used at more than 100 universities in the United States and around the world. In 1971, he and Joel Ferziger initiated the highly successful turbulence simulation program at Stanford. Bill pioneered the introduction of the LES technique in engineering analysis, which is widely used today .

Bill's honors included fellowships of the American Society of Mechanical Engineers (ASME) (1979) and the American Physical Society (APS) (1982), election to the National Academy of Engineering (1979) and the American Academy of Arts and Sciences (1995), and the Fluid Engineering Award of ASME (1989) and Otto Laporte Award from APS (1992).

Bill was an outstanding teacher. His knowledge was deep, his ability to explain difficult concepts was exceptional, and his passion and enthusiasm in the classroom were legendary. With unusual clarity of thought and "out-of-the-box" design of problems, his textbooks on thermodynamics are standouts in the field. Strongly physics-based and very fundamental in their approach, his textbooks reveal a depth of understanding that makes for both solid teaching and a satisfying read.

Besides being an outstanding research scientist and teacher, Bill Reynolds was a classic do-it-yourselfer in the great tradition of American engineering. He could often be seen in the department workshop on weekends, working on a piece of hardware, academic or domestic. He designed and built his Los Altos home, had it re-engineered after it was severely damaged in the 1989 Loma Prieta earthquake, and took on many of the rebuilding tasks himself. He wrote his own word processor program, which could elegantly display mathematical equations. If he needed something in his work, he invented it, and he managed to get into everything: computer science, electronics, MEMS, optical instrumentation, and complex mechanical transmissions. He took on all problems, figured them out, and solved them.

Bill was never intimidated by technical challenges. After traditional cannons were banned in Stanford Stadium because of a misfiring accident in 1970, Bill and one of his graduate students built an "impulse horn" to be sounded at the 1971 Rose Bowl game after every Stanford score and at the appropriate moment during "The Star-Spangled Banner." Bill's horn reverberates through the stadium to this day.

Music was an important part of his life. He played the trumpet and arranged music for his own and other dance bands while a student at Stanford and enjoyed jazz concerts throughout his life. After his official retirement in 2000, even while he was still active in academic life, he took up music again, playing trumpet and arranging music for an amateur big band group.

At a memorial service for Bill in the Stanford Memorial Church on January 20, 2004, the church was overflowing. An estimated 700 people attended, an indication of the deep respect and affection for him in the Stanford community and beyond. After the service, in a moving salute, a small group of student band members fired his cannon three times while another student played "Taps" on the trumpet.

His departure surely represents the end of an era at Stanford. The editors of the *International Journal of Heat and Fluid Flow*, who dedicated an issue to his memory, wrote that the world of fluid mechanics had lost "one of its strongest and most inventive and charismatic leaders."

Bill is survived by his wife of 50 years, Janice Reynolds, sons Russell and Peter Reynolds, and daughter Margery Reynolds.

Herman P Schwan

HERMAN PAUL SCHWAN

1915–2005

Elected in 1975

*"For contributions in biomedical engineering research,
education and the development of this field."*

BY KENNETH R. FOSTER AND JOHN A. QUINN

Herman PAUL SCHWAN, a renowned scientist and pioneer
in biomedical engineering, died at his home in Radnor, Pennsylvania, on March 17, 2005.

Schwan was born in Aachen, Germany, in 1915. As a gymnasium (high school) student, he found himself under a political
cloud because of his liberal political views. He served briefly in
the Reich Labor Service, an organization that combined quasi-
military training and forced labor in an attempt to rehabilitate
"politically immature" individuals. Certified as politically mature
(a requirement for entry to a university), Schwan entered the
University of Frankfurt, then, driven by the search for financial
support, he moved to the Universities of Goettingen and Breslau,
where he studied physics, mathematics, and engineering.

Unable to win a tuition waiver for graduate study because of
his political views, he became a technician for Boris Rajewsky,
the famous radiation biologist at the Kaiser Wilhelm (now Max
Planck) Institute in Frankfurt. Rajewsky was a member of the
Nazi party (Schwan thought for career reasons) and had sufficient political clout to keep Schwan out of the army. He assigned
Schwan to study the electrical properties of tissues for the development of therapeutic applications of radio-frequency energy,
an interest that Schwan pursued for the rest of his career. Schwan
obtained his Ph.D., with distinction, in biophysics from the Uni-

versity of Frankfurt in 1940 and his professional doctorate (Dr. Habil.) in physics and biophysics in 1946.

After the war, Rajewsky was obliged to step down as institute director pending his appearance before a de-Nazification court, and Schwan, who had not joined any Nazi-related organizations, took over as associate director of the institute, now renamed the Max Planck Institute. In 1947, Schwan came to the United States, where his first job was at the Aeromedical Equipment Laboratory at the U.S. Naval Base in Philadelphia. He joined the faculty at the University of Pennsylvania in 1950. In 1952, he was appointed head of the Electromedical Division of the Moore School, and, in 1961, he became chairman of the Graduate School of Arts and Sciences Group on Biomedical Electronic Engineering. In 1972, he became chairman of the Bioengineering Department. He retired as the Alfred Fitler Moore Professor Emeritus in 1983.

Over the course of his long career, Schwan published more than 300 scientific papers, gave countless lectures, and received many honors. These included fellowships in the Institute of Electrical and Electronic Engineers (IEEE) and the American Association for Advancement of Science, membership in the National Academy of Engineering, and election as foreign member of the Max Planck Institute for Biophysics. He received three honorary doctorates (Universities of Pennsylvania, 1986; Kuopio, Finland, 2000; and Graz, 2001). He was awarded the Boris Rajewsky Prize for Biophysics (1974), IEEE Edison Medal (1983), IEEE Centennial Medal (1984), and d'Arsonval Medal of the Bioelectromagnetics Society (1985), as well as the first Otto H. Schmitt Award of the International Federation for Medical and Biological Engineering (2000). He was also an honorary member of the German Biophysical Society. An extended biography of Schwan can be found at *http://repository.upenn.edu/be_papers/52/*.

As a scientist, Schwan is best known for his many studies of the electrical properties of cells and tissues and the nonthermal mechanisms of interaction between fields and biological systems. He discovered or provided important theoretical insights into the large, low-frequency dielectric dispersion in biological material, electrically induced forces on cells, and other such phenomena.

Schwan was also deeply concerned about the possible health effects of nonionizing electromagnetic fields. In 1953, he sent a letter to the U.S. Navy proposing a safe limit for human exposure to microwave energy of $100 \, \text{W/m}^2$ (based on thermal analysis). This letter became the basis for exposure standards in the United States and elsewhere. In 1965, Schwan chaired the committee that established the first U.S. exposure limit for radio-frequency energy for the American National Standards Institute, which evolved into the present IEEE C95.1 standard. The U.S. standard was influential in the development of exposure limits around the world.

Schwan also played an important role in the development of the fields of biomedical engineering and biophysics. In the early 1950s, he served on numerous national and international committees helping to organize and promote professional societies. He was chair (1960) of the Institute of Radio Engineers Professional Group on Medical Electronics, the largest biomedical engineering society of its time, and helped guide the evolution of this and other groups into the present IEEE Society on Engineering in Medicine and Biology. Schwan held many leadership positions in the biomedical engineering sections of the American Institute of Electrical Engineering and Institute for Radio Engineering, the two engineering societies that eventually merged to form the IEEE. He was a founding member of the Biophysical Society, Bioelectromagnetics Society, and Biomedical Engineering Society and chairman of the American National Standards Institute committee that developed the first limit for human exposure to radio-frequency energy in the United States.

Schwan is survived by his wife (since 1949), Anne Marie Del Borrello, of Philadelphia, five children, and six grandchildren. He was a mentor to all of them, teaching them first and foremost to think for themselves and never to simply follow the crowd. A man of integrity, Schwan influenced not only his wife and children, but also his many students and colleagues.

CHESTER P. SIESS

1916–2004

Elected in 1967

"For reinforced concrete construction."

BY METE A. SOZEN

CHESTER PAUL SIESS was born in Alexandria, Louisiana, in 1916, to Leo Chester Siess and Adele Liebreich Siess. In time, he attended Rosenthal Grammar School and Bolton High School, both in Alexandria. He continued his education at the Baton Rouge campus of Louisiana State University where he was a member of the Reserve Officers' Training Corps. In those years, when Huey Long rarely missed a football weekend in Baton Rouge, the young Siess was within earshot of Long almost every week during the football season.

When Siess graduated in 1936 with a B.S. in civil engineering, he had the highest scholastic record in the engineering school and was named the Outstanding Civil Engineering Graduate by the Louisiana Section of the American Society of Civil Engineers. Besides being gifted in mathematics, he developed a keen sensitivity to writing and grammar, evidenced by his only teenage rebellion against his father, who had a sign identifying his drug store as "Siess' Pharmacy." His son would have none of it! He insisted on "Siess's Pharmacy." That was one argument he did not win.

Chester entered the profession during the Depression, and his first job was survey party chief in the Rural Road Inventory Program of the Louisiana Highway Commission, where he spent his time documenting the layout and condition of the road sys-

275

tem in several Louisiana parishes. After six months, when a soil-testing laboratory was established in the Highway Commission, he became a soils engineer.

In September 1937, he began graduate studies at the University of Illinois, Urbana, with a half-time appointment as a special research graduate assistant in the Department of Theoretical and Applied Mechanics (T&AM). There he had the opportunity to work on a research project with Dr. N.M. Newmark, then an assistant professor, Dr. V.P. Jensen, and Professor Frank E. Richart. Chester's M.Sc. thesis, "Moments in I-Beam Bridges," which he completed in 1939, was the centerpiece of *Illinois Engineering Experiment Station Bulletin* No. 336, produced by him and N.M. Newmark.

In June 1939, he joined Dr. Ralph B. Peck in the Chicago Subway Soils Laboratory. When construction of the subway was completed in April 1941, he started working as an engineer-draftsman in the Bridge Office of the New York Central Railroad in Chicago. While in Chicago, he met Helen Kranson from Marshall, Texas, who had come to Chicago to work after her freshman year in Urbana.

In September 1941, Chester returned to Urbana as a special research associate in T&AM and was put in charge of experimental research, replacing Professor Ralph Kluge, who had taken a position at the University of Florida. While working full time running the laboratory, he began work on his doctorate. He married Helen soon thereafter, in October 1941; their daughter, Judith, was born in 1947.

By 1948, Dr. Siess had not only extended the moment-distribution method, developed by Hardy Cross, to apply to two-way slabs, but had also completed his Ph.D. dissertation. In 1949, he transferred to the Department of Civil Engineering as a special research assistant professor. He became a full professor in 1955 and served as head of the department from 1973 to 1978, when he retired. Upon his retirement, some of his former students established the Chester P. Siess Graduate Award.

In the late 1950s, the Structural Engineering Laboratory of the Department of Civil Engineering was the scene of a number of exciting developments in reinforced concrete. At that time, several experienced, creative researchers, such as Eivind Hognestad and Ivan Viest, were members of the Department of T&AM. A friendly, but intense, competition between the staffs of the Departments of Civil Engineering and T&AM led to many advances in structural analysis and the design of reinforced and pre-stressed concrete that ultimately transformed the structural design in that medium, not only in the United States but throughout the world.

Dr. Siess's stewardship of much of this research was recognized in his many awards. The Ernest E. Howard citation from the American Society of Civil Engineers reads, "Through his extensive research in reinforced concrete and pre-stressed concrete, the translation of his research results to practice, his informative writings, his effective teaching and stimulation of his students and co-workers, Chester P. Siess has made significant contributions to structural engineering with worldwide influence."

Chester joined both the American Society of Civil Engineers (ASCE) and the American Concrete Institute (ACI) in 1936 and served on nine ACI committees over the years. From 1980 to 1983, he was chairman of the Standard Building Code Committee, of which he was a member from 1953 to 1995. He served on the board of ACI from 1961–63 and 1972–1977 and was president in 1974–1975. From 1968 to 1980, he was chair of the Reinforced Concrete Research Council of ASCE and was secretary of the organization from 1961 to 1968. He was appointed to the Advisory Committee on Reactor Safeguards of the U.S. Nuclear Regulatory Commission in 1968, served as committee chair in 1972, and retired from the committee in 1992. Dr. Siess was also a consultant to the Army, Navy, and Atomic Energy Commission.

In 1949, he and N.M. Newmark were awarded the ACI Wason Medal for a paper based on Chester's doctoral dissertation on reinforced concrete slabs. For contributions in the same field, he received the Concrete Reinforcing Steel Institute Award in 1956. He received the Boase Award from the Reinforced Concrete Research Committee in 1975 for research related to behavior and design, the Turner Medal (1964), the Howard Award

(1968), and the Reese Award (1970), the latter with M.A. Sozen and J.O. Jirsa. He was made an honorary member of the American Concrete Institute in 1969 and of ASCE in 1978.

Dr. Siess was elected a member of the National Academy of Engineering in 1967, its third year, and was made a charter member of the Louisiana State University Engineering Hall of Distinction and the Civil Engineering Hall of Distinction. In 1985, the University of Illinois College of Engineering presented him with the Alumni Honor Award for Distinguished Service. In 2001, the Structural Engineers Association of Illinois honored him with the Parmer Award. In 2006, the American Concrete Institute Board of Direction established in his memory the Chester P. Siess Award for excellence in structural engineering research.

Dr. Siess was a member of Tau Beta Pi, Sigma Xi, Phi Kappa Phi, and Omicron Delta Kappa. He was also a member Chi Epsilon, the civil engineering honorary society. He was made a Chapter Honor Member of the University of Illinois Alpha Chapter in 1987 and the 51st National Honor Member in 1994, the sixth from the University of Illinois, which has more National Honor Members than any other institution.

In an interview in *Concrete International* in 1998, Dr. Siess was asked about safety in the building code. He responded that, "Theory says that 1.2 is plenty [for dead load]. But the engineer is not thinking entirely in terms of low probability of overload [versus] a low probability of understrength. The engineer is thinking about mistakes .... and a safety factor of 1.2 will not do to cover mistakes if it is all dead load." Perhaps this statement provides a glimpse of his rare ability to bridge theory and practice. It is generally agreed that the ACI Building Code of 1982, which he directed, is the last one that was written with a concern for the practitioner.

Dr. Siess demanded the highest standards of economy, correctness, and expression from his students. The University of Illinois has been blessed with a number of great teacher-researchers in structural engineering over the years, including Newmark, Richart, Wilson, Westergaard, and Talbot. The most important recognition that Dr. Siess received is the firm belief of students who knew him in the classroom and in endless discussions in his office (where, as in the old saying, if the pistol of his argument misfired, he beat you down with its butt end) that he belonged in that select class. On the occasion of the establishment of the Chester and Helen Siess Professorship in Civil Engineering at the University of Illinois, he said, "If someone asks me what I think was my most important contribution to the profession, I will cite the engineers I have taught."

Dr. Siess passed away in Savoy, Illinois, a suburb of Urbana-Champaign, on January 14, 2004. He is survived by his daughter and son-in-law, Judith Ann and Stephen Bremseth of Cleveland, Ohio, and an "adopted" son, Larry Jackson. Larry, the grandson of a long-time cleaning lady, attended the University of Illinois through the generosity of Chester and Helen Siess. The Siesses considered Larry the son they never had, and Larry regarded them as his own parents.

A. W. Skempton

ALEC W. SKEMPTON

1914–2001

Elected in 1976

"For leadership in the study and practice of geotechnical engineering."

BY T. WILLIAM LAMBE

PROFESSOR ALEC W. SKEMPTON, one of the most influential British civil engineers of the 20th century and a world-renowned civil engineer, died on August 9, 2001, at the age of 87.

Alec studied civil engineering at Imperial College in London, where he developed an interest in geology and an ambition to conduct research. In 1937, he became interested in soil mechanics, the application of engineering science to geotechnical problems, when he participated in the investigation of the collapse of the embankment of the Chingford Reservoir, directed by Karl Terzaghi, the acknowledged "father" of soil mechanics.

Alec Skempton was an unusual man. An academic and scholar who considered research his first priority, he believed that first-rate research required an intimate association with practical engineering and real structures in the field. Not surprisingly, therefore, most of his research originated from problems that arose in the field, such as bearing capacity; slope stability; engineering geology; pore pressures and effective stresses in soil, rock, and concrete; and foundation engineering. His work on the fundamentals of soil mechanics and geotechnical engineering are still widely used as a basis for many design methods. For example, his work on settlements is the basis for current criteria for allowable settlements of structures. In addition, slopes in stiff clays are generally designed according to Alec's methods.

Alec demonstrated a rare versatility—as scientist, engineer, historian, and musician. Through his writings and lectures, he had a major impact on geotechnical engineering around the world, and he won many awards and held many important positions—Rankine Lecturer, 1964; fellow of the Royal Society; and president of the International Society of Soil Mechanics and Foundation Engineering, 1957 through 1961.

In 2000, Alec was awarded a knighthood in the New Year's Honors List for service to engineering. He was nominated by *New Civil Engineering* magazine as one of the greatest civil engineers of the 20th century.

Over the years, I corresponded and had personal contact with Alec Skempton from time to time. During my leadership of the Geotechnical Division at the Massachusetts Institute of Technology (MIT), I brought him to give lectures, and he proved to be the most popular lecturer I ever brought to MIT. In 1983, when I investigated the stability of a river bank at an industrial plant at Jarrow, England, I enlisted the assistance of Professor Peter Vaughan, a former student of Alec's. When Alec heard of our investigation, he joined in purely out of interest in the problem.

Civil engineers around the world will mourn the passing of Alec Skempton.

FRED NOEL SPIESS

1919–2006

Elected in 1985

*"For significant breakthroughs in ocean engineering, including FLIP,
Deep Tow, precision benthic navigation, and exotic platforms."*

BY ROBERT A. FROSCH AND WILLIAM KUPERMAN

FRED NOEL SPIESS, husband, father of five, grandfather of eight, great grandfather of three, U.S. Navy submariner, deep-sea explorer and inventor, and Professor Emeritus of Oceanography at the Marine Physical Laboratory at the Scripps Institution of Oceanography (MPL/SIO) at the University of California, San Diego, died on September 8, 2006. He was 86 years old.

Born in 1919, Fred earned his A.B. from the University of California, Berkeley, with a major in physics. From 1941 to 1946, he served in the U.S. Navy submarine force; he was awarded the Silver Star and Bronze Star for participating in 13 war patrols in enemy waters, the highest number of patrols by any individual. He remained a captain (retired) in the U.S. Naval Reserve until his death.

He left the Navy after the war "to study oceanography and make the Navy smarter," he told a friend. He earned an M.S. in communications engineering from Harvard University (1946) and returned to the University of California, Berkeley, where he earned a Ph.D. in physics (1951). After a short stint as a nuclear engineer at Knolls Atomic Power Laboratory, Schenectady, New York, he joined MPL/SIO, where he continued to work for the rest of his career. He was director of MPL from 1958 to 1980. He spent the year 1962–1963 as acting director of SIO and was director from 1964–1965. He then was an associate director of SIO until 1980. He also served as chairman of the Scripps Graduate

Department in 1963–1964 and 1976–1977. During 1974–1975, while on leave from Scripps, he was a scientific liaison officer for the Office of Naval Research in London. He was professor of oceanography at SIO from 1961 to 1990, when he became Professor of Oceanography Emeritus. He also served from 1980 to 1988, as director of the Institute of Marine Resources, University of California.

Fred was not only a leader in oceanography, but also a deep-sea scientist, seagoing technologist, and explorer who led the development and use of new technologies for investigating the deep ocean and seafloor. He not only developed new technologies and the instruments for their implementation, but also took them to sea and used them to explore the oceans and their underlying geology. Among the instruments he developed were Deep Tow, a device that tows instruments for looking closely at the deep ocean, measuring its acoustics, and examining the seafloor, and Floating Instrument Platform (FLIP), a research platform developed by Fred (and the late Fred Fisher). Deep Tow was used in the search for the *USS Thresher*, and the platforms, vehicles, and acoustic-transponder technology he developed enabled ocean scientists to make the first accurate measurements of the deep ocean.

One example of the combination of new ocean technology and science was the discovery, under the leadership of Fred and K. McDonald, of the first superheated "black smoker" vents on the seafloor. This discovery completely revolutionized scientific models of the chemistry of seawater and introduced the idea of life-forms that could survive (perhaps even originated) in extreme conditions, temperatures as high as ~400°C and very high pressures. The resulting paper by Fred (the lead author) and others was published in *Science* and was awarded the Newcomb-Cleveland Prize of the American Academy for the Advancement of Science (AAAS) for the most important contribution to *Science* in 1980.

Precision measurement is central to the very definition of experimental physics. Fred led a team of scientists (including Chadwell and Hildebrand) that was able to measure directly the absolute motion of an oceanic plate. Their amazing, and reassuring, result was that plate motion measured on a timescale of months and years was very close to the motion measured indirectly based on marine magnetic anomalies, averages of motion over hundreds of thousands of years.

FLIP is a 700-ton research platform that can be towed to sea, upended, and ballasted with seawater. It then becomes a large spar buoy with a 300-foot draft and incredible stability in very high waves and swells. For example, in 30-meter swells, it has a vertical motion of less than 1 meter. Carrying a crew of five and a research team of 11, FLIP can operate for 30 days without resupply. Moored or adrift, it provides an extremely stable, acoustically quiet platform for ocean observation and experiments and has been particularly useful for acoustic studies. This unique vessel remains in use as "a wonderfully successful and quiet platform, which was built for virtually nothing and has enriched our knowledge of the oceans for four decades," said Walter Munk, an emeritus professor of oceanography at Scripps Institution of Oceanography.

In 1989 Fred led the development of a wireline re-entry system to carry research instruments from the deck of a ship through 5,000 meters of seawater and into seafloor boreholes previously drilled as part of deep-sea scientific drilling programs. He continued to lead the refinement and use of this capability, with a 2001 expedition on *R/V Revelle* installing the first wireline thermistor strings in drill holes to study the circulation of fluids in the Earth's crust.

Fred Spiess was elected to the National Academy of Engineering (NAE) in 1985 "for significant breakthroughs in ocean engineering, including FLIP, Deep Tow, precision benthic navigation, and exotic platforms." He was a fellow of the American Geophysical Union (AGU), the Acoustical Society of America (ASA), and the Marine Technical Society (MTS). He served as president of the Ocean Science Section of the AGU and served on the Ocean Studies Board of the National Research Council. He was also a member of the Maritime Historical Society, the Society for Industrial Archaeology, the Scholia Club of Sand Diego, Sigma Xi, and Phi Beta Kappa.

Fred was awarded the John Price Wetherill Medal by the

Franklin Institute in 1965, the Distinguished Achievement Award
by MTS in 1971, the Robert Dexter Conrad Award by the U.S.
Navy in 1974, the Newcomb-Cleveland Prize (mentioned above)
by AAAS in 1980, the Maurice Ewing Medal by AGU and the
U.S. Navy in 1983, the Pioneers of Underwater Acoustics Medal
by ASA in 1985, the MTS/Lockheed Award for Ocean Science
and Engineering in 1985, the Secretary of the Navy Distinguished
Public Service Award in 1991, and the Distinguished Technical
Achievement Award of the IEEE Oceanic Engineering Society
in 2006.

After 20 years as director of MPL, Fred assumed other senior
management positions in the University of California system. In
his eighth decade, he was asked to lead the planning of the academic program at the new University of California campus at
Merced, a task he performed most effectively—a testament to
his unending energy and sense of service to the academic community. Just a few months before his death, he undertook an
NSF proposal to reinvent FLIP as a large-platform prototype for
the future ocean observing system.

Fred resided in La Jolla, California. He was married for 60
years to the late Sally Whitton Spiess who was a tireless supporter
of his work at Scripps, the Marine Physical Laboratory, UC San
Diego, and the community at large. One of their last joint projects
was the restoration of the historic Old Scripps Building, which
was designed by Irving Gill and was one of the original buildings
of the institution. Both Fred and Sally were active members of
their church, the Union Congregational Church of La Jolla. Sally
was the mainstay of the social ministries of the church, and Fred
was moderator during 1984–1985 and financial secretary for
many years. They are survived by their five children: Katherine
Dallaire of Chester, New Hampshire; Mary Elizabeth De Jong of
San Francisco, California; Morgen Spiess of Seattle, Washington; Helen Spiess Shamble of Santa Clara, California; and Peggy
DeLigio Spiess of Eugene, Oregon; four sons-in-law; eight grandchildren; and three great grandchildren.

Fred Spiess will be remembered and missed by his many
colleagues in oceanographic science, technology, and
engineering. He was not only an ingenious inventor and a

pathbreaking contributor to ocean science and technology, but also a gentle, smiling, wise, and witty colleague and friend who was always ready to help. Of all his accomplishments, Fred was most proud of his students, postdoctoral students, and the three generations of ocean scientists he mentored. The words of Tom Brokaw in his book, *The Greatest Generation*, aptly apply to Fred Spiess, "....duty, honor, love of family and country, service, achievement and courage gave us the world we have today ...." If we continue that tradition, those values can also lead to the world we want tomorrow.

Warren E. Stewart

WARREN EARL STEWART

1924–2006

Elected in 1992

"For leadership in chemical engineering research and the application of advanced mathematical and numerical methods."

BY R. BYRON BIRD, W. HARMON RAY,
AND EDWIN N. LIGHTFOOT

WARREN EARL STEWART, McFarland-Bascom Professor Emeritus of Chemical and Biological Engineering at the University of Wisconsin, died on March 27, 2006, after a long and distinguished career. Warren was born in Whitewater, Wisconsin, on July 3, 1924, to Earl and Avis Stewart. He received both B.S. and M.S. degrees at Wisconsin, in 1945 and 1947, and the Sc.D. in 1951 at Massachusetts Institute of Technology (MIT). All of his degrees were in chemical engineering. While an undergraduate at Wisconsin, he gained fame as the first student in the history of the College of Engineering to graduate with a straight-A academic record. His MIT experience introduced him to numerical analysis and computational techniques, which proved to be essential at the dawn of the electronic computer age.

In World War II, Warren enlisted in the U.S. Naval Reserve (1944–1946). He returned to Wisconsin as a Navy engineering trainee under the V-12 Program, and after graduation served as a communications officer on the aircraft carrier *USS Midway*. In 1947 he married Jean Durham Potter, who later was alderman for the city of Madison for 16 years (1977–1993). They had six children and 18 grandchildren.

After five years at the Sinclair Research Laboratories, Warren Stewart joined the faculty of the Department of Chemical Engineering at the University of Wisconsin in 1956, where he taught until 1997. As chairman of the department (1973–1978), he recruited and nurtured several young faculty members who went on to become international leaders in their fields as well as NAE members. He supervised many Ph.D. students and postdoctoral fellows who today hold responsible positions in universities and industrial research laboratories around the world.

His research publications are indicative of the breadth of his interests and knowledge. How many chemical engineers could write significant contributions on such widely varying topics as prediction of vapor pressures, reciprocal variational principles, kinetics of benzene hydrogenation, chemical kinetics and reaction engineering, multicomponent diffusion, orthogonal collocation, measurement of diffusivities, droplet vaporization, kinetic theory of rigid dumbbell suspensions, tokamak reactors, thermal diffusion, catalysis, corrosion, parameter estimation, Bayesian statistics, strategics for process modeling and parameter estimation, viscoelastic fluid dynamics, insulation qualities of animal fur, sensitivity analysis, and distillation column design? Whereas most professors tend to become very specialized, Warren Stewart was an impressive generalist. When he served as department chairman, he was able to discuss with all faculty members the details of their ongoing research programs. No other department chairman in the last half-century has been able to do that.

Warren published well over 100 research papers, many containing an impressive amount of detail. He wrote several systematically organized series of reviews of many important transport problems, invariably using his facility in applied mathematics. The first of these series dealt with the boundary-layer theory for momentum, heat, and mass transfer in laminar, multicomponent systems. Then came a series of papers in *AIChE Journal* dealing with forced convection in three-dimensional flows: I (1963); II (1970); III (1983); IV (1988); the second of these is the famous paper dealing with transport across mobile interfaces, coauthored with J.B. Angelo and E.N. Lightfoot. Then in 1974, there was a series of four papers with J.P. Sørensen dealing with computation of forced convection in slow flow through ducts and packed beds, published in *Chemical Engineering Science*.

Among Warren Stewart's most important technical contributions was his development of new mathematical and computational methods for modeling chemical phenomena and chemical processes. His work in this area led to better design and safer operation of chemical processes involving chemical reactions, transport of heat and mass, and the complex flow of fluids. His research results, which have been adopted around the world, increased the fundamental understanding of chemical phenomena and significantly influenced industrial practice.

In addition, there were many publications dealing with the analysis of diffusion experiments and the collection and correlation of diffusivities for various gaseous and liquid systems. In 1964 he and Richard Prober wrote a paper about the matrix approximations for multicomponent mass transport in *Industrial and Engineering Chemistry Fundamentals*; this work was followed by an article in *AIChE Journal* dealing with multicomponent diffusion in turbulent flow in 1973. An analytical solution of which he was particularly proud was that of the Fourier analysis of energy transport in turbulent tube flow at large Prandtl numbers, which appeared in *AIChE Journal* in 1987. The work on multicomponent diffusion and on turbulent heat transfer were included in the second edition of *Transport Phenomena*, by R.B. Bird, Warren E. Stewart, and E.N. Lightfoot (2002), §22.9 and §13.6, respectively.

Beyond influencing his own research students, he was an inspiring teacher and valuable consultant for many students and professors in the Chemical Engineering Department. Furthermore, Warren was a co-author of the 1958 green paperback, *Notes on Transport Phenomena*, which served as a preliminary edition for the 1960 textbook, *Transport Phenomena* (published by John Wiley & Sons). This textbook changed the direction of chemical engineering teaching everywhere in the world. It was translated into Spanish, Russian, Italian, Czech, and Chinese. After 64 printings of the first English edition, a second edition was prepared by the same trio of authors. The new edition appeared in 2002 and has been translated into Chinese, Portuguese, and Spanish.

In the preparation of this textbook, Warren displayed important characteristics that were invaluable: very high standards for writing technical material, a photographic memory of the technical literature, and an insistence that there be no spelling or grammatical errors (this last quality earned him the nickname "gimlet eye"). Furthermore he didn't allow any question marks to be missed (he would say "I think we've missed a little 'buttonhook' at the end of the penultimate sentence").

At the time of his death, Warren had almost completed *Computer-Aided Modeling of Chemically Reactive Systems* (by Warren E. Stewart and Michael Caracotsios), along with accompanying software. This book provides an overview of chemical kinetics and reactor modeling, as well as an extensive description of strategies for parameter estimation based on noisy and incomplete data sets. An interactive software package is included that can perform modeling and parameter estimation calculations based on the problem details supplied by the user.

Despite his quiet demeanor and modesty, Warren received many awards for his research and teaching: Elected Fellow of the American Institute of Chemical Engineers (AIChE) (1973); Citation Classic status for *Transport Phenomena* (see *Current Contents*, 17 September 1979); Citation Classic status for "Solution of Boundary Value Problems by Orthogonal Collocation" (see *Current Contents*, 21 September 1981); Alpha Chi Sigma Research Award of AIChE (1981); Benjamin Smith Reynolds Award for Excellence in Teaching, University of Wisconsin College of Engineering (1981); Chemical Engineering Division Lectureship Award, American Society of Engineering Education (1983); Honorary Member of Phi Beta Kappa (1983); McFarland-Bascom Professorship (1983); Computing in Chemical Engineering Award, CAST Division of AIChE (1984); E.V. Murphree Award in Industrial and Engineering Chemistry, American Chemical Society (1989); Byron Bird Award for Outstanding Research Publication, University of Wisconsin College of Engineering (1991); and membership in the National Academy of Engineering (1992). The hallmark of Warren's career was understated excellence in his work and unfailing kindness to students and colleagues.

He was given honorary membership in Phi Beta Kappa for his exceptional scholarship and his extensive contributions to

Chemical Engineering in Mexico and South America. He was a visiting professor at the Universidad Nacional de La Plata in Argentina in 1962, at the Universidad Nacional Tecnológico de Celaya in Mexico in 1983, and at the Universidad Autónoma de México in 1985. At these institutions he lectured in Spanish. For 18 years he was an editorial advisor for the *Latin-American Journal of Chemical Engineering and Applied Chemistry*. Following that, he held a similar position for *Latin-American Applied Research*.

Warren Stewart was well known for his sly sense of humor and his ability to produce, instantly, jokes on just about any topic. He loved puns and had a warning sign on his desk given to him by colleagues: "Incorrigible punster—don't incorrige."

Warren loved his family and was devoted to them. He is survived by his wife, Jean; six children, Marilyn (Jim) Weaver, David, Douglas, Carol (David) Ray, Margaret (Kurt) Straus, and Maru Jean (Bruce) Glasgow; 18 grandchildren, Katherine, Thomas, and Rebecca Weaver, Jenny Kershner-Stewart, Joanna, Andrea, Rachel, Daniel, Susanna, and Abigail Ray, Gretchen, Eric, Madeline, and Zachary Straus, Johathan, Caroline, Andrew, and Jeffrey Glasgow. He is also survived by two sisters-in-law, Virginia and Helen Stewart, and one brother-in-law, John Potter; many nieces and nephews, cousins, and other relatives.

Jerome J. Tiemann

JEROME J. TIEMANN

1932–2006

Elected in 1984

"For his creativity and leadership in developing advanced electronics for communications, medical diagnostics, radar, and video information processing."

WRITTEN BY JAMES B. COMLY
SUBMITTED BY THE NAE HOME SECRETARY

JEROME J. TIEMANN, retired physicist at General Electric (GE) Global Research for more than 44 years, died of a heart attack at his home in Schenectady, New York, on April 25, 2006. He was 74 years old.

Born on February 21, 1932, in Yonkers, New York, Jerry grew up in Hastings on Hudson, New York. He graduated from the Fieldston School in Riverdale, New York (1949), the Massachusetts Institute of Technology (B.Sc., 1953), and earned his Ph.D. in theoretical nuclear physics from Stanford University. While at Stanford, he was invited to work at Los Alamos Scientific Laboratory and the University of California Lawrence Radiation Laboratory.

Jerry came to the GE Corporate Research Laboratory (now GE Global Research) in 1957, the year the integrated circuit was patented. That was also the year he married Adrian Rooke, his wife of 49 years. Jerry was an inspired scientist and engineer who lived and worked during a golden age of scientific advancement, brought about in part by competition after the launch of Sputnik by the Soviet Union.

His early fundamental studies on interband electron tunneling (1959–1964) led to the first practical method of manufacturing commercial tunneling diode devices. This work was cited by Leo Esaki in his 1973 Nobel Lecture for physics. Jerry then helped design circuits incorporating these devices, including the first "vest-pocket transmitter" (1959). He did pioneering work on piezo-optics, and, in the mid-1960s, turned his attention to the optical properties of semiconductors and developed new experimental techniques for studying piezo-reflectivity. His work on thin-film magnetic heads anticipated the application of semiconductor manufacturing processes to hard disk head design (1966).

In 1970, Jerry and colleagues co-invented the surface-charge transistor, which Bell Labs had independently invented as the charge coupled device (CCD). Jerry's patents contributed to the subsequent development of the CCD. He was also a leader in the early program at GE Global Research on a real-time ultrasonic imaging system for medical diagnostics. In February 1971, Intel co-founder Gordon Moore wrote to Jerry commending his work. "Your paper at the Solid State Circuits Conference was far and away the best of [those] relating to charge coupled devices," Moore wrote.

In 1972, Jerry published an important paper on random access memory (RAM). In 1974, he co-developed and demonstrated the surface-charge correlator, which was 100 times faster than existing processors. In 1979, Nobel Laureate Leo Esaki honored Jerry by inviting him to give a series of lectures in Japan. Jerry won many industry awards, including IR-100 Awards in 1971 and 1974, and became a Coolidge Fellow in 1975 (GE's highest honor for research and development). In 1976, he was elected a fellow of the American Physical Society and the Institute of Electrical and Electronic Engineers (for clarifying the understanding of interband tunneling and surface-charge transport and for their application to new devices). In 1984, he was elected to the National Academy of Engineering; his citation reads, "For his creativity and leadership in developing advanced electronics for communications, medical diagnostics, radar, and video information processing." He joined the Whitney Gallery of Technical Achievers at General Electric in 1990.

Jerry was a natural problem solver. His 135 patents ranged from a super-pure laboratory-made diamond to a mirror that reflected without the "mirror image," from a fail-safe circuit breaker to an automatic ice maker that produced ice cubes that would not freeze together. But perhaps more important, he was a patient teacher and an enthusiastic mentor who paid special attention to younger scientists and used his uncanny ability to simplify complex ideas to make them accessible to novices and laypeople.

At home and among his many friends, Jerry's talents were varied. He played jazz piano with a style of chord voicing that earned him the nickname "mittens." His knowledge of chemistry translated seamlessly to candy and fudge-making. With his artistic design and craft skills, he produced elegant silver jewelry of his own design, often featuring stones he had found at locations across the country that had been cut and polished with tools of his own making. He designed and made furniture for his family out of wood from trees he felled on his own property. Captain of the 1953 MIT varsity cross-country team, Jerry won a track medal for GE's corporate relay team (in the 50-to 59-year-age category) in 1990.

He also loved the outdoors. When his boys Michael and Bruce were young, he and Adrian organized overnight hikes in the Adirondack Mountains, where they had a summer residence. With his love of science and prodigious memory, Jerry could identify and discuss plants along the way with a botanist's exactitude and depth. The rich diversity of mountains and streams tapped into his equally impressive knowledge of geology and mineralogy.

Jerry is survived by his wife, Adrian Rooke Tiemann, Ph.D.; his brother, Karl Tiemann, of Owego, New York; his sister, Lydia Lynn, of Big Flats, New York; two sons, Michael Damian Tiemann, and wife Amy Page Tiemann, Ph.D., of Chapel Hill, North Carolina, and Bruce Gregory Tiemann, Ph.D., and wife Valeria Bassi Damiao, Ph.D., of Longmont, Colorado; three grandchildren, Miranda Page Tiemann of Chapel Hill and Jai Damian Tiemann and Shay Julian Tiemann of Longmont. Jerry is also survived by several nieces and nephews.

He was preceded in death by his parents, Ruth Darling Johnson Tiemann, aged 94, and Roland Wilfrid Tiemann, aged 96, and by his father-in-law, Denis Morley Rooke, aged 86, and mother-in-law, Velma Howell Rooke, who died at age 100 in 2005.

Jerry's *joie de vivre* was apparent in everything he did, and his personal charm endeared him to his many friends and associates. One always came away with different, interesting, and clearer insights into the world when Jerry was around. His scientific and technical expertise, his creativity in all matters, his enthusiasm and buoyancy, and his warm and active friendship will be missed by everyone who knew him.

CHANG-LIN TIEN

1935–2002

Elected in 1976

*"For contributions to the theory of heat transfer and for its
application to difficult contemporary engineering problems."*

BY ERNEST S. KUH AND RALPH GREIF

CHANG-LIN TIEN, a world leader in heat transfer and thermodynamics, died in Hillsborough, California, on October 29,
2002, at the age of 67. He was a creative researcher, a master
teacher, and, above all, a distinguished and enthusiastic educator and leader.

Born in Wuhan, China, on July 24, 1935, Chang-Lin was a
high school student in Shanghai when he followed his family to
Taiwan in 1949 to escape civil war in China. He received his B.S.
degree from National Taiwan University in 1955. After one year
of military service, he came to the United States, first to Louisville, Kentucky. He later earned his M.A. and Ph.D. from
Princeton University in 1959. Immediately afterward, he came
to the University of California, Berkeley, as acting assistant professor; he became full professor in 1968. Chang-Lin was chairman of the Department of Mechanical Engineering, vice chancellor of research, and then, from 1988 to 1990, executive vice
chancellor at UC Irvine. From 1990 to 1997, he was chancellor
at Berkeley. He was appointed NEC Distinguished Professor in
1997, and in the same year he was appointed University Professor.

Chang-Lin Tien was a visionary who identified new, critical
fields and then proceeded to carry out pioneering research in
those disciplines, elucidating essential elements and phenom-

ena. He also recognized and reported on important applications of his research. One of the first investigators of heat transfer to focus on thermal radiation in gases, he provided a basis for quantifying the infrared radiation properties of gases and for generalizing these properties so that gases could be characterized in terms of fundamental variables, thus providing a foundation for current engineering approaches. Tien also made significant contributions to the understanding and determination of radiation transport in solids in the form of particulates and surfaces. He was also the first to provide a sound theoretical basis for determining dependent scattering, and his experimental results delineated the region of applicability.

In the area of thermal insulation, he studied all modes of energy transport to determine the critical and controlling phenomena governing transport in multilayer, cryogenic, and microsphere insulations. His work on porous insulation encompassed general analysis and experiments in porous media.

Tien also made pioneering contributions on microscale thermal phenomena—phonon transport in nanostructures and semiconductor superlattices, non-Fourier heat conduction in thin films, femtosecond laser interactions with thin films and micromechanical structures, heat transport in random media, picosecond optical properties of porous silicon, and microscale laser interactions with liquids. His contributions to the field, which include research, supervision of students and postdoctoral scholars, and the founding of a new journal, *Microscale Thermophysical Engineering*, changed the field and led to the new discipline of microscale heat transfer.

Chang-Lin was the recipient of numerous teaching honors. In 1962, he became the youngest professor to win Berkeley's prestigious Distinguished Teaching Award. In 1976, at the age of 41, he was elected a member of the National Academy of Engineering (NAE). He was elected a fellow of the American Academy of Arts and Sciences in 1991. In 1997, he was given the Presidential Medal by the University of California Systemwide. In 2001 he was awarded the NAE Founders Medal. He was also a member of the Academia Sinica and a foreign member of the Chinese Academy of Sciences.

In 1990, when Chang-Lin Tien was appointed chancellor at Berkeley, he was the first Asian scholar ever appointed to the top position of a major research university. His enormous energy, optimism, hard work, and excellent judgment made him an outstanding chancellor who was loved by students and respected by faculty. An excellent fund raiser during a time of severe budget restrictions, he was able to generate great support from alumni all over the world. After Proposition 209 was passed in California, he contributed significantly to affirmative action policies through a creative program called the "Berkeley Pledge."

An avid supporter of the athletic programs at Berkeley, Chang-Lin Tien often attended the home games of the California Bears, cheering on the basketball and football teams and following the careers of Jason Kidd and other stars. Although he was only 5'7", basketball was his passion and hobby, both as a student and later in his life.

Chang-Lin was a very disciplined individual, and he always kept a clean desk. This meant that after every trip he would come to his office, sometimes after midnight, to complete his tasks. This action typified his enthusiasm and energy. He was a warm, joyous human being who was universally admired and respected among his peers throughout the world and was recognized as a leader in higher education.

Chang-Lin published one book, edited 16 volumes, and published more than 300 research papers and monographs. His many honors and awards include 12 honorary doctoral degrees. He served on a number of boards of major universities, including his alma mater, Princeton University.

Tien's contributions and accomplishments extend beyond science, engineering, and education. He was an ambassador to many countries, especially in Asia, in terms of public service. He was a member of the Board of Trustees of the Asian Foundation, advisor to the governor of Hong Kong, chairman of the San Francisco Bay Area Economic Forum, a member of the board of directors of Kaiser Foundation Hospitals, a Charter Member of the Council of the Oakland Museum, and a member of the Aspen Institute Domestic Strategy Group, just to name a few of his affiliations. In business, he served on the Board of Directors of

Chevron Corporation, Wells Fargo Bank, Raychem Corporation, and Air Touch Corporation.

Although he was deeply involved in many fields and activities, Chang-Lin was devoted to his family and friends. He is survived by his wife, Di Hwa, of Hillsborough, California; son Norman, and his wife, of Cleveland, Ohio; two daughters—Phyllis, of Hillsborough, California, and her husband, and Christine, of Stockton, California, and her husband. He was extremely proud of his six grandchildren. Chang-Lin's untimely death was a great loss to his family, his friends, his colleagues, and the nation.

Keith W. Christopher

KEITH W. UNCAPHER

1922–2002

Elected in 1998

"For information technology on the national level."

BY ANITA JONES

KEITH WILLIAM UNCAPHER, founder and Executive Director Emeritus of Information Sciences Institute, Associate Dean for Information Sciences Emeritus of the University of Southern California, and senior vice president of the Corporation for National Research Initiatives, died at the age of 80 on October 10, 2002. He died in mid-air while returning to the West Coast after attending an NAE meeting.

Keith was born in Denver, Colorado, on April 1, 1922, one of three children of Wayne Samuel and Alice Clague Uncapher; the family moved to California when he was six months old. After high school graduation in Glendale, California, he joined the Navy and became a radar technician. Although he was prone to seasickness, he never hesitated when he had to climb the mast of his ship to fix the radar. When he left the service in 1946, Keith studied electronics and mathematics at Glendale College. In 1950, he graduated from the California Polytechnic Institute with a B.S. in mathematics and electrical engineering.

At the recommendation of one of his professors, Keith applied for a job at the RAND Corporation in Santa Monica, California, which was a fairly new organization at the time. He was readily accepted at RAND and soon began to conduct fundamental research on digital-memory technology (before the time of core memory). His talent for managing research was evident early on, and he was soon put in charge of the Computer Engineering Group, where he led the development of a digital-memory subsystem for the Johnniac computer, based on the use of Selectron tubes. This system broke the previous world record for reliability, running for 10 hours without an error.

Keith also participated in the development of several early interactive computing systems, including JOSS, Grail, and the RAND Tablet. Under his leadership, RAND conducted pioneering research on survivable communications, which introduced a concept that eventually became known as packet switching, a fundamental technique that was used in the Advanced Research Projects Agency Network (ARPANET) only a few years later. Packet switching was later widely adopted by the telecommunications industry and remains a key element of the Internet to this day.

In 1972, Keith left the RAND Corporation to found the Information Sciences Institute (ISI), which he hoped would have close university connections. After one California university told him it would take many months to get approval to establish the institute, he contacted the provost of the University of Southern California (USC), who welcomed the idea and rapidly established ISI as part of the university. Keith located ISI on the beautiful marina of Marina del Rey and served as executive director until 1988. Under his leadership, the institute flourished and grew to have a staff of several hundred.

During the 1970s, when the relevancy of university research was being questioned by the U.S. Department of Defense (DoD), he showed that university computer-science research could be directly relevant to military needs. The Military Message Experiment, for example, demonstrated the first use of interactive computing, electronic mail, and networks for military communications. Other projects included reliable, network-based time-sharing services and rapid turnaround fabrication of very large scale integration (VLSI) designs using an online brokerage service called MOSIS (metal-oxide semiconductor implementation service). MOSIS provided a vehicle for the fast, low-cost fabrication of semiconductor designs for university students and faculty; researchers in government and not-for-profit laboratories; as well as for researchers in large and small corporations. By making hands-on experimentation with early VLSI design, implementation, and testing widely accessible, MOSIS was an important factor in establishing and maintaining the U.S. lead in microelectronics.

For decades, Keith served as a trusted advisor to senior government officials, especially officials in DoD and the Defense Advanced Research Projects Agency (DARPA). Keith exerted a profound influence by encouraging reliance on digital communications and information systems. He personally sought out excellent researchers, broadened their horizons, and, in some cases, convinced them to move for a period of time from their research laboratories into key government staff positions (e.g., to act as DARPA program officers to initiate programs in critical areas of research). He was untiring in his determination to ensure that these positions be filled by individuals who were knowledgeable in state-of-the-art hardware and software—at a time when the information technology field was expanding and changing rapidly—to ensure that DoD-funded research would be creative and effective.

After 15 years as head of ISI, Keith became Executive Director Emeritus so he could focus on two other activities. In 1980, he had become the Associate Dean of Engineering for information sciences at USC. He now had time to help USC discover applications of information technology and how it could be used to improve the university's academic research programs, as well as its administrative processes. In 1993, he became Associate Dean Emeritus. Keith was also a founder and senior vice president of the Corporation for National Research Initiatives (CNRI), a not-for-profit corporation he and Robert Kahn established in 1986. CNRI determines priorities for critical applications of information technology and fosters research and development on information infrastructure on a national scale.

Microelectromechanical systems (MEMS) is one example of a technology Keith recognized early on as important to U.S. economic leadership and national security. He recognized that MEMS, which combine sensors, actuators, and some computational capability, could lead to the development of low-cost, small devices that could be mass produced for myriad applications. In the 1990s, Keith worked directly with the university research community to stimulate interest in solving technical problems related to the design and manufacture of MEMS devices. He also championed DARPA's efforts to develop a MEMS-focused brokerage service modeled on the MOSIS approach, so that researchers and developers in universities, laboratories, and small companies could have their designs fabricated rapidly and affordably. The service gave thousands of designers working in many scientific and engineering disciplines access to MEMS fabrication resources. Thanks to Keith's leadership, investment by DoD in MEMS research was doubled, and the United States rapidly developed military applications for MEMS devices. In addition, for a time at least, U.S. industry had a technical lead thanks to the availability of students trained in this technology in university research laboratories.

Keith also served the technical community in other ways. He helped orchestrate a merger between the American Institute of Electrical Engineers and the Institute of Radio Engineers to create the Institute of Electrical and Electronic Engineers (IEEE). He facilitated the emergence of a single national computer-engineering professional society in the United States, the IEEE Computer Group, and in 1964, was its first chair. The Computer Group became the IEEE Computer Society in 1971. In 1970, Keith was elected president of the American Federation of Information Processing Societies (AFIPS). He was also a member of the Air Force Science Advisory Board for 15 years.

Keith Uncapher's contributions have been recognized and celebrated many times over. In 1979, he was awarded the AFIPS Distinguished Service Award. The Air Force granted him the Air Force Meritorious Civilian Service Award in 1981. In 1983, he received the IEEE Centennial Award. And in 1998, he was elected a member of the National Academy of Engineering.

Keith was a man of high integrity with a sunny disposition, a genuine love of humanity, an engaging sense of humor, and a taste for fine food, travel, and natty clothes. He had an uncanny ability to identify promising areas of technology and to facilitate the rapid advancement of those technologies at a national level. Thus, he influenced the pattern and pace of research in universities, government laboratories, and industry. He ensured that a broad community would have access to semiconductor fabrication and to interactive, time-shared computing so that researchers could explore these technologies. He identified individuals with the vision and knowledge to advance a technology and was instrumental in putting them into key roles where they could advance that technology. His efforts changed the face of technology, and his insights, wisdom, and dedication to his nation inspired everyone who had the privilege of working with him.

Keith is survived by his wife Doris Uncapher and two sons, Jeffrey Keith Uncapher and William Bradley Uncapher. His two sisters predeceased him.

FERNANDO VASCO COSTA

1913–1996

Elected in 1989

"For distinguished contributions to the theory and practice of ship berthing, mooring, and maritime structure design."

BY THORNDIKE SAVILLE JR. AND ROBERT L. WIEGEL

FERNANDO VASCO COSTA, educator, researcher, consultant engineer, and internationally recognized authority on port engineering and the design of marine structures, died October 20, 1996, at the age of 83. He is survived by his wife of 52 years, Fernanda da Silveira Vasco Costa, and three children and eight grandsons. His son Augusto and three of his grandsons became architects.

Elected to the National Academy of Engineering in 1989 as the first (and, so far, only) Foreign Associate from Portugal, Fernando Vasco Costa was cited for his contributions to ocean and marine engineering, particularly in the mooring and berthing of ships. He had a distinguished career as a professor of civil engineering at the Instituto Superior Tecnico in Lisbon, where he was a tenured professor, and at the Technical University of Lisbon, where he also served as rector from 1969 to 1971. In addition, for many years he was an active researcher at the Centro de Estudios de Engenharia Civil (Civil Engineering Research Center) and the Laboratorio Nacional de Engenharia Civil (Portuguese National Laboratory for Civil Engineering). In 1985, he was awarded the Manuel Rocha Research Prize by the latter institution.

Vasco Costa was born in Lisbon in 1913, the eldest son of Ines Vasco Serra Costa and Augusto Serra Costa, a maritime officer. After graduating as a civil engineer from the Instituto Superior

315

Tecnico in 1936 at the age of 22, he went to work as a design and site engineer in charge of foundations and harbor projects for a German firm, Gruen and Bilfinger, A.G. From 1941 to 1943, he served in the Engineer Corps of the Portuguese Army. While stationed in the Azores, he met his future wife. The couple was married in 1944.

Vasco Costa held various academic positions at the two universities (they are affiliated) through 1980, when he became a full-time consulting engineer for harbor works in Lisbon. During his early years in academia (1946–1947), he was awarded a one-year scholarship in the United States—one semester at Cornell and one at the Bureau of Reclamation in Denver. In 1960, he was awarded a scholarship at the Hydraulics Research Station in Wallingford, England, where he worked on a thesis on the impact of vessels with berthing structures. During this period, he also founded CONSULMAR, an engineering consulting company; Fernando was director-general of the company from 1972 to 1980, and he worked there until his death in 1996. As a consultant, he participated in studies for all of the main Portuguese ports (Lisbon, Leixoes, Setubal, Sines, Viana do Castelo, Aveiro, Figueira da Foz, Portimao, Ponta Delgada, Funchal) and many foreign ports, such as Bissau (Guinea-Bissau), Ana Chaves (San Tome and Principe), Tenerife (Canary Islands), Mormugoa (India), Mocamedes (Angola), Maputo (Mozambique), and Ka-Ho (Macao).

The author of more than 50 papers and five books, mostly on various aspects of port engineering, Vasco Costa also wrote several papers on hydraulic modeling, another subject of great interest to him. He authored the *Tabelas Tecnicas,* a technical reference book used in Portugal by engineers for many years. He had a remarkable ability to combine a theoretical understanding of the physics of natural problems with the simplifications necessary to arrive at usable solutions—and an even more remarkable ability to express this understanding in terms that could be understood by others. His papers on the dynamics of berthing and mooring ships, including very large ships, were both theoretical and practical.

He was very involved in risk analysis of structures and structural systems. As he said, "We must recognize and accept the fact that risks are inherent to any kind of human activity and refrain from designing structures as if we could ignore the gravity of the consequences of their possible modes and degrees of failure." He made important advances in how to treat the consequences of a structural failure from the standpoint of both direct cost and social cost. He used the concept of "utility" to compare and order alternative options without having to assign monetary values to human and social values. He asked, "How safe is safe enough? How grave is the failure?"

Vasco Costa was an invited lecturer at a number of foreign laboratories and institutions (Wallingford, Delft, Trondheim, Hanover, Buenos Aires, New York, Athens, and Paris), was active in professional societies, and was a leader in the international community. He was the representative from Portugal during the formation of the Engineering Commission on Oceanic Resources (ECOR), an advisory body to the Intergovernmental Oceanographic Commission (IOC) of UNESCO. Founded in 1971, ECOR was advisory to the international community on engineering aspects of protecting and exploring ocean resources and on marine affairs in general. At the Permanent International Association of Navigation Congresses (PIANC), he was a Portuguese delegate (1965–1981) and chief delegate and chairman of the Portuguese Section (1977–1981). He headed several PIANC working groups and was responsible for issuing their reports. Because of his diplomatic skills in working out corresponding, mutually acceptable, French and English translations (he was fluent in both languages), he was a frequent choice for editing committees charged with formulating conclusions at PIANC meetings. He organized and gave lectures at two NATO Advanced Courses, one on ship berthing and mooring in 1965 and another on application of the statistical theory of extremes to engineering in 1967.

Vasco Costa's international activities were officially recognized with the establishment in 1993 of the Professor Vasco Costa Scholarship, which provides funds to encourage young researchers to present papers at international scientific meetings at the Portuguese Institute for Marine Science and Technology. He was always enthusiastic about the spread of knowledge and the development of engineering assistance and practice through international relations. He was a fellow of the American Society of Civil Engineers and an assistant editor of two international journals, *Coastal Engineering* and *The Journal of Coastal Research.*

Vasco Costa was an accomplished equestrian who took every opportunity to ride and an ardent photographer who was never without his Pentax. His technical photographs added much to his professional presentations, and his personal photographs provided many happy moments for his friends and family. He also took great pleasure in music, an interest he shared with his wife, who came from a musical family and was an accomplished pianist. His friends abroad always looked forward to his annual Christmas gift of a bottle of vintage port. A gentleman of the old school, Vasco Costa was always courteous, polite, and considerate in making his point, but deliberate in making sure he was understood.

Arthur R. von Hippel

ARTHUR R. VON HIPPEL

1898–2003

Elected in 1977

*"For pioneering in molecular engineering and in setting a
pattern for interdisciplinary materials research."*

BY RUSTUM ROY

PROFESSOR ARTHUR R. VON HIPPEL, professor of
electrophysics, founder and director of the Laboratory for Insulation Research, and Institute Professor at the Massachusetts
Institute of Technology (MIT), died on December 31, 2003, in
Weston, Massachusetts. He was a pioneer and champion of interdisciplinary studies at MIT, and his laboratory was an existence theorem for the value of interdisciplinary study and research
in academia.

Dr. von Hippel was born in Rostock, Germany, on November
19, 1898. He married Dagmar Franck, daughter of the German
physicist James Franck, in 1930; the von Hippels became naturalized American citizens on April 21, 1942. They had five children, Peter Hans, Arndt Robert, Frank Niels, Eric Arthur, and
Marianne Margaret.

Professor von Hippel studied at the University of Göttingen,
where he received the degree of doctor of philosophy in 1924.
He spent three years doing research at the University of Jena,
under Professor Max Wien, and then a year as a Rockefeller Fellow in physics at the University of California. He then returned
to Jena for a year as Privat-Dozent. From 1929 to 1933, he was
Privat-Dozent in Professor James Franck's Institute at the University of Göttingen. In 1935, he spent a year as professor at the
University of Istanbul. From there, he went to the Niels Bohr
Institute in Copenhagen, where he worked with Professor Bohr
on dielectric breakdown.

In 1936, Dr. von Hippel moved to MIT as assistant professor of electrical engineering; he became associate professor in 1940 and full professor in 1947. In 1940, he founded the Laboratory for Insulation Research, which he directed until 1962, when it was merged into the APPA-funded, MIT Centre for Materials Science and Engineering. He retired officially in 1964 but continued working at MIT until 1980.

During World War II, von Hippel was a staff member of the MIT Radiation Laboratory and a member of its Coordination Committee and a member-at-large of the Office of Scientific Research and Development (OSRD). He was also the representative of OSRD on the War Committee for Dielectrics, which acted as an advisory board on service and supply problems. In 1948, in recognition of "outstanding services to his country," he was awarded the President's Certificate of Merit, the second highest civilian award.

Professor von Hippel was a fellow of the American Academy of Arts and Sciences, American Physical Society, American Association for the Advancement of Science, New York Academy of Sciences, and Washington Academy of Sciences and a member of the American Chemical Society. In 1952, he was appointed chair of the Conference on Electrical Insulation of the National Research Council. From 1964 to 1965, he was scientific advisor for the Office of Naval Research in Washington, D.C., and on October 27, 1965, he received the Superior Civilian Service Award from the Department of the Navy.

He was an active supporter of the founding of the first major interdisciplinary society, the Materials Research Society (MRS), by his MIT colleague, Professor Harry Gatos, and Professor Rustum Roy of Pennsylvania State University. Von Hippel participated in the organization's annual meetings in Boston until 1984. In 1976, MRS named its highest honor the von Hippel Award and named Arthur von Hippel the first recipient. Professor von Hippel was elected to the National Academy of Engineering in 1977.

Arthur von Hippel's academic and other interests were grounded in his family history, which has been traced back to the 14th century. Many of his ancestors were large land-holders or served in the military. His grandfather Arthur was one of the first professors of ophthalmology, and his father Robert was a professor of criminal law at the University of Göttingen. Von Hippel had two older brothers, Ernst and Fritz, and a younger sister, Olga.

After grammar school, the young Arthur attended the Humanistische Gymnasium in Göttingen, for nine years, where he received a solid classical education that included nine years of Latin and six years of Greek, in addition to French and English, and an excellent background in science and mathematics. A teacher introduced von Hippel to a pre-WWI youth movement—the Wandervogel (migrant birds), a group that expressed its differences with the "class state." Members hiked through Germany and neighboring countries, sleeping in barns, helping with farm chores, rediscovering and collecting folk songs, cooking outdoors, and playing musical instruments. Abandoned houses and later, even old castles, were fixed up as homes for these transient groups of young people, who took a solemn pledge to live a life of purity, responsibility, and mutual helpfulness.

The first large-scale test of this oath came during World War I. Members of the Wandervogel, who were immediately identifiable by a colored string on their uniforms, made friends with each other, independent of rank. About 10,000 members of the youth movement, half its men, were killed in combat. Had they lived, von Hippel believed, World War II and the assumption of power by the Nazis might have been avoided. As university students, von Hippel, his brothers, and some of their friends organized what they called the Akademische Gilde, an alternative to the singing-drinking-dueling student fraternities of the time. In addition to creating a positive social environment and lifelong friendships for themselves, members also tried to enrich the lives of working-class children.

These formative experiences of his youth influenced von Hippel's motto, "We shall not be intimidated," a principle he lived up to throughout his life. He was both anti-Communist (he requisitioned an artillery battery to help put down a local Communist uprising during the post-World War I revolutionary period in Germany) and openly anti-Nazi after they came to power (he once publicly refused to salute Hitler). And, despite the disapproval of some in his family (who later apologized), he married Dagmar Franck, who was Jewish, in 1930—a time when anti-Jewish feeling was already very strong in Germany. His professional models were James Franck and Niels Bohr, nonhierarchical academic leaders and socially responsible scientists. Another model was MIT president Karl Taylor Compton, whom von Hippel considered an ideal administrator.

Professor von Hippel pursued extensive studies in the fields of ferroelectrics and ferromagnetics, electric breakdown, dielectric polarization, rectifiers and photocells, gas discharges, and solid-state physics. He conducted pioneering research in the field of molecular science and molecular engineering, which he described as a "broad new discipline .... comprising the structure, formation, and properties of atoms, molecules and ions; of gases, liquids, solids and their interfaces; the designing of materials and properties on the basis of this molecular understanding; and their imaginative application for devices." Dr. von Hippel was particularly concerned with the future of this vital science and with the establishment of laboratories to promote its study by workers in industry as well as by university students.

Professor von Hippel was the author of *Dielectrics and Waves* (1954) and editor of several books on materials research, *Dielectric Materials and Applications* (1954), *Molecular Science and Molecular Engineering* (1959), and *The Molecular Designing of Materials and Devices* (1965). His final research was focused on identifying the role of water as a solvent in biological systems. This included the precise molecular meaning of terms applied to the liquid state (e.g., activity coefficients, hydration clouds, structure makers, and breakers).

Arthur von Hippel was much more than an academic. In 1919, when he left the German army, and, before turning to science, studied Renaissance art in Munich. Later, he drew on this background to visualize atomic and molecular structures (helped by his draftsman John Mara). He was intrigued, indeed "thunderstruck," by the art of Maurits Escher and its similarities to crystal structures. He championed the use of Lichtenberg figures, the patterns assumed by electrical discharges. (One is on display on the wall of the MIT/Kendall Square subway station in Boston.)

He was also in love with the American wilderness. After World War II, he realized a dream when he had a log cabin built on the bank of the Swift River at the edge of the White Mountains National Forest in New Hampshire. Contact with the natural world helped him retain his realistic outlook. In a 1969 interview, published two years later in the *Czech Journal of Physics*, the interviewer finished by asking von Hippel's views about the ethics of molecular engineering. He responded in part:

> Ours should be a "Golden Age." Instead, everywhere enters the jealousy of competition and the abuse of new knowledge. This is a major cause of the unhappiness of the present student generation in all parts of the world. They feel and we feel that there is not only matter and antimatter in the universe but spirit and antispirit and that we have to side with the spirit!

ACKNOWLEDGMENTS
Some of this material is taken from the NAE files and papers by Frank von Hippel and Markus Zahn.

APPENDIX

Members	Elected	Born	Deceased
Hubert I. Aaronson	1997	July 10, 1924	December 13, 2005
James G. Baker	1979	November 11, 1914	June 29, 2005
Lynn S. Beedle	1972	December 7, 1917	October 30, 2003
Donald S. Berry	1966	January 1, 1911	December 16, 2002
John L. Bogdanoff	1975	May 25, 1916	July 20, 2003
Bruce Alan Bolt	1978	February 15, 1930	July 21, 2005
Harvey Brooks	1968	August 5, 1915	May 28, 2004
Richard M. Carlson	1990	February 4, 1925	July 12, 2004
George F. Carrier	1974	May 4, 1918	March 8, 2002
Marvin Chodorow	1967	July 16, 1913	October 17, 2005
Leland C. Clark Jr.	1995	December 4, 1918	September 25, 2005
Franklin S. Cooper	1976	April 29, 1908	February 20, 1999
L. Stanley Crane	1978	September 7, 1915	July 15, 2003
Wilbur B. Davenport Jr.	1975	July 27, 1920	August 28, 2003
W. Kenneth Davis	1970	July 26, 1918	July 29, 2005
Leslie C. Dirks	1980	March 7, 1936	August 7, 2001
Harry George Drickamer	1979	November 19, 1918	May 6, 2002
Robert C. Duncan	1981	November 21, 1923	May 17, 2003
Carroll Hilton Dunn Sr.	1998	August 11, 1916	January 31, 2003
Ernst R.G. Eckert	1970	September 13, 1904	July 8, 2004
Ralph E. Fadum	1975	July 19, 1912	July 12, 2000
P. Ole Fanger	2001	July 16, 1934	September 18, 2006
Robert Bruce Fridley	1985	June 6, 1934	March 19, 2006
Bernard Gold	1982	March 31, 1923	January 15, 2005
William A.J. Golomski	1996	October 14, 1924	February 17, 2002
Donald R.F. Harleman	1974	December 5, 1922	September 28, 2005
Willis M. Hawkins	1966	December 1, 1913	September 28, 2004
Edward Graham Jefferson	1986	July 15, 1921	February 9, 2006
Howard St. Claire Jones Jr.	1999	August 18, 1921	February 26, 2005
J. Erik Jonsson	1971	September 6, 1901	September 1, 1995
Richard C. Jordan	1975	April 16, 1909	June 14, 2002
Thomas J. Kelly	1991	June 14, 1929	March 23, 2002
Jack St. Clair Kilby	1967	November 8, 1923	June 20, 2005
R. Peter King	2003	March 12, 1938	September 11, 2006
Leon K. Kirchmayer	1979	July 24, 1924	November 12, 1995
Jerome Fox Lederer	1967	September 26, 1902	February 6, 2004
Plato Malozemoff	1969	August 28, 1909	August 8, 1997
I. Harry Mandil	1998	December 11, 1919	April 27, 2006
John S. McNown	1987	January 15, 1916	February 19, 1998
M. Eugene Merchant	1975	May 6, 1913	August 19, 2006
Arthur B. Metzner	1979	April 13, 1927	May 4, 2006

continued on next page

Members	Elected	Born	Deceased
Russell G. Meyerand Jr.	1978	December 2, 1933	November 23, 2003
Rene Harcourt Miller	1968	May 19, 1916	January 28, 2003
Herbert Louis Misch	1976	December 7, 1917	June 23, 2003
Rocco A. Petrone	1975	March 31, 1926	August 24, 2006
Frederick George Pohland	1993	May 3, 1931	January 9, 2004
A. Alan B. Pritsker	1985	February 5, 1933	August 24, 2000
Alvin Radkowsky	1991	June 30, 1915	February 17, 2002
William C. Reynolds	1979	March 16, 1933	January 3, 2004
Herman Paul Schwan	1975	August 7, 1915	March 17, 2005
Chester P. Siess	1967	July 28, 1916	January 14, 2004
Alec W. Skempton	1976	June 4, 1914	August 9, 2001
Fred Noel Spiess	1985	December 25, 1919	September 8, 2006
Warren Earl Stewart	1992	July 3, 1924	March 27, 2006
Jerome J. Tiemann	1984	February 21, 1932	April 25, 2006
Chang-Lin Tien	1976	July 24, 1935	October 29, 2002
Keith W. Uncapher	1998	April 1, 1922	October 10, 2002
Fernando Vasco Costa	1989	June 8, 1913	October 20, 1996
Arthur R. von Hippel	1977	November 19, 1898	December 31, 2003

ACKNOWLEDGMENTS FOR
THE PHOTOGRAPHS

FRANKLIN S. COOPER, by Earl Colter Studio

FERNANDO VASCO COSTA, by Foto Aurea

329